DR. CHARLIE BURRY, JR.

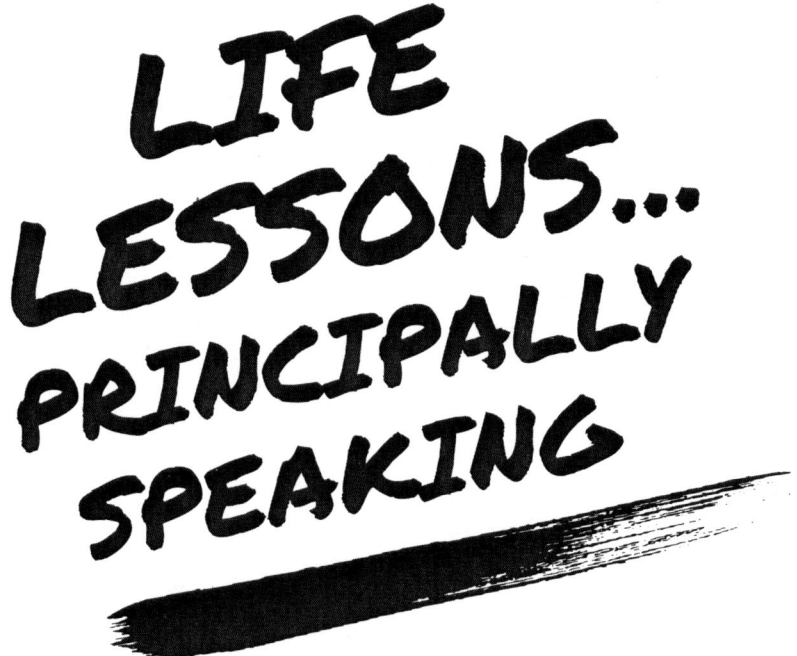

LIFE LESSONS... PRINCIPALLY SPEAKING

Memoirs from the Life of a
High School Teacher, Counselor,
Coach, and Principal

BookBaby

7905 North Crescent Boulevard

Pennsauken, NJ 08110

www.BookBaby.com

Print ISBN: 978-1-09830-515-4

eBook ISBN: 978-1-09830-516-1

Printed in the United States of America on
SFI Certified paper.

First Edition

CONTENTS

Quote Lessons 118

Acknowledgements

"Each one should use whatever gift he has received to serve others, faithfully administering God's grace in its various forms."

1 Peter 4:10

Foreword

Writing is something most anybody can learn to some degree. Then there are those people who are especially gifted with the ability to express themselves with words that not only convey facts, but also express feelings. My friend, Dr. Charlie Burry, has this uncommon gift.

In *Life Lessons . . . Principally Speaking*, you will become absorbed in his world. In some places you'll say to yourself, "Aha, now I get it!" because he saved the punch line until last, or you'll laugh at his self-deprecating humor. In other places you'll fight back tears because you've been moved by something good that made a difference. You'll find nuggets of wisdom that will not only help you become a better person, but will enable you to impact others in a similar manner to Dr. Burry's influence in the Hartsville community. The book begins on a tender note as Charlie reflects on the impact of family and other important people in his life in the small town of Hartsville that became home to him at a young age. It builds toward a fitting conclusion in the final section where Dr. Burry shares the richly pointed "last lessons" from the graduation ceremonies at Hartsville High School during his tenure as principal. I think we all want to grow a little wiser as we go along and make difference wherever we've been. If that describes you as it does me, then I invite you to join Dr. Burry on a journey of real-life experiences that yield life lessons that will help us do both.

Being in a collegiate environment, I understand how important it is to read as much as possible. I keep an annual "top read" list of those books that I consider to be the best

I've encountered in the past year. Especially in recent years, I can quickly name the book that I consider the best one from that year, in terms of enjoyment and benefit. *Life Lessons... Principally Speaking* stands out as my best read of 2019!

Dr. Bob Cline

Vice-President of Church Relations and Senior Campus Pastor

Anderson University

Former Pastor Hartsville First Baptist Church

Gone, but Not Forgotten

As I read *Life Lessons . . . Principally Speaking*, I smiled and I cried, for I was with Dr. Burry for those fourteen years as he served as principal of the high school in which I taught. His words brought back many memories (since I sat through all fourteen first-day speeches and all fourteen graduation speeches). I found those speeches inspiring at the time and still inspiring to this day. His words reminded me of the admiration which I always possessed for him, as both a principal and a human being.

My admiration runs deep because I knew Charlie Burry as a coach and teacher when I was a high school student, but my most valuable experience has been working for him as a teacher while he was principal of my alma mater. A good principal is capable of bringing numerous unique individuals together to work for a common cause, and Dr. Burry did just that. He always had an open-door policy and was accessible to faculty and students. Students and adults alike knew that he believed in what he was doing and that he had their best interests at heart.

I have remained at Hartsville High School since Dr. Burry retired, and to this day students fondly remember him. One of the more whimsical honors that Dr. Burry received was the screensaver that I observed on a student's computer the year after he retired. This image was a rather serious photo of Dr. Burry with a silly king's crown photo-shopped atop his head with the caption "Gone, but not forgotten!" To me this was the highest form of compliment from a student.

No one can ever deny that Dr. Charlie Burry had an impact on the lives of those he encountered as principal of Hartsville High School. Likewise, *Life Lessons . . . Principally Speaking* will impact the lives of those who read it and will give them a glimpse into the heart and mind of this outstanding individual.

Mrs. Ashley Burchfield

English Teacher

International Baccalaureate EE and CAS Coordinator

Hartsville High School

Prologue

When did I become a writer? It was a lifetime ago in Hartsville, South Carolina, because parts of this book were written in my mind when I was in Boy Scouts, playing little league baseball, and working in my dad's dime store. A few sections were written on my heart when I was in Sunday school and when I was in high school and college. Most of it was written at 2210 Oak Avenue and 1016 Edgewood Drive in Hartsville. I say this because those were my formative years at home, when my parents and others were teaching me about character, values, responsibility, and how to live life. It was during that time that I began to form a philosophy of living that became the basis, much later in my life, for the physical act of putting these words on paper. A few of the selections were written as devotions when I was on the Deacon Board at Hartsville First Baptist Church, and a couple were written in response to significant events that took place in our nation while I was a guidance counselor at Hartsville High School. Much of the writing took place during the time that I was principal of Hartsville High School. The rest has been written during the last eighteen months as I adjusted to retirement and wrestled with my identity and purpose in life. The process involved reflection on a forty-five-year career in public education, remembering people in my life who led me down that path, and recollection of events that shaped me. Nearly one-third of my career (2004-2018) was devoted to serving as principal of my high school alma mater, hence, the title - *Life Lessons . . . Principally Speaking*.

To begin, I've written about a few of the important people in my life - some who showed me the way, held my hand, motivated me, and upon whose shoulders I stand. Following that is a section about life lessons that I learned from some of those people, from others who were also important in my life, and from my own experiences. The third section is a sampling of "Character Education Quotes of the Day" that I used during the morning announcements while I was principal of Hartsville High School, and how those quotes relate to learning experiences in my life. The chapters in the fourth section tell of life lessons learned through athletics during my coaching career. The fifth section is about key philosophical pieces of The Red Fox Renaissance that made Hartsville High School a great school again and "a better place for everyone." The chapters in the final section are bits of advice that I offered while I was principal to the graduating classes during their commencement exercises. Some folks who have heard me speak in church, at faculty meetings or staff development sessions, or at graduations may recognize some of these compositions. I've tweaked most of them just a bit from the original presentations in order to better fit book format.

I've again been deeply moved and inspired while pulling this book together, reliving some of the most significant, joyous, and difficult moments of my life, and remembering people and places that I love dearly. My hope is that others will enjoy reading these memoirs, and maybe learn at least a little of what I did by living them.

Dr. Charlie Burry, Jr.

About the Author

Dr. Charlie Burry, Jr., is a native of Nevada, Missouri, born in 1951 to Charles and Wilma Burry. The Burry family also lived in Grand Junction, Colorado, and Biloxi, Mississippi, before moving to Hartsville, South Carolina, in 1959. As a child of avid readers, young Charlie also developed a love for books which was nourished further when his father opened Burry Bookstore in 1972. The Burry family has been influential in the growth and development of the Hartsville community for sixty years. As a self-professed wordsmith, Burry enjoys the process of sharing his thoughts through the written word.

Dr. Burry is a 1969 graduate of Hartsville High School. He received his B.A. degree in History in 1973 from Furman University, a Master of Education (M.Ed.) degree from Francis Marion University (College) in 1976, and in 1993 completed his Doctor of Education (Ed.D.) degree in Curriculum and Instruction from the University of South Carolina. Burry began his teaching and coaching career in 1973 with the Department of Juvenile Justice at the South Carolina School for Boys in Florence, South Carolina, as a physical education teacher and at Francis Marion College as a graduate assistant basketball coach. He taught social studies and coached basketball and football at Gilbert High School in Lexington County, South Carolina, for two years before returning to Hartsville in 1978. Burry taught US History and Sociology for nine years at Hartsville High School, was a guidance counselor for seventeen years, and became principal of Hartsville High School in July 2004. He coached in the Red Fox football program for twenty-six years, working as a varsity assistant from 1987 through 2003, and coached basketball and tennis at other times during a thirty-one-year coaching career prior to becoming principal. Burry served as the AAAA Representative on the Executive Committee of the South Carolina High School League from 2014 until 2018, and was recognized by the South Carolina Athletic Administrators Association as the 2018 AAAA Principal of the Year. He was also honored with the 2014-15 Distinguished Principal Award by the Darlington County School District. Burry retired in June 2018 after forty-five years in public education - forty of which were at Hartsville High School - and completed the last fourteen years of his career as principal of the school.

Dr. Burry is a member of First Baptist Church in Hartsville, taught Sunday school for a number of years, and chaired the Board of Deacons on three occasions. He enjoys watching sports, listening to music, reading, writing, kayaking on Black Creek near Hartsville, South Carolina, and spending time in the Blue Ridge Mountains near Saluda, North Carolina. Burry is married to the former Debby Sturgeon of Columbia, South Carolina, who is a retired registered nurse. They have two daughters, Beth and Caye - both graduates of Hartsville High School and Furman University - who are both highly successful in their own personal and professional lives.

People in My Life

There is a story about a boy coming upon a turtle on a fencepost, and the boy wondering about how the turtle got there. We must come to the conclusion, as the boy did, that the turtle had some help ascending to such a lofty perch. The same is true in every person's life story. We all achieve our goals, mark our accomplishments, and owe our stations in life - at least to some degree - to others. If we are fortunate, we have parents who set good examples for us. Others might teach, inspire, and challenge us. There might be those who discipline us when our behavior warrants such action, and who allow us to learn lessons the hard way instead of giving us an easy way out. Hopefully, there are friends in our lives with whom we can share our hopes and dreams, our darkest secrets, our deepest sorrows and our greatest joys, and who love us unconditionally.

I have been blessed to have a number of those people in my life: parents and a spouse, Sunday school teachers, Boy Scout leaders, little league baseball coaches, high school teachers, counselors and coaches, professional colleagues, a former player who is a better man than his old coach will ever be, and a college roommate who became the best friend of my life.

I'll be telling you more about just a few of these folks - there are many others too numerous to write about - in the next few chapters.

Charles and Wilma Burry

Following are the remarks that I made at the dedication of Burry Park, named for my father - Charles E. Burry, Sr. - in Hartsville, South Carolina, on October 2, 2008. These anecdotes illustrate not only the lessons of right living that my parents taught me and my brother and my sister, but also the manner in which they - and especially my dad - impacted the Hartsville community. It is a story of courage and hard work that led to prosperity in the form of an iconic small-town independent bookstore. More importantly, it is a story of giving back.

Good afternoon. On behalf of my mom, my brother Brent, my sister Emily, our spouses and children, and other members of the extended Burry family, I want to express our appreciation to everyone who has contributed to making this event possible. Our family is also deeply grateful that this wonderful addition to our city, which will ultimately honor the service of many deserving people, will be named in memory of our beloved and dedicated husband, father, and grandfather - Charles E. Burry. I am humbled by the opportunity to speak for our family and to tell you a little bit about my dad. The first thing I can tell you is that he never would have dreamed that such a place as this would bear his name, and I doubt that he would have allowed it. As hard as he worked and as much as he contributed to the Hartsville community, I guarantee you that personal recognition never crossed his mind. As he looks down and listens to us today, though, I do think he'll probably allow himself a little smile, but it will be more because he's pleased with the park itself rather than its name. I'll get back to that idea later.

My dad was born and raised in Greenville, South Carolina, and was the second youngest of five children, two boys and three girls. As a teenager he worked as a typesetter for the Baptist Courier, was a Golden Gloves boxer, and graduated from Greenville High School. He went to work for S. H. Kress Company when he was seventeen years old, and then during World War II earned the rank of first lieutenant and qualified as a multi-engine pilot in the Army Air Corp. During that war, both of my parents lost older brothers in Europe. Their brothers, James Burry and Carroll Boyd, were B-17 pilots just like my dad. Today my nephew, Sgt. Duncan Burry, is twenty-three days away from completing his second tour of duty in Iraq with the United States Army's 2nd Stryker Cavalry Regiment. My parents shared in the sacrifices made by the men and women that Tom Brokaw calls "the greatest generation," and they know firsthand what we all owe to the military veterans - of every generation - who are honored by this park.

My dad met Wilma Boyd when he was stationed in basic training at Clemson College, and she was a student at Furman University. They were married on September 3, 1946, and after my dad went back to work for Kress, they spent time in the Carolinas in Fayetteville, Wilmington, and Columbia. He managed his first store in Nevada, Missouri, and he also managed stores in Grand Junction, Colorado, and Biloxi, Mississippi. Our family came to Hartsville in the summer of 1959 when he bought Brown's Variety Store, which was where the Wachovia Bank parking lot is now on North Fifth Street and turned it into the Hartsville 5 & 10. Within a couple of years, he moved the dime store to a new and bigger building on Carolina Avenue, and in 1972, he opened Burry Bookstore next door. He owned and managed both businesses for five years until he sold the dime store so that he could concentrate his efforts on the bookstore. He operated that business with a tremendous amount of success and satisfaction for twenty-two years, finally selling it to my sister, Emily, a couple of years before his death at the age of seventy-two on October 25, 1996. I've just told you, although very briefly, about a few of the things my dad did in his life. That's not what brought us here today, though. The reason we're here today is not what he did, but why he did it.

When I remember my dad, I think of the courage it must have taken to leave a promising career with a national retail chain when he was thirty-five years old, pack up everything that he and my mom owned (including two little boys), pull a U-Haul trailer across four states, and sink his entire life's savings - except for what he spent in Atlanta when our car's transmission went bad - into a small variety store. In the early years, he put every bit of money that he made back into the store, except what we needed for basic necessities and what he gave to the church. I remember some of the lyrics from the song *Sixteen Tons* that we'd hear him singing around the house during those years: "Sixteen tons and what do I get, another day older and deeper in debt." Another memory from the early days was when he'd bring home a box of candy or nuts from the store's candy counter on Saturday night after a sixty or seventy-hour week, and if it had been a good week, it would be a box of cashews. If it had been a bad week, it would be Spanish pea-nuts. And then after that long week of work, he'd go back to the bedroom and finish preparing the Sunday school lesson that he would teach the next morning to a group of high school boys that included guys like Jimmy Bell and Marty Driggers. Another of the life lessons he taught me was when he'd take me with him to play golf. That was back in the days when all the stores downtown closed at one o'clock on Wednesday afternoons. I was about ten years old, and I had four little sawed-off clubs in my canvas golf bag - a driver, two irons, and a putter - and he'd tell me, "Boy, you don't have to hit it far, just keep it straight down the middle." Another thing I remember is how very deter-mined he was that Emily and Brent and I would go to college.

There was never any question about that, due in large part I think - and this may surprise some of you - because he never had the opportunity to do that himself. My dad told me right before he died, though, that it had been one of his dreams to have his own business on the main street in a small town, and how blessed he'd been to bring his family to Hartsville and, in his own words, "not have one regret."

You can tell from what I've said so far that my dad worked awfully hard and spent a lot of hours at the store. That's where our mom came in, and their marriage provided us with a wonderful example of Christian love and solid family values. She fed us and kept us in clean clothes, took care of us when we were sick, got us to school and ball practice on time, made us do our homework, managed to work at the First Baptist Church kindergarten for a number of years, and discipline-wise it was only on rare occasions that she resorted to "Just wait 'til your daddy gets home." She stood faithfully beside her husband for fifty years and made her own significant civic contribution by serving for seventeen years as a member and chair of Hartsville's Planning and Zoning Commission. She, too, worked to ensure the orderly development of Hartsville, protecting its beauty, heritage, and livability, while promoting its modernization and growth. But it's really been in the last twelve years that her children have more clearly seen their mother's incredible strengths and abilities. There is no doubt that mom and dad were a team when it came to the success and good fortune that our family has enjoyed in Hartsville, and this is a great day for Wilma Burry as well.

As you've heard other people say today, my dad worked just as hard for the community - and especially downtown Hartsville - as he did for his family. That's illustrated in a newspaper article from the *Florence Morning News* about him and the bookstore that I have on the wall in my office at school.

The headline reads "Charlie Burry Is at Home in Hartsville," and the article ends with his being quoted as saying, "You have to put something back." On the surface, the idea that you have to put something back might seem to be just an expression of gratitude for what Hartsville had meant to him and his family, and I'm sure that thinking was part of it. There's much more to it than that, though. To really know Charles E. Burry is to know that he had the wisdom and the character to develop a philosophy of business and life that allowed him to combine his life's work as a merchant with his service as a humanitarian. That was one of the keys to his success. Make no mistake about it, he was an astute businessman and knew how to turn a profit. That's how he built two successful businesses from scratch. More importantly, he understood that if he ran a successful business the way he thought it should be done, that it could do more than provide a good living for his family; it could make downtown a better place and serve the community, too. He also understood that his time and efforts in improving the community went hand-in-hand with creating a better business climate. He realized that his efforts in both areas served the purpose of the greater good for everyone, not just himself, and I believe that is the best reason of all for the very existence of Burry Park.

As a Hartsvillian, my dad would be so proud of this today, and so pleased that there is another generation of selfless people who love Hartsville and who are perpetuating his philosophy of doing things for the greater good. Every aspect, civilian or military, of this wonderful addition to our city epitomizes his belief that "You have to put something back." I think I can speak for our entire family when I tell you it is that ideal, above all else and more important than any individual, that is what Burry Park should represent and inspire others to do.

Wilma and Charles Burry

BURRY PARK
IN LOVING MEMORY OF
CHARLES E. BURRY, SR.
(1924 - 1996)
WHOSE HUMANITARIAN EFFORTS AND FORESIGHT
WERE SIGNIFICANT IN SPURRING THE GROWTH AND
DEVELOPMENT OF

Emily, Brent, Wilma, and Charlie Burry

2

Debby Sturgeon Burry

Family is a true blessing of life, and the family of Charles and Wilma Burry was - and continues to be - one of my most special blessings. I was blessed with loving parents who provided me with a Christian home, and who guided me, disciplined me, and set a wonderful example of right living for me. I was blessed with a brother and a sister with whom, although there is six years between each of us, I've shared the special love, comfort, and support that only siblings have in life. When a person grows up in such a home, one naturally begins to think, and hope, and pray for the blessings of a similar home in one's adult life. The foundation of such a home is a partnership based on a romantic love that grows and matures through the years. It is a love that values mutual respect and faithful support, and develops to include infinite patience and deep forgiveness. While I was a student at Furman University, I found Debby Sturgeon, and she became my partner in life - and for life - on August 24, 1974.

Debby was a student at the Greenville General Hospital School of Nursing when we met in 1971 on the Furman campus. After graduating in 1973 as a registered nurse, she worked as a hospital nurse, was a nurse in a doctor's office, and worked as a school nurse (she's smart enough to have become a doctor herself had she been encouraged to set her sights a little higher while she was in high school). After we moved to Hartsville, she enjoyed working for my dad at Burry Bookstore until an ear problem developed into a situation that forced her to become a stay-at-home mom. It was then that I began to know

Debby Sturgeon as someone who makes the best from life's tough circumstances.

Beginning in 1981 and over a period of about two years, Debby had multiple ear surgeries - initially corrective in nature - that resulted in a total loss of hearing in her left ear, necessitated the removal of all balance tubes in that ear, and left her with severe tinnitus, which is commonly known as "ringing in the ears." Those conditions not only ended any possibility of her returning to a nursing career, but also severely impacted her quality of life. The loss of hearing actually became a lesser concern when compared to the dizziness that is exacerbated by travel, and the tinnitus that became almost intolerable as a result of such things as crowd noise at a ball game or even in a restaurant or organ music in church. She once described the tinnitus to me as hearing a combination of monks chanting and the roar of a jet engine in her head. Debby made the best of that situation, though - emotionally and financially - by calling on a skill that she began learning as a child from her grandmother. She became widely known as an expert seamstress, not only for difficult and precise alterations, but also for making bridesmaid dresses, and even wedding gowns. She enjoyed a sense of satisfaction and accomplishment, the rewards of helping others, and making new friends as the customer base of *Exclusively for You* grew. Unfortunately, as her sewing business developed, so did a new health challenge.

Fibromyalgia is a mysterious and cruel disease. Despite years of research that finally led to an official diagnosis, the cause remains unknown, and so does a cure. The symptoms include widespread pain and tenderness to touch, stiffness, fatigue, and exhaustion and are often accompanied by problems with sleep, memory, and thinking processes. Some of the symptoms are similar to those of arthritis, and research indicates that fibromyalgia amplifies painful sensations by affecting the way the brain processes pain signals. Debby began experiencing these symptoms about twenty years ago. This further compromised her quality of life, and on some days is almost debilitating. Most mornings when I left for work, even a hug and a quick kiss were painful for her to tolerate. With her medical background, she has researched fibromyalgia almost obsessively, and she knows more about it than most doctors. She has tried multiple medications and treatments, some of which have intolerable side effects, and none of which have provided any measure of relief. Publicly and among friends, she puts up an incredibly courageous front, and most people never suspect the relentless discomfort and pain that she hides. I have tried to be understanding, and often failed at that, but I don't think anyone who does not actually have fibromyalgia can imagine living with it.

Through these cruel twists of fate and exceptionally difficult circumstances, Debby has given me the family that I prayed for years ago. Most importantly, she's given us the two greatest treasures of our lives - our daughters, Beth and Caye. They are both intelligent, personable, and successful. We love them unconditionally and could not be prouder of who they are, what they are, and how they live their lives. Debby deserves most of the credit for the way they turned out because she raised them while I was away coaching other people's children. While her medical issues forced her to be a stay-at-home mom - and I would not wish those on anyone - that turned out to be a blessing in disguise. She was always there to play with them, teach them to talk and walk, read to them, and watch a million episodes of *Sesame Street* and *Mr. Rogers' Neighborhood* with them. She was there to pick them up from school and help them with their homework. She was there to have the talks with them that only moms can have with daughters. She provided the example that they needed to become the wonderful young women that they are now.

Family is one of the true blessings of life, and my family is a special blessing. I've been a teacher, counselor, coach, and principal, but being a husband and a father are by far the greatest accomplishments of my life. Those accomplishments were partnerships, though, and Debby Sturgeon Burry has been at the center of our family as my partner for more than forty-five years. How could a man be more blessed?

Beth, Debby, and Caye Burry

3

William Jesse Sturgeon

William Jesse Sturgeon was my father-in-law. By example, he also taught his family lessons about right living, how to be a good husband, father, and grandfather, and the benefits of hard work. Following is the eulogy that I was privileged to give at his funeral on January 10, 2009.

I am humbled and honored by the opportunity to speak today. To Donna, Billy, and Patti, and to my dear wife Debby - thank you for trusting me with that responsibility. What do you say in a just few minutes about a man who lived for ninety years? How do you summarize what he did in his life, find words to express the love and devotion that he gave to and received from his family, and tell even just a little bit about what kind of man he was? One of the most meaningful things that has helped us through the last few days has been talking and hearing about his relationships with his grandchildren, and I think that speaks volumes about him. Wendy was the very first apple of his eye, and she called him Sam. Eric and Kelly and Cole knew him as Granddaddy, but his little buddy Chris had some trouble saying that, so he just called him Dey. Laura, I wish your children would have had more of an opportunity to know him; they'd have loved him, too. As I've thought about what to say about William Jesse Sturgeon today, though, I kept coming back to what Beth began calling him when she was little, and what she and Caye have called him all their lives. They called him Big Bill.

The word "big" can mean a lot of different things. People can be big and strong physically, and I won't forget the first time I saw the man that I always respectfully addressed as Mr. Sturgeon. Sometime during the first few months that Debby and I had been dating, she'd told me one of her childhood stories about her daddy breaking a baseball bat over his knee, and I'd been pretty impressed by that. So, as I pulled in the driveway at 2100 Chippewa Drive for the very first time with that story in mind, out from under the hood of a car came a big, broad-shouldered man in a white tank-top t-shirt with these huge, hairy forearms that looked like Popeye's. As I introduced myself and shook his hand and felt the strength in his grip, I decided right then that if Debby and I ever broke up, it wouldn't be at her house while her daddy was around. As I got to know him better, though, I found him to be a quiet man with a very gentle spirit, but at that time I was not going to risk getting on the wrong side of Big Bill.

Mr. Sturgeon also had a huge talent for building and fixing things. I don't know that he ever had to call a carpenter or a painter, a plumber or an electrician, or a roofer or a brick mason; he did all those things himself. He cooked supper for his family when he got home from work in the afternoon, grew his own vegetables, cut and split his own firewood, built his family's first pop-up camper from the wheels up, and Debby and I have furniture and craft items in our house today that he made. He worked at the Post Office and other jobs that required hard, physical labor and were dangerous, breaking his jaw and his back in a couple of different accidents. I've never known a man who was more self-sufficient and independent, or with a stronger work ethic. If you ever needed something built, or repaired, or replaced, you didn't need the Yellow Pages, you just called Big Bill.

People can also be big-hearted, and that's another characteristic that I associate with Mr. Sturgeon. He sure wasn't much of a talker, but his actions were those of a generous and giving man, especially when his family was concerned. I never knew him to be outwardly demonstrative either, but he had a subtle sense of humor and teased his children and grandchildren with these quirky little mannerisms and noises. When he wasn't "checking his eyelids for cracks," it was easy to see the twinkle in his blue eyes that was a sure giveaway to the way he loved his family. Most of the stories that I've heard Donna, Debby, Patti, and Billy share about their childhood have been family oriented - the old house in Eau Claire, camping trips to the beach and the mountains, the way they spent holidays, and other things that they did together. Even after Mrs. Sturgeon died and up until the last few years, it was always understood that Thanksgiving and Christmas for the Sturgeon family would be at Big Bill's house, just as it was for the last time this year. Just as it was Wednesday night when he finally found comfort and peace in the house of the Lord, his family was there . . . with Big Bill.

As Alzheimer's and other physical problems took their toll on Mr. Sturgeon in the last couple of years, I think one of the deepest core values that stayed with him the longest was his devotion to his family. One image of him that sticks in my mind is from 1991 when Mrs. Sturgeon was fighting through the last hours of her life at Lexington Medical Center. He didn't know it, but I watched him for a long time that night, standing there motionless by her bed - a classic picture of a husband's unconditional love and devotion to his wife - never wavering, never leaving. In these last couple of years when I'd see him, he had begun to repeat the same stories to me, usually about his military service; he was very proud of that. But every time before he finished and would get quiet again, he would always talk about his marriage, and each time he would use these exact same words: "My wife died in 1991. We were married for forty-six years." And he'd pause, and then he would say, "I loved my wife dearly."

The last couple of years have been really difficult for Mr. Sturgeon, and especially for Donna as well. He hasn't been the man that he used to be in a long time, and her efforts in caring for him have been the ultimate in love and devotion. I think we all know that he's been "ready Freddy" for his trip to Heaven for quite some time. But now that those tough times are behind him, and behind us, let's do our best to forget all that. That's not who Big Bill was. Let's remember and celebrate and cherish the better times we had with a good, good man who was a wonderful husband, father, and grandfather.

He loved us, and we loved him . . . dearly.

Beth, Big Bill, and Caye

Tim Watson

Tim Watson was my basketball coach during my senior year of high school. During the eight years that began in 1968, he and Mrs. Watson became a second set of parents to me. When I got married in August 1974, Coach Watson was a groomsman, and they unofficially adopted my wife, Debby. Mrs. Watson began to teach her how to be a coach's wife, and Debby developed a special relationship with them as well. Nearly forty years later, on July 8, 2007, it became one of the great responsibilities and privileges of my life to give the eulogy at my coach's funeral. My words are in the paragraphs that follow.

The Scripture that I'd like for you to think about again today - just as we did about six years ago at Coach Watson's ordination as a minister - comes from John 20:21-22, when Jesus, after His crucifixion, appeared to the disciples behind locked doors: "Again Jesus said, 'Peace be with you! As the Father has sent me, I am sending you.' And with that He breathed on them and said, 'receive the Holy Spirit.'"

Many of you know that those verses and that hymn, *Breathe on Me*, have a special story connected with them. In July of 2000 when Coach Watson's recovery from heart surgery was complicated by a stroke, he became desperate one night for breath - he said he just couldn't breathe. He prayed for the Holy Spirit to breathe on him and help him, and he asked Aubrey Floyd to pray the same prayer and to sing the hymn *Breathe on Me* to him. Well, I'm not sure that Aubrey did such a good job singing, as a matter of fact the story goes that he had to hum a good part of it because he couldn't remember all the words. But he must have done a lot better job praying, because Coach Watson made it through that crisis, and I think that event was a big part of his call to the ministry back in the spring of 2001. I am deeply honored to be here today to tell you how my coach - through the Holy Spirit - breathed on me.

Giving the eulogy for Coach Tim Watson is one of the greatest privileges and one of the most awesome responsibilities of my life, and I'd like to thank his family for allowing me to speak. Others of you are probably wondering who I am, and what my connection is. I'm the principal at Hartsville High School now, but Coach Watson came into my life thirty-nine years ago when he became the basketball coach at Hartsville High School. I played for him during my senior season and then left to go off to college. Four years later I was looking for a start in the coaching profession, and he helped me get my first job - teaching physical education at the South Carolina School for Boys in Florence - where Mrs. Watson was teaching music. Coach Watson had just been named as the head men's basketball coach at Francis Marion College, and he allowed me to work with him that season as a graduate assistant coach. We were there for three years together, and then our professional careers took us in different directions. I was single during that first year in Florence, and I spent more time at the Watsons' house than I did my own place at Gregg Apartments. I became a big brother to their children, Jay and JoEllyn, and I even sat with them in church. I think they were pretty relieved when I finally got married, realizing that would get me out of their house some and cut down on their grocery bill. A couple of years earlier Coach Watson had really tried to help me out in the romance department when I introduced my bride-to-be to him, and the first thing he said - right in front of her - was "What kind of seeing-eye dog does she have, Burry?" And when Mrs. Watson died the week after Thanksgiving in 2003, he said the same thing he said every time Debby and I visited: "Cha(r)lie, I don't know how an ugly rascal like you could get so lucky." And then I answered the same way I always did - telling him that I just looked for a girl like Mrs. Watson until I finally found one, and I figured if somebody like him could get that lucky, maybe I could, too.

So, why me? Why, right before he went to the operating room for that heart surgery seven years ago, did he completely baffle Mrs. Watson by telling her that he wanted Charlie Burry to do his eulogy, and then remind me of that nearly every time I saw him from then on? Why is there a voice speaking today from almost forty years ago? Why do I have the honor today of representing the hundreds of boys he coached and loved, and who loved him? How in the world can I put into a few words what he has meant to so many people? What have I gotten myself into?

That's exactly the same thought I had when Coach Watson dropped by my daddy's dime store to introduce himself one summer day in 1968, wearing a crew cut and looking like he'd come straight off Parris Island. What have I gotten myself into? And it's the same thought I had when he met with our basketball team for the first time, and - to make a point about playing tough defense - spit his false front teeth out right there on the gym floor and said with a gap-toothed snarl, "Boys, that's what I mean when I say nobody shoots a layup against us without paying the price." What have I gotten myself into? And it's the very same thought I had during that first pre-season conditioning session when he ran us so much and so hard that I threw up and my legs were so rubbery that I could barely stand. What have I gotten myself into?

Well, I'll tell you what I got myself into. I got to play for and coach with a man who was honored by the South Carolina Athletic Coaches Association by being selected as a head coach in the North-South All-Star Game in both basketball and baseball, and who was a great football coach as well. I got myself into a friendship with a man that I grew to love like a second father. I got myself into a thirty-one-year coaching career because I admired a man so much that I wanted to be just like him, and to mean to other boys what he meant to me. I got myself into a great marriage because I wanted a wife and family just like he had. And most importantly, I got myself into a deeper Christian commitment because I wanted to be a man of strong faith, just like he was. What did I get myself into? I got myself into a wonderful relationship that began with a great love for athletics and coaching, but developed into so much more - a love for my coach and all he stood for that made me a better man, a better husband, a better father, and a better child of God. Most of you got yourselves into the same thing when he became your coach, or colleague, or Sunday school teacher, or your friend, because Coach Watson meant those same things to you.

Today we can put away the basketballs, pack up the bats, and take off the pads. Coach Watson has gone on to his eternal reward with our Heavenly Father, and he's walking the grassy fields and the polished hardwood in Heaven. He and Joanne are together again even though I don't believe those perfect soul mates have ever really been apart. He's seen Billy Hodge again by now, and the next time he sees me, my coach isn't going to be in a wheelchair or in bed. He's going to greet me by picking me up almost off my feet with that big bear hug of his, just like he used to. He's probably been really surprised by now to learn that in Heaven, even the referees and umpires are perfect. And anyway, once you get to Heaven, there aren't any technical fouls, and you can't get tossed out.

But Coach Watson has an everlasting life here on earth, too. He'll always be a part of me, and the hundreds of other boys he coached at Hanahan and Berkeley, in Hartsville, Florence, Darlington, and Pamplico. The things he taught us about "hustle, scrap, and a keen desire to win" are part of our work ethic, and others see those things in us. His marriage and family life showed us how that's supposed to be done, and we're showing our children how to do it. His ministry and contributions to his church have been tremendous examples of Christian faith and service, and have inspired others to do likewise. There's not a day that goes by when I don't recall, consciously or subconsciously, something that he taught me about coaching, or work, or life, or being a Christian. Coach Watson coached us to win in basketball, and football, and baseball. More important than all that though, is this: he coached us to win in the game of life. And by doing that . . . by coaching us to win in the game of life . . . He breathed on them . . . and said, "receive the Holy Spirit."

Thanks be to God for the life of Tim Watson, and everything he has meant to all of us who called him Coach. Amen, and peace be with you.

Tim Watson

5

Ray Petty

It is not unusual for a young person to struggle with determining a career goal. When I graduated from Hartsville High School in 1969, however, I knew what I wanted to do with my life. I wanted to be a high school guidance counselor and a coach because I wanted to be like Ray Petty.

I became aware of Coach Petty when I was eight or nine years old, and our family lived on Oak Avenue in Hartsville. The Petty family lived just a few houses down the street from our house on the corner of Oak Avenue and Barefoot Street. I knew that Coach Petty was the varsity baseball coach at Hartsville High School and that he also coached the junior varsity football team. My first memory of him is seeing him in his front yard catching for one of his team's baseball pitchers - Dennis Adams, I believe. Little did I know then that the native of Buffalo, South Carolina, had pitched professionally himself before becoming a high school teacher and coach. During their early years in Hartsville, Coach Petty and his wife, Francis, were in the process of becoming the proud parents of four girls - Susan, Beth, Kerry and Amy. They eventually built their current residence just a short distance away from Oak and Barefoot on what was then Miller Road, but is now known as Fourteenth Street. By the time I was a student at Hartsville High School, Coach Petty had given up coaching and become Mr. Petty, one of the school's guidance counselors.

As it happened, Mr. Petty became my guidance counselor during my junior and senior years in high school. I went into that relationship knowing of his reputation as a tough, but fair, coach who was greatly respected by his players and loved by all of his students. I knew of his Christian faith and that he lived his life according to those high standards. I knew that he loved his wife and children and that he was the kind of husband and father that Francis and their girls loved back in equal measure. I saw first-hand the kind of job that Mr. Petty did, and I admired the manner in which he did it. So, early in my freshman year when I met with my academic advisor at Furman, Dr. James Smart, I told him that I wanted to be a high school guidance counselor and coach. Dr. Smart did some research on the requirements to become certified as a school counselor, we met again to develop a plan, and I declared a history major. My intention was to become another Ray Petty - I even began losing my hair so that our physical resemblance might be greater.

Eighteen years after that meeting with Dr. Smart, and after fourteen years of teaching and coaching, I became a member of the Hartsville High School guidance department. The other members of the department during that 1987-88 school year were Juanita McFarland, Paula Terry, and . . . Ray Petty. What a tremendous experience it was for me, personally and professionally, to become a colleague with my old high school guidance counselor and have him mentor me for three years before he retired. I watched and listened closely as he worked with his students, and I learned to be attentive and compassionate. I saw him meet his students' academic and personal needs, and gain their respect and affection. My own respect and love for him became even greater.

In his retirement, he played more tennis, watched more TV movies, and continued his service to his church. As the years passed by, he also became a front-row fixture at the softball field when his granddaughters played for the Red Foxes. He regularly attended our annual retired teachers' luncheons at which his unmistakably shrill whistle got everyone's attention for the blessing that he was usually asked to give. And he continued his role as the patriarch of the ever-growing Petty clan.

While we didn't see as much of him after his retirement, I continued to witness the love that his former players and students had for him, his exemplary leadership as a father, and especially the steadfast love that he possessed for Francis. That was clearly evident to me one afternoon at Kelleytown Stadium, which was the site for that year's *Relay for Life* fundraising event for fighting cancer. He and Francis were there that day because she is a cancer survivor. As the afternoon wore on, Mr. Petty and I were standing around talking, catching up, and he was probably telling me about winning his latest tennis match. Suddenly in mid-sentence, he was gone - off like a shot - and was jogging across the field. It took me a few seconds to figure out what had caused him to leave so abruptly, and then I understood. The cancer survivors' lap to begin the event had just started, and Francis was walking that lap. In a moment, Mr. Petty was there at her side, on the grass just off the track, and walking about a half step behind her left shoulder. And he stayed there with her, stride for stride, all the way around the track. My thought as I watched them, that I have remembered in all the years since, was about how symbolic that was - a perfect example of a man's steadfast love for his wife in their walk through life together. Watching their walk that day taught me to be a better husband and father.

Ray Petty has walked the walk in every part of his life. One of my greatest hopes is that he might see - through my own walk in a career in education - how he has paid those ideals forward.

Charlie Burry and Ray Petty

Dr. Charlie Burry, Jr.

6

Hubert Twitty

Hubert Twitty was my Dixie Youth League baseball coach for four years (1960-64) beginning when I was eight years old. Our team was sponsored by the local Exchange Civic Club, and we competed in Hartsville's National League with three teams sponsored by the Civitan, Lions, and Rotary Clubs. The American League teams were Hal's Esso, Moose, Sonoco, and Pee Dee Poultry. We played on a manicured diamond behind Carolina Elementary School that was unusual because of its grass (not clay) infield. Dixie Youth baseball was such a big deal in town that many of the games were broadcast over the local radio station, WHSC. Many of the men who managed the teams during those years worked at Sonoco Products Company. They were good men who knew baseball and kept the game in the proper perspective for the young boys whom they were coaching. They volunteered their time, and came to practice after they got off work to teach us how to field, throw, hit, and run the bases. Today, most men who played little league baseball during the 1950s and 1960s in Hartsville have fond memories of those times and recall their coaches with great respect. While Hubert Twitty certainly fits well in that category, he became truly legendary in youth baseball circles in Hartsville and in South Carolina. His teams always won, and his ageless legacy was firmly established when he coached a group of Hartsville National All-Stars to the 1967 Dixie Youth World Series Championship in Red Bank, Tennessee. It was one of the great good fortunes of my life when Hubert Twitty saw enough potential in me at tryouts as an eight-year-old to draft me to play on his Exchange team.

While Mr. Twitty established an exceptional record, he went about his coaching in a very unassuming manner. He arrived at practice in his work clothes, his physical presence tall and lanky, and his ball cap perched on the back of his head. None of us knew it at the time, but I had a very credible Hartsville old-timer tell me a few years ago that "Hubert Twitty was probably the best all-around athlete to ever come through Hartsville High School." While he was probably still in his early forties when he coached our team, his prowess as a ballplayer was shown only by an easy and fluid motion as he pitched batting practice and hit fly balls and grounders to us. He taught us the fundamentals of the game - to keep our eye on the ball and swing level, to get behind ground balls and stay down on them, to catch fly balls with both hands, and to never question an umpire's call. He did all of this in a low-key manner, and I can't ever recall hearing him raise his voice. Seeing him smile when you got on base, scored, or made a good play in the field made a young boy's heart smile, too. And if anyone made a poor play, Mr. Twitty might drop his head for just a brief moment, but then you saw nothing but a positive expression - never disappointment - on his face as he quickly looked back up, encouraging you to do better next time. I can see him in my mind's eye now, sitting by the corner of the dugout on a cement block, holding a bat ready to give the bunt or the steal sign. Just his calm presence would be saying "Son, you can do this," even when I was batting against guys like "Wild Bill" Shelley or Jimmy "Two-Ton" Lunn. If you haven't figured it out by now, I grew to love Hubert Twitty.

As a baseball coach, Mr. Twitty was one of my real-life boyhood heroes and someone that I wanted to emulate. I also saw him on Sundays throughout the year as he and his family attended First Baptist Church, so he provided a Christian example for me as well. As you also might have guessed by now, Mr. Twitty is one of the reasons that I wanted to become a coach. Little did I know that about fifteen years after he coached me, during my first year as the head boys' varsity basketball coach at Hartsville High School, I would have one of the most awesome responsibilities of my career. I would have the opportunity to coach my coach's son, Randy, who was a senior that year. Mr. Twitty was graciously supportive during that season. We talked occasionally, and he offered some advice, but he never put any pressure on a young coach that I wasn't already putting on myself. Today, Randy Twitty is a successful baseball coach himself at Sumter High School and has a wonderful family. We see each other at ball games and other events from time to time, and he recently visited our house to give me two pictures of his dad's teams on which I played. He also gave me copies of our team's stat sheets - in his dad's own handwriting - from the 1963 and 1964 seasons. After a close examination of my batting averages, he allowed that I "might have been a pretty good player." I consider Randy to be a very good friend, and I believe the feeling is mutual. I hope that means I pleased his dad.

Youth baseball is still very popular in Hartsville, has won more championships, and has provided a strong foundation for a successful program at Hartsville High School. Other men have come along to provide opportunities for youngsters to learn and respect the game, just as we did. They have created their own memories and carved their own places in the culture and history of Hartsville's boys of summer. There will always be a special bond and fellowship, though, among those of us who were blessed to be one of "Hubert Twitty's boys."

Hubert Twitty

Dr. Charlie Burry, Jr.

7

J. T. Alford

My scoutmaster during the first few years that I was in Boy Scout Troop 522 in Hartsville was J. T. Alford. We were a newly organized troop when I joined after being in Cub Scouts, and we did not have a scout hut for our meetings like some of the more established troops. West Hartsville Baptist Church sponsored our troop, and we met in the basement boiler room at the rear of the church building. At different times, Wilmont Berry, R. L. Clanton, Marion Humphries, Jim Rose, Orell Smith, Milton Turnage, and others assisted Mr. Alford. Jimmy Gregory was also an assistant scoutmaster, and he eventually became scoutmaster of Troop 522. Most of the neighborhood boys close to my age made up the membership of the troop. We enjoyed being mentored by all of the men who helped our troop, and we respected the different skills and knowledge that each of them shared with us. Mr. Alford was special, though, and he became one of the most impactful men in my life. I'll try to tell you why.

During my formative years as a young boy and in my early teenage years, scouting was one of the best activities in which I participated. We learned the twelve points of the Scout Law, the Scout Motto, and the Scout Oath. We not only memorized and recited these tenets at every meeting, but we discussed their meanings and life-applications. Progression through the various Boy Scout ranks was encouraged by involvement in projects that were also character lessons. Moving through the ranks required the earning of merit badges which taught a wide variety of specialized skills, such as archery, cooking, electricity, first aid, and swimming. Earning twenty-one merit badges from different categories was the main requirement for achieving Boy Scout's highest rank of Eagle Scout. I eventually became an Eagle Scout, probably due more to my father's persistent encouragement than my own initiative, but I am proud of that accomplishment. In recent years, rarely have I had occasion to talk about my scouting experience in everyday conversation, but when I do, mention of the Eagle Scout rank never fails to bring an acknowledgement of respect, especially when speaking with someone who was also involved in Boy Scouts. Scouting taught life lessons that built good character, and no one better epitomized that than J. T. Alford.

The highlight of the scouting experience for us was camping trips. Mr. Alford's house on Miller Road (Fourteenth Street) had a large wooded area behind it. Mr. Alford was an expert outdoorsman although he didn't hunt. He knew the name of every tree and plant imaginable, and he frequently hiked in those woods. When we camped there, not only did we enjoy sleeping in tents and cooking over a campfire, but those woods were his classroom for the study of nature and the outdoors. A special treat was toasting marshmallows and listening to a ghost story that one of the men always seemed to be able to conjure up. And, yes, we did do some singing around the campfire. We also traveled to other areas for camping, and an annual camporee in which the troops competed against each other in different camping skills was always eagerly anticipated. Mr. Alford always led with the quiet confidence that was one of the trademarks of his personality. He was not a tall man, but he was stocky and strong, barrel-chested, with big forearms and thick wrists. He could run, too, and would challenge us to races around the outside of the church building. He always won, laughing as he eased up at the end of the lap. What I remember most about him, though, was his voice. It was deep with a distinctive mellow tone, and no matter how much we tried his patience, it was always pleasant and encouraging. I could hear that voice today and recognize it instantly as his.

Some years after my scouting experience, Mr. Alford and his wife, Betty, moved next door to our house on Miller Road Circle (now Edgewood Drive), and my family cultivated and enjoyed a close relationship with them. They were wonderful neighbors, and our dog - a beagle named Scamp - wore a path in the grass between our houses because they fed him, too. As time passed and I became heavily involved in my career, I saw less and less of the Alfords. Finally, one day not many months after my father died, I was driving into Magnolia Cemetery to visit his grave. In the distance I saw a man walking with an unmistakably familiar stride. As the man approached my truck, I stopped and rolled down the window, and he looked a bit alarmed before I said, "Mr. Alford, I'm Charlie Burry." His face broke into a smile, and that deep, mellow voice once again said, "Well, hello friend." We had a nice reunion that day, and I saw him several other times on his walks though the cemetery, and we always had time for a chat.

Mr. Alford passed away in June 2003 leaving a legacy of young boys who admired him, and who - later in life as grown men - fully realized what he meant to them. He lived by the Scout Laws without even trying. That was just natural to him. He enjoyed and respected God's beautiful world and taught others to do the same. He's hiked the woods in Heaven for a number of years now, naming all the trees and plants and flowers as he passes by. I want to walk with him again one day to be sure he knows how much he meant to me, and how much I loved him. I still do. Scout's Honor.

J. T. Alford

Dr. Charlie Burry, Jr.

8

Bucky Goudelock

One of my Sunday school teachers at First Baptist Church when I was growing up was Mr. Bucky Goudelock. He and his wife, Nelle, were faithful members of the church, serving in a variety of ways for many years. They were perfect examples of folks who were at church every time the doors opened. Mr. Goudelock worked at Sonoco Products Company and was a Clemson alumnus and a huge supporter of Tiger athletics. He played on the Clemson tennis team during his time there, was an exceptional player for many years afterward, and was known for a long time as one of the best tennis players in Hartsville. My memories of him as a Sunday school teacher are that we all liked him very much although he did have a bit of a gruff voice. That voice was tempered, though, by a wry sense of humor that you saw when the corner of his mouth turned up just a bit. As I grew older, I continued to see a lot of him, not only at church, but at the Prestwood Club tennis courts because I played on the high school tennis team with his son, George. George was an outstanding player as well, and even though he attended Erskine College on a tennis scholarship and graduated there, he inherited his dad's love for the Clemson Tigers. At some point in my adult life, Mr. Goudelock became "Buck" to me - which was what most people called him - and that went against my upbringing of always referring to my elders as "Mr." and "Mrs." I think that "Buck" is what his grandchildren called him, though, and I guess it reflected my level of comfort in our relationship. Some of my best memories as an adult of times with Buck and George are of attending Clemson football games.

Let's change gears at this point to a Sunday school lesson that I was teaching to a group of fifth and sixth graders in June 2002. The lesson was on perseverance, the Scripture was about Samuel's birth to Hannah as God's answer to her prayers, and the memory verse was from the first chapter of James where he says that our perseverance through tough times and difficulties makes us mature and complete. As a means of explaining this, I used several quotes, one of them being from my coaching repertoire: "Tough times don't last. Tough people do." Then, we started talking about what makes people tough - personality, the way they grow up, the kind of work they do, and so forth. But then we talked about the fact that there are some things in life that are so hard to deal with that no matter how tough people are, they still need some help with it. And then the key question in the lesson was "Where can we get that help?" And the answer, obviously, was that the toughness, the patience, the persistence - whatever it takes to overcome the greatest difficulty - that attitude is one of the fruits of the Spirit. People can persevere in life's ultimate tests because of their faith in God.

A teacher always needs an example to illustrate the major point of the lesson, and it was then that I told those fifth and sixth graders about one of the most faithful men I knew and his wife. A man and his wife who had been tested far beyond what any of us would likely experience and yet continued to be wonderful Christian examples in our church and community, never questioning God's love and goodness and plan for their lives even during the toughest times. I told those boys and girls that if they ever wanted to see an absolutely perfect example of the kind of perseverance that can be built through a person's faith in God, that he sat right there in our church every Sunday morning. That all they needed to do was just take a look over to the right-hand side of the sanctuary at Mr. Bucky Goudelock and his wife, Nelle . . . two of the most gracious, and faithful - and toughest - people I knew.

The rest of the story that will make your understanding of that Sunday school lesson complete is this. When he was seventy-three years old, Bucky Goudelock suffered a stroke that resulted in both of his legs being amputated just above his knees. A man who still led an active life suddenly was physically crippled. A man who still loved to play tennis spent the rest of his life in a wheelchair. A man and his wife who had every right to be bitter about life's circumstances and feel sorry for themselves remained faithful Christians, spiritually whole and strong every step of the way. For most of those Clemson games we attended, George drove a van that was equipped to handle Buck's physical limitations, and we sat with him in a handicapped section. The van was bought with donations from men who Buck had taught as boys in Sunday school and Royal Ambassador's, and others who had worked with him at Sonoco - just one indication of how well-respected and loved he was. I heard a lot of stories on those trips about legendary figures in Clemson's athletic history whom Buck knew personally. He was a big supporter of Hartsville High School athletics, too, but no longer attended our football games. As an assistant coach, I had videotapes of our games, and every Monday night of the season after practice I dropped by Buck and Nelle's house to bring him a tape of the previous week's game. He liked that because the game tape didn't have any lag time between plays, there were obviously no commercial time-outs, and he could watch a game in less than an hour even with rewinding and watching the outstanding plays several times. We'd talk about sports and church and life, and it was one of the great pleasures and privileges of my life to be able to visit with Buck and Nelle.

Bucky Goudelock taught me Sunday school lessons, but he taught me by example a lot more about living a Christian life. He set an example of toughness and perseverance that I will never forget. During the years that I was principal of Hartsville

High School, part of my weekday routine was to set my alarm for a 4:30 AM workout. That wasn't easy to do, especially if I'd had to work late the night before, and there were many days when I hated the sound of that alarm. But then I would open my eyes, lie there for a moment, and think, "I'll bet Buck would love to be able swing his legs over the side of the bed and feel his feet hit the floor." That was all the motivation I needed to remind me of what a blessing good health is, and how fortunate I was to have had Bucky Goudelock in my life to teach me to keep my feet on solid ground.

Bucky Goudelock

9

Kaye McElveen

Kaye McElveen has been a part of my life as a teacher, colleague, boss, and friend for nearly as long as I can remember. I've had a lot of good people touch my life in wonderful ways personally and professionally, and you've met some of them in the earlier chapters of this book. But I don't know that there's anyone who has done that for as long and in as many ways as she has. It started in junior high school with a schoolboy crush (along with every other boy in the eighth grade) on that new, drop-dead gorgeous South Carolina History teacher and continued (although in a more appropriate manner) for more than fifty years. She is a part of my high school memories, too, and at some point in time she transitioned from being a teacher to a guidance counselor. When I came back to Hartsville High School as a teacher and coach in 1978, it didn't take me long to figure out that if I couldn't be the next John Wooden or Dean Smith, then I wanted to join her and Ray Petty in the guidance department one day. Seeing the way that she and the other counselors worked together, helped people, and had fun doing it just made me even more sure that was what I wanted to do.

That goal really began to take shape when I was fired after seven years as the boys' varsity basketball coach in the spring of 1985. I was lost professionally and personally, couldn't get a basketball job at another school, and didn't know who I was if I wasn't a basketball coach. I had to continue to provide for my family, though, and I stayed at Hartsville High School as a social studies teacher. It was at that point that a hurt, mixed-up young coach began to take advantage of free therapy sessions in the guidance department, most of them in Kaye McElveen's office. One of the first questions she asked me was "What do you need to do to get certified as a guidance counselor?" I contacted the State Department of Education and obtained a worksheet outlining the twenty-four hours of graduate credit that I would need to meet those requirements. Then came even more advice and encouragement while I completed those graduate courses over a two-year period. Now, with the benefit of more experience to aid my perspective on those days, I know that there must have been many times when she was busy and hated to see me come to her door, but she always invited me in and listened to me.

If you've never believed that God's timing is everything, this is what happened next. In the spring of 1987, just as I was finishing the last course that I needed to become certified as a guidance counselor, Kaye McElveen was appointed as an assistant principal at Hartsville Junior High School. The vacancy in the Hartsville High School guidance department was advertised, and I quickly applied. Obviously, by that time I had some pretty good references from that department, and I'm fairly sure that Dr. McElveen lobbied for me with Dr. Duke Hucks, who was principal. A few weeks later Dr. Hucks called me into his office and told me that if I'd promise not to spend too much time talking sports with Ray Petty, he would recommend me for the position. I told Dr. Hucks that we could make that work. At about the same time, head football coach Lewis Lineberger was looking for a varsity assistant coach, and he hired me to coach offensive and defensive backs. That began what was probably the happiest seventeen years of my career in education. I had what I still describe today as the best job in the school. It all came together because of Kaye McElveen.

A couple of years later, being a glutton for punishment, I began working on my doctoral degree at the University of

South Carolina. I made good progress through that program, but as I reached the end of my coursework and prepared to begin work on my dissertation, one of the four members of my doctoral committee left USC. I needed a replacement, and the regulations specified that as long as three members of a doctoral committee were USC professors, that there could be one outside member if that person held a doctoral degree. That being the case, the paths of Charlie Burry and Dr. Kaye McElveen crossed again, and she agreed to join my committee. Part of her responsibilities in that role included reading my dissertation, and there is no greater test of a friendship than to plow through something like that.

But I wasn't done with Dr. Kaye McElveen, or to put it more accurately, she wasn't done with me. In 1995 she became my boss when she was named principal of Hartsville High School. That began a seven-year period of working for someone who cared passionately about educating young people, realized as a professional the value of her faculty and staff, and with whom I had a very special, long-term bond. She would summon me to her office occasionally to ask for information or my thoughts on a situation. I would offer my input, and she would sometimes attempt to pin me down on what my decision might be if I were principal. As I would get up to walk out the door, I'd smile and say, "That's why you're making the big bucks." At that time, I never dreamed that in 2004 I'd be sitting in the big chair on the other side of the desk facing similar decisions.

One of the things I've admired most about Kaye McElveen is her love for Hartsville and Hartsville High School. I'll never forget what she would tell me during some of the times that I interviewed for other positions at other schools. She'd say, "Charlie, we're Red Foxes, and Hartsville will always be part of us." She is one of that loyal guard who grew up in Hartsville and then came back full circle to make it a better place by helping young people. There can be no greater calling and contribution than what she did and accomplished so well in our hometown. There is absolutely no one who has meant more to me in my professional career than Kaye McElveen. We are, and we will always be . . . Red Foxes.

Kaye McElveen, Duke Hucks, and Charlie Burry

10

Danny Nicholson

I was Danny Nicholson's basketball coach during his junior and senior years in high school. He was a very good player, coachable and conscientious about getting better, and was a great teammate. His involvement in pre-season conditioning for high school basketball evolved into an outstanding college career in track as a distance runner and paid for his education at Charleston Southern University (then known as Baptist College of Charleston). It was a pleasure to coach Danny, and I knew that his character and values would undoubtedly provide a solid foundation for success in whatever career he chose to pursue. We didn't have winning records during either of those seasons, but I got a letter from Danny a couple of years after he graduated from Hartsville High School that affirmed some of the ideas about attitude, character, and persistence that we were trying to instill in our basketball program. He mentioned that I'd coached him in basketball, but that I'd coached him in the game of life as well. That letter meant the world to me, and I still have it today. It was at that point in my coaching career that one of my former players began coaching me.

In 1984 Danny began a thirty-three-year career in higher education that primarily involved administrative duties and fundraising. He served in those capacities at Charleston Southern University, Coker University, the Medical University of South Carolina, Coastal Carolina University, Glenville State College, Carson-Newman University, and Winthrop University. In those roles, his purpose, passion, and personality fueled fundraising campaigns that raised over one hundred million dollars.

During those years, his musical talent evolved as he became a songwriter, and he completed four original albums. Proceeds from sales of those albums were used to support children's ministries and mission work. He also wrote poetry and in 2019 became a published author with the debut of his autobiography, *My Own Backyard*, which contains many of his songs, poems, and stories. Danny has now found the true calling in his life as president of the Connie Maxwell Children's Home in Greenwood, South Carolina. No matter where he was on his career journey, though, he would still find time occasionally to come home to Hartsville to speak at churches, civic clubs, and special events. Every time that I heard him give his testimony and sing, my heart just burst with pride over the man and witness for Christ that he had become. My former player continued to coach his old coach.

Danny also became involved with Jamie Morphis in the Darlington County Education Foundation (DCEF) during the time he was in Hartsville and working at Coker. DCEF is an organization whose purpose is to provide financial support for the Darlington County School District. For a number of years, DCEF also hosted a pig pickin' at the Darlington Raceway for all employees of the school district. A highlight of the event was the presentation of *Making a Difference* awards to people who had made significant contributions to their schools or the school district. When I arrived at the event in October 2003, I was pleased to learn that Danny Nicholson would be the keynote speaker for the presentation of the awards. Little did I know that my former player was going to coach me again that afternoon.

Here's how that happened. My dad passed away in October 1996. One of my most prized possessions is a hand-written letter from him to our oldest daughter, Beth, for her thirteenth birthday in 1992. While my dad gave the letter to my wife and me not long after he wrote it, his instructions were to give it to Beth when she had her first child. The letter is about a Sunday school lesson that he taught on November 11, 1979 - the morning that Beth was born. As a means of illustrating the lesson, my dad used some passages from a book by Margery Williams entitled *The Velveteen Rabbit*. He used a conversation between two toys in a child's playroom - the Velveteen Rabbit and the Skin Horse - about how a toy becomes loved as an analogy to illustrate how people are saved by God's love through Jesus Christ. I'd read that letter a number of times over the years since my dad gave it to us, especially after his death, and practically had the passages from *The Velveteen Rabbit* memorized.

Danny started speaking that day and about two minutes into his remarks, I nearly fell out of my chair. I was stunned, because he was using - as a means of illustrating his main point - the exact same passage from *The Velveteen Rabbit* that my dad had used in his letter to Beth eleven years earlier. As I recovered a bit, I found myself - with tears in my eyes - whispering the lines from the book with Danny as he read them to the audience. After the event concluded, I found Danny in the crowd, shook his hand, hugged him and said, "You don't have time for me to explain right now, but our stars have crossed again. I'll write to you and tell you about it." That night I wrote Danny a letter telling him the story that I just told you, and I included a copy of my dad's letter when I mailed it. My former player had coached his old coach again.

In most of the player-coach relationships in my life where I've been the player, it's been my ambition to try to measure up to the standards set by my coaches (such as Tim Watson and Hubert Twitty). Out of respect, I always called all of them Coach, even in my adult life. Danny Nicholson, my former player, is a better man and servant of God than I will ever hope to be. He always calls me Coach, and he says that he loves to do that. Seems like it ought to be the other way around.

Randy Twitty, Brooks Shumake, Charlie Burry, and Danny Nicholson

Rusty Harter

I met Rusty Harter during the fall of our junior year at Furman University at a Kappa Alpha fraternity rush party. He had just transferred to Furman and was exploring the possibility of joining a fraternity. He was offered a KA bid, accepted, and became one of my fraternity brothers. He would become much more. Rusty and I discovered that we both enjoyed basketball, plotting the flight trajectory of water balloons, and Rainbow Drive-In jumbo cheeseburgers. We became such good friends that we decided to room together during our senior year.

As his roommate on the third floor of Geer Hall, it did not take me long to determine that Rusty Harter was a slob. I was not the best housekeeper in the world, but in comparison to him, I was like Felix Unger (Jack Lemmon) in *The Odd Couple* and later, *Grumpy Old Men*. Rusty, of course, was Oscar Madison (Walter Matthau). We had a linen service that would supply us with fresh bedsheets and towels weekly, and all you had to do was deliver the dirty ones to the truck parked at the curb beside the dorm and pick up clean ones. Rusty did business with them twice a year, once at the beginning of the school year and then again in January. I'm sure that when he turned his sheets in after five months, the linen service company just burned them. He took his dress shirts to the cleaners on a similar schedule. By December, there would be shirts at the bottom of a pile in his closet that he had not been cleaned since September. When he ran out of shirts after three or four weeks, he just turned the pile over and started over again. That pile of shirts emitted such a foul odor that I once threw them down the trash chute.

I don't think he ever wore socks. Rusty had an 8:00 AM Latin class during winter term that year. It took eight minutes to walk from Geer Hall to his classroom. He set his alarm for 7:50 every morning, rolled out of bed, pulled on a pair of corduroy pants, put a wool sport coat on over the white t-shirt that he'd slept in, and stumbled off to class. His long hair was fairly normal since nobody got haircuts very often in 1973. So, how did we make it through that year and actually become even better friends? I suppose it can be described as the odd couple phenomenon.

Our love for the game of basketball was also an interesting relationship. We spent probably too many hours in Alley Gym, just a short walk from our dorm, playing one-on-one, pick-up games, and HORSE. We argue to this day about who was (and is) the better shooter, and we occasionally have to find a ball and a goal in a driveway so that I can remind him. Rusty was a huge Pistol Pete Maravich fan, and my favorite player - being a Boston Celtic fan - was John Havlicek. Many of our one-on-one games were Hondo against The Pistol, and the recent SEC Storied documentary on Pete Maravich brought back many memories for both of us. Pistol Pete was playing for the Atlanta Hawks during our time at Furman, and we made several trips to Atlanta when the Celtics were in town.

The strangest twist in our basketball one-upmanship occurred on two successive nights. We were playing ball on a Saturday afternoon, and Rusty went down with a sprained ankle. By the next morning he was on crutches, and I was giving him an unmercifully hard time about being such a klutz and spraining his ankle. I went back to the gym to play ball Sunday night, and karma became my opponent. By the time I hobbled back to our room on my own sprained ankle, the word had already reached Rusty, and he was ready for me with the same stream of insults that I'd been giving him twelve hours earlier. So, when we both headed to class Monday morning on our crutches - because we were so close and went everywhere and did everything together - our friends thought it was a joke. An odd-looking couple, indeed.

Being the handsome, suave, and sophisticated young men that we were, Rusty and I naturally attracted plenty of interest from members of the opposite sex. By that time, I was dating Debby Sturgeon, a Greenville General Hospital nursing student who became my wife. Rusty was dating Cindy Franklin, a high school sweetheart who became his wife. Debby and Cindy developed a close relationship as they tolerated whatever shenanigans that Rusty and I had in mind for ourselves on Friday nights, and then we took them out for dinner and a movie on Saturday nights. There was a constant debate between Rusty and me over the issue of which of us was more controlled by his girlfriend and which was the more free-wheelin' and side-steppin' casanova. We made a bet about which of us would get married first, and the first one to walk down the aisle would owe the other a hundred dollars. Rusty, already an aspiring attorney, had the agreement drawn up, signed and notarized. We had the document framed and kept it on the wall of our dorm room during our senior year. When Cindy and Rusty got married three months before Debby and I did, I gift wrapped the framed bet and gave it to them - a $100 wedding present.

Lives and marriages sometimes take odd and unexpected turns. Some of them are absolutely heartbreaking, and others are truly heartwarming. The trick, as the song by The Amazing Rhythm Aces goes, is to "keep your hand upon the throttle and your eye upon the rail." During one of those difficult turns a number of years ago, I happened to show up unexpectedly at Rusty's house. We had a long talk about an issue that he was dealing with and just before I departed, he looked at me as we were shaking hands and said, "Jessie, you always know just when to call." Those are song lyrics by Joshua Kadison that - in that song - don't quite match the context of that evening's conversation. But I knew what he meant, and what he said got right to the heart of our relationship. There have been a number of times since then - especially when a parent died, and they're all gone now - when we each knew just when to call. There was another time though, nearly thirty years into our friendship, that was Jessie's most heartbreaking call ever.

Cindy Harter was diagnosed with a cancerous melanoma in early 1999, and her funeral was on November 1, 2000. As I sat across the aisle from Rusty at that funeral, unable to even imagine his grief, I kept thinking about our friendship. How you think you've done everything in the world with a guy - been up the creek and around the bend and back again - and then are struck nearly dumb by the realization that there's one more thing to do. The hardest thing of all . . . to help him bury his wife, who hadn't even reached her fiftieth birthday. Rusty Harter kept his hand on the throttle and his eye on the rail, though, and had faith that somehow Cindy's death was part of God's plan for his life. I don't know that it ever brought him understanding, but it eventually brought him healing and wonderful memories of Cindy. Rusty Harter kept his eye on the rail, stayed true to his Christian faith, set a wonderful example for his children - Trad, Rhett, and Carly - and today he is one of the most Godly men that I know. That faith, and a surely kinder version of fate, brought him to another oddly coincidental turn in his life several years ago on the night that he attended a St. Andrews High School reunion in Charleston. He reconnected with the lovely Cathy Matthewes, and they are now happily married. Between them, they have more grandchildren than I can count, and Rusty - with snow-white hair just like his father had - is the perfect grandfather.

Russell W. Harter, Jr., Esq., has been successfully practicing law in Greenville, South Carolina, for more than forty-three years and is a highly regarded and esteemed member of the legal profession. His intellect, character, demeanor, and distinctive low-country accent make him the perfect modern-day Atticus Finch. His legacy will be more than just the practice of law, though. He still logs long hours and travels frequently because he enjoys his work. But Rusty Harter's legacy will be that he helped hundreds of people better their lives. His daughter, Carly, is now practicing with him in the firm of Chapman, Harter & Harter, P.A., and will carry that legacy forward, personally, and professionally.

And the last, at least for now, heartwarming turn in the story of our friendship is that in November 2019, Rusty Harter - my old college roommate - officiated at the wedding of our oldest daughter, Beth. That was entirely fitting because he's known Beth since the day she was born, and just recently he compassionately counseled her with good advice, comfort, and encouragement during a difficult turn in her life. Uncle Rusty has meant a lot to both Beth and Caye over the years, but if you had told me forty-seven years ago that he would officiate at one of their weddings, I'd have bet a lot more than a hundred dollars against it. I'd have lost, though, because Jessie always knows just when to call.

Charlie Burry and Rusty Harter

Dr. Charlie Burry, Jr.

Lessons from My Life

One of the main reasons that the people whom I wrote about in the first section are important to me is that I learned about life from them. Some of their instruction was intentional, but much of it was just the manner in which they went about their business and lived their lives. There were also lessons taught to me by other remarkable people whose paths I was fortunate to cross in my life's journey. Then, there have been lessons that I managed to figure out for myself after life hit me over the head a few times. There's certainly nothing earth-shattering in this section, as I'm not smart or innovative enough to come up with anything of that significance. Also, while some of the selections are devotions that I wrote when I was a church deacon, I don't mean to be preachy, either. I'm not a good enough Christian to do that. So, dear reader, please be patient with me. While many of the life lessons in this section are as old as time, I'm hopeful that the manner in which I learned them and have related them to you is a little different and maybe even interesting and meaningful.

12

Out by a Country Mile

During the time that I was a classroom teacher, I'd occasionally tell my students a joke or a quick story. Sometimes it would be for the purpose of taking a break from a class discussion, or other times it was just to inject some levity into the student-teacher relationship. I liked stories and jokes that had clever punchlines, and occasionally - okay, maybe frequently - my students justifiably accused me of being downright corny. That worked, too, because student eyerolls can also build rapport. From time to time, though, I would learn that my sense of humor was so incredibly clever that a story would just sail right over the heads of everyone. Like this time.

One afternoon, I was playing center field in a bush-league baseball game on a make-shift field way out in the country. The diamond's dimensions were pretty close to regulation, and the chalk foul lines were almost straight. The chicken-wire backstop caught a few of the foul balls, and that was important because we only had three baseballs. Some of the players wore hats and pieces from a variety of uniforms, and there was one umpire - standing behind the pitcher's mound - who called the game. Fifty or so fans strained the structural integrity of a rickety set of bleachers. There was no outfield fence, and the field of play - roughly cut by a tractor bush hog about once a month - just transitioned into a heavily wooded area about three hundred and fifty feet from home plate. There were no ground rules, so on a batted ball that ended up in the woods, the hitter and any other baserunners just kept running.

With two outs in the bottom half of the last inning, my team was ahead by one run. The batter lifted a deep fly ball into the gap between left field and my position in center. As I gave chase, I saw the ball hit the ground, bounce a couple more times, and roll into the woods. As the left fielder and I frantically searched for the baseball, we knew that the tying run was sprinting around the bases. We were pawing through weeds and stalks of broom straw, and I finally grabbed a small tan-colored object thinking that it was the ball. To my surprise, the "ball" turned out to be a baby rabbit. With no more time to continue looking, I turned and fired that baby rabbit on a line toward the catcher waiting at home plate. The runner and the rabbit arrived at exactly the same time. The catcher snagged my throw, the runner slid into home in a cloud of dust, and the catcher applied the tag. The umpire, peering into the cloud of dust, hesitated for a suspenseful couple of seconds and then made his call: "Out, by a hare!"

As you can see, I'd done a great job telling the story, and after delivering the punch line, I awaited the expected screams of laughter and knee-slapping from my students. Instead, I was met by thirty-five blank stares and complete quiet. After about five seconds of total silence, the deep voice of a male student from the back of the room said, "Cain't nobody throw a rabbit that far."

As nods of affirmation spread around the room, I just dropped my head. I knew that not only had my story failed to score, but I was out - not just by a hair - but by a country mile.

13

If You Don't Know Where You're Going, Be Careful . . . You Might Get There

The title to this chapter is an idea that I used quite a bit in my seventeen years as a guidance counselor and also when I occasionally continued to counsel students in a different capacity as that of principal for Hartsville High School. A large part of my work as a guidance counselor was helping students plan and execute their four-year academic course of study in conjunction with whatever they thought they might want to do after high school. We addressed personal and social issues as well, but the two main areas of focus were (a) getting them graduated and (b) having them prepared for whatever they wanted to do after graduation. While realizing that it is not unusual for high school students to be unclear about what they ultimately want to be doing with their lives, I did encourage them to at least give those prospects some thought and begin to explore some avenues. It also was my practice, even if asked, never to make a choice for them. I don't believe that it's a parent's right to make such a choice for a child, either. It is important, even as a teenager, to take ownership of that responsibility.

The theory behind the establishment of goals is the same as taking a trip, whether it's to the grocery store or across the United States. One first determines a destination, and then one plans how to get there. With a person's life, it's usually advisable that it be more than just a Sunday afternoon drive where one can end up almost anywhere. The problem in life with lacking a destination is the increased likelihood of just wasting time wandering from place to place, but also - fifty years down the road - realizing that you're not at all where you want to be in terms of happiness, fulfillment, and standard of living. Worst case scenario that could result from a life without direction is the possibility of ending up someplace where, with the benefit of hindsight, you realize that it's where you absolutely don't want to be and from which there's no escape.

I had some fun with this idea when I was principal and was asked to make a few opening remarks at an event organized by our school counseling department called *Jump Start Breakfast*. The event was for juniors and their parents, and the program - after serving them breakfast - was to provide information about the college admissions process, financial aid for college or technical school, and other tasks that they would need to accomplish during their senior year in high school. I would greet everyone and then tell everyone about what an exciting day it was going to be and that by the end of the morning they would all know where they'd be going to college. I would then ask everyone to recall childhood memories of a party game called *Pin the Tail on the Donkey*. I would explain that we were going to play a form of that game to decide where everyone was going to college. Juniors would write their names on sticky notes. We'd then project a map of the United States on a screen at the front of the room. The students, one at a time, would come to the front of the room, be blindfolded, turned around three times, and then given a gentle push toward the map. When they arrived at the screen, as their parents held their breaths, the students would affix their names somewhere - anywhere - on the map. The blindfold would then be removed, and the students would - at the very least - discover in which state their future college was located. By the time I'd finished explaining the game and asked for a volunteer to be first, everyone would know that I was joking. Hopefully, though, my point would be made: they shouldn't let their college choice, or any other major decision in their lives, be a game of *Pin the Tail on the Donkey*. I then encouraged them to begin gathering the information that they'd need to make a plan rather than have four years of their lives depend on blind chance.

I think that it's wise to know where you're going, but in reality, the plans that most people have for their lives change as time passes. There's an old saying: "If you want to make God laugh, tell Him your plans." While realizing that faith in God's plan for our lives should be the foundation for whatever we do and wherever we go in life, I don't think that it hurts to help Him out a little bit with a few ideas of our own.

14

The Rubber Band Man

Educators attend a lot of meetings - staff meetings, department meetings, faculty meetings, professional development
meetings, and meetings in the community. Every organization
has meetings to disseminate information, focus resources and
effort, and motivate. Meetings come with the territory. While
realizing that it was important to be a contributor in meetings
when it was appropriate and when it could be of value to
the group, I generally made it a practice to keep my mouth
shut. That was a lesson that I learned from my dad about his
experience in meetings. He would say, "I don't talk because
I already know what I'm going to say. I want to listen to other
people so that I can learn what they know." I thought that was
pretty good advice.

I also learned to listen from my own professional experience. I didn't become a principal until I was in my thirty-second
year in education because I'd always wanted to coach, and
at most places you can't do both. I told each superintendent
for whom I worked that I'd never had a course in school law or
school finance, but that the best preparation for being a principal I'd had was seventeen years as a guidance counselor and
learning to listen to people. People want to be heard even if
you can't solve their problems or give them what they want,
and most left my office at least somewhat content because I'd
allowed them to speak their minds. Another piece of advice
that I would give to teachers about parent/teacher conferences was to try to sense when a parent was winding down and
just let that happen rather than prolonging the conference.

Also, an important piece of counseling or investigative technique to understand is that silence is uncomfortable, and people will sometimes try to alleviate discomfort by telling you more than they really want to. As a principal, one of the most important things to realize about making decisions is that there's more than one way to skin a cat, and the way to find out about different approaches to situations is to listen to the opinions and ideas of others. Dr. Eddie Ingram, former superintendent in the Darlington County School District, used to tell his principals that "All of us are a lot smarter than one of us." From an emotional standpoint, one of the hardest lessons that I learned was that sometimes in controversial and stressful situations when you'd really like to verbally blast someone, it's better in the long run just to stay quiet and let it pass. Harsh comments made only for the purpose of self-satisfaction or just because you're angry usually make the situation worse. Finally, a piece of wisdom comes from Yogi Berra, the New York Yankees Hall of Fame catcher, who once said, "You can hear a lot just by listening."

There is some pretty good advice in the previous paragraph, but sometimes people need a reminder that the best course of action is to stay quiet. A technique that I would use in counseling teenagers (and adults, too) in conflict resolution situations was to suggest that they wear a rubber band around their wrist. The rubber band would serve as a reminder for them to keep their emotions under control. If the situation escalated, they could stretch the rubber band out and quickly release it to feel the sting of a stronger reminder. I used this technique myself for a number of years when attending district office meetings both as a guidance counselor and principal. Those meetings would occasionally involve getting unpleasant news, hearing things that were objectionable, or receiving directives for which compliance was disagreeable. While I almost always felt that these issues were open to discussion and that my opinions were respected and valued, I also learned to recognize when something was a lost cause and that the best course of action was just to grin and bear it. That's when my rubber band would save me. If I was expecting a particularly difficult meeting, I'd wear several. Usually, when I would check out of the school office to travel to a district meeting, at least one of our administrative assistants or assistant principals would ask me, "Got your rubber band?" Over the course of my career, I found that it was always better at the end of a meeting to have a red wrist rather than a red face.

15

Listening to Old People

Listening to the voice of experience is a valuable lesson. If we're smart, experience teaches us about life, and we become better for having learned those lessons, although sometimes painfully. We become better parents, and our children are the beneficiaries of that whether they like it or not. When we're in a marriage with a solid foundation, or even if it's only tolerable and salvageable, we sometimes turn into better spouses when we're patient and try hard enough. We develop recreational skills - becoming better skiers, tennis players, and musicians - that help us to enjoy life more. We learn occupational and professional skills to become better teachers, welders, and physicians that make us more valuable in the marketplace. However, one of the frustrating things about navigating the job market when you're young is that employers are looking for people with experience. And, one of the sadly conflicting things about the world of work is that as you gain experience you also get older, sometimes to the point where age becomes a liability. Experience in most forms is a valuable commodity that is obtained by going through the fire, and that metaphor is not necessarily meant in a negative sense. Fire shapes beautiful glassware, is essential to the manufacture of steel, and cooks a steak to perfection. Fire also leaves scars that remind us of times in our lives when we've been burned. But regardless of how it's described, the only way to get experience is by getting experience. Sounds frustrating doesn't it, especially to younger people?

But wait, wouldn't it be nice if there was a quicker and easier way to get experience while you're still young? Well, there is, and that is to learn from the experiences of others. In order to do that, though, younger people have to understand the value of being told about someone else's life experiences, even if comes in a slow, halting manner. Younger people have to be patient with older people, which is another characteristic that usually comes with age. People of all ages should value the opportunities to read about the experiences of others, especially if it was written by a soldier fighting in the Battle of the Bulge, or in someone's journal or a diary from the period of the Great Depression, or even in old love letters. It is said that history repeats itself and that it is wise to learn from it. If that's true, who has seen more history and change than older people? Who else has seen the evolution of telephones, from party lines to smart phones? Who else has experienced World War II, the Korean War, the Vietnam Conflict, and our country's involvement in Afghanistan? Who else has witnessed the assassination and resignation of United States presidents? There is another old saying: "Fool me once, shame on you. Fool me twice, shame on me." Well, shame on us if we don't respect and value the experiences of others and use them to become better people and a better society.

Finally, do an old guy - and yourself - a favor. Make an effort to visit regularly with someone who is a couple of generations ahead of you. Grandparents, uncles or aunts, or older neighbors are excellent resources. Ask them about their daily lives when they were younger . . . what it was like to get only three channels on a black and white television, and when gas was twenty-five cents a gallon. Have them tell you about their early working lives . . . what it was like to crop tobacco or pull third shift in the cone department at Sonoco. Ask them about their military service . . . what it was like in Korea or Vietnam, if you can get them to talk about it. Question them about their children . . . yes, their children - your parents or cousins. You'll be surprised at what you might learn from a different perspective about people that you thought you knew well. During the last six months of my mother's life, she told me about things that had happened to her and her family seventy years before that I had never heard her mention - like whom she'd dated before she met my father. It was one of the most interesting experiences of my life, and I wish that I'd spent more time with her.

If you'll take my advice, what you'll learn is that old people know a lot of stuff even if their opinions on religion, politics, and social issues are different from your own. Listening to them speak is like going through the museums of their minds. When you sit patiently and listen to an old person, you'll also often sense a calmness and a peace that comes from the perspective of recalling events from long ago. We can learn from that. They might pause occasionally, and you'll see a brief faraway look in their eyes, and you'll wonder what else is there. More often than not, you'll see a small smile on their faces that tells you it's not only a pleasant memory, but they enjoyed telling you about it. The other benefit you'll receive is knowing that they enjoyed having you visit, and you've given them something - your time - that might be the highlight of their day. You will have given them your respect by listening to them and indicating that you value their words. You will have shown an old person kindness, for which both the giving and the receiving is a wonderful experience.

Dr. Charlie Burry, Jr.

16

O Captain! My Captain!

I believe that the fundamental key to teaching and learning is the relationship between the teacher and the student. As principal of Hartsville High School, I told our teachers that such a relationship was grounded in mutual respect, would begin to grow as the students sensed that the teacher cared about them as a student and a person, and would flourish as the teacher and student got to know each other in the proper manner. I also told our faculty that the teacher-student relationship, particularly with teenagers, was a slippery slope. Our teachers were advised never to physically touch a student, particularly one of the opposite gender, in either anger or affection. I emphasized to our teachers that attempting to gain the cooperation of students by becoming a buddy to them was like fool's gold - that what might appear to be a friendly rapport on the surface was only a false sense of respect. A question pertaining to that idea was always asked during my interviews with prospective teachers, and the manner in which a candidate answered that question was weighed heavily as I determined their suitability for Hartsville High School. I told our teachers that, if the teacher-student relationship was proper and genuine to the core, you could teach them anything, and they'd follow you anywhere.

One year during teacher in-service training prior to the beginning of school, I illustrated the type of relationship of which I was speaking by showing our faculty and staff a video clip from the 1989 movie *Dead Poets Society* starring Robin Williams. The movie setting is an elite boarding school for boys, and it tells the story of an English teacher who inspires his students through the teaching of poetry. Williams plays the role of the teacher, John Keating, who endears himself to his students with his unorthodox teaching methods and encourages them to make their lives extraordinary. Keating also resurrects the Dead Poets Society, a student club of which he was a member when he was a student at the school. Keating soon finds himself in conflict with the school administration and also at odds with the parents of some of his students. Parental pressure forces the suicide of one of the boys, and the circumstances become twisted so that Keating is forced to take the blame. His students, succumbing to school administration and parental pressure, agonizingly betray Keating. Keating is fired, and on his last day at the school he stops by his classroom to pick up his personal belongings. His visit interrupts his old English class, which is being taught by the headmaster who orchestrated Keating's dismissal. As Keating is preparing to leave, his former students, one-by-one, stand up on top of their desks. Defying the headmaster's furious orders to sit down, they each salute their beloved former teacher with the words, "O Captain! My Captain!" At that point in the video, I had tears in my eyes and a lump in my throat, as did many of our teachers. I then told our teachers that if they could foster the same kind of relationship with their students as John Keating did with his, they could teach their students anything, and they would follow them anywhere.

At the end of that school year, *Dead Poets Society* came up again unexpectedly. We were having our end-of-the-year luncheon at which each of the faculty members who would not be returning to Hartsville High School the next year were recognized. I spoke briefly about the departing faculty members, presented them with a parting gift, and they were given the opportunity to say a few words to their colleagues. Kenneth Stokes, a member of our school counseling department, was leaving our school to return to Columbia to work with his dad. He spoke with fondness and gratitude about his time at Hartsville High School. Then, as he finished and prepared to sit down, he turned and saluted me with these parting words, "O Captain! My Captain!" It was one of the most rewarding moments of my career.

17

You Always Get Caught

"You Always Get Caught" is a devotion that I gave on July 12, 1999, at a meeting of the Board of Deacons of Hartsville First Baptist Church. I used it again when I spoke on Layman's Sunday at Wesley Chapel United Methodist Church in Lydia, South Carolina, on September 19, 1999.

Part of our Scripture comes from Psalm 139:1-5:

O Lord, Thou has searched me and known me. Thou dost know when I sit down and when I rise up; Thou dost understand my thought from afar. Thou dost scrutinize my path and my lying down, and art intimately acquainted with all my ways. Even before there is a word on my tongue, behold, O Lord, Thou dost know it all. Thou hast enclosed me behind and before, and laid Thy hand upon me.

For a number of years, Lewis Grizzard was one of my favorite authors. I liked his earlier books best, the ones that described his childhood and adolescence, his family, his career as a young sportswriter, and his three stormy voyages into the sea of matrimony. Those were the ones with titles like *Kathy Sue Lowdermilk I Love You*, *Don't Sit Under the Grits Tree with Anyone Else but Me*, *Elvis Is Dead and I Don't Feel So Good Myself*, and *If Love Was Oil I'd Be About a Quart Low*. Some of his publicists described him as a "modern day Mark Twain," and I think that's a stretch for anyone. But Lewis Grizzard, like Mark Twain, could make you laugh until you hurt. I truly mourned when he died on March 20, 1994, at the age of forty-seven, and I pay my respects to him every time I watch a University of Georgia home football game. You see, Grizzard was cremated, and some of his ashes were spread on the fifty yard-line at Sanford Stadium. No one that I've ever read though, matches Twain's combination of sarcastic wit and common sense as a critic of the social and political figures of his day, or his philosophy of life in general. Mark Twain would have skewered Bill Clinton in the Lewinski affair and wouldn't even have considered it good sport. I'm sure Grizzard would have taken his shots, too, but perhaps our president would have been better off had he taken some advice of a more somber tone offered by the good ol' boy from Moreland, Georgia. Grizzard, who in his books often ridiculed his own futile attempts at marriage, was relating several tales of marital infidelity which - depending on your point of view - had taken twists which were quite humorous. But his concluding thought to those stories, to be read with whatever degree of seriousness one chose, was this: "Boys, if you're thinking about having an affair, remember one thing. You always get caught."

You always get caught. Was Grizzard being biblical when he made that statement? I seriously doubt it. But in all the stories about his ex-wives, no matter how funny they were, one always sensed a tone of very honest regret that he hadn't been able to do it right. That he'd gotten caught . . . every time. Now understand me; I'm not saying that his failed marriages were caused by extra marital affairs. He never admits or even implies that in any of his books, and despite his many other vices I think that he was probably honorable in that regard. So, what's my point here? Was Grizzard only talking about the affairs of others, or is there more meaning to that statement? What is getting caught?

With this thought expanded to the broad spectrum of general wrongdoings, I've gotten caught at just about every wrong thing I've ever done. I think that for me, that life pattern was established very early. I was about six years old, and we were living in Biloxi, Mississippi. I'd done something really bad one day, and my mother was after me with the business end of a big, flat wooden hair brush that my parents used for major-offense spankings. Well, I'd made up my mind that I wasn't going to take that anymore . . . so I decided to run. And, if you can picture this, I took off down the street with my mother in hot pursuit. Our house was about half a block from the Gulf of Mexico, and my original thought may have been to swim to Cancun, but instead I veered off into Miramar Park, which was a playground down at the end of the block right across the street from the beach. By that time my mom, who was running a little faster than she can now, was closing in on me. It was then that I decided that my escape route should be up the ladder of a nearby sliding board. Seconds later, as I zoomed down the slide believing that I'd broken away again, my mother - thinking a little further ahead than my six-year-old mind - was waiting for me at the bottom with that hairbrush cocked and fire in her eyes. She didn't even wait until we got home. We set a world record that day for however many licks a little boy can get in a half-block, double-time, forced march. I don't think that I sat down for a week.

So, does the story that I've just related to you accurately represent what getting caught is? Is it getting caught redhanded or, no pun intended, getting caught with your pants down? Is it dreading the thought of sitting on your daddy's knees when he comes home from work and having to look him in the eyes and tell him what you did wrong? Is it finally having to show those F's on your report card to your parents after weeks of telling them that you'd been studying? Is it seeing those blue lights flashing in your rearview mirror? Is it seeing your name in the headlines as the subject of a nation-wide scandal? Is it being convicted in a court of law? If nobody ever finds out about it, and the statute of limitations passes, do you still get caught? The question that I want us to think about is this: Do you have to get caught to get caught?

Maybe getting caught is just knowing that you've done something wrong. Maybe it's having to look someone in their eyes while knowing deep down in your heart that you've deceived him or her. It might be showing that grade of A on a term paper to your parents, but knowing that it's someone else's work. Could it be knowing that, despite what the insurance report says, if you'd been going the speed limit, the accident wouldn't have happened? Is it reading the morning newspaper and not being able to concentrate because of the noise of your own skeletons rattling in the closet? Maybe it's walking out of a courtroom with a not-guilty verdict, but admitting to yourself that your freedom is the result of a legal technicality and the skill of your attorney, rather than your own innocence. Is it knowing that as far as anyone else on earth is concerned you've gotten away with compromising your professional ethics but being nagged by the unsettling realization that God doesn't have a statute of limitations? Again, the question is this: Do you have to get caught to get caught?

Although I've probably provided a little more context to Grizzard's quote than he ever intended, I think he answers our question. You always get caught. Just because you seem to have gotten away with something, that doesn't mean you aren't caught. That's because of something God gives us called a conscience. It's developed, to varying degrees, through the morals and values instilled by one's parents and the other guiding influences of childhood, adolescence, and early adulthood. The conscience, I believe, is a major part of a person's spiritual make-up. It can be a mere nuisance, like a gnat buzzing around your eyes, or it can be a major psychological hang-up. Mine, for instance, is a bear, and I mean one of those fifteen-hundred-pound Kodiak Alaskan brown bears.

You'd think it would make me a better person and a better Christian, but it doesn't always work that way. That's because a lot of times I rationalize that old bear right into his cage, slam the door shut behind him, and get as far away from him as I can. The psychological term for that is compartmentalization, when a person puts the different parts of his life - spiritual, family, professional, social, recreational, and so forth - into separate compartments. Kind of like leaving God at church when we drive out of the parking lot - a theory espoused by Mark Twain when he said, "It is best not to use our morals on weekdays, it gets them out of repair for Sundays." Of course, the reason we do this is so that the values and standards from one life compartment, despite being in conflict with the others, remain separate in our minds and don't actually cause us any psychological conflict and discomfort. We're playing games with our conscience. But getting back to that bear - sooner or later he manages to escape from that cage, or occasionally some preacher lets him out. And then, just when I'm zooming down that sliding board, there's that big, old Kodiak at the bottom waiting for me. And I'm caught again.

So, if our consciences are always catching us, how do we deal with that? One day I was out on a pond fishing, obviously without enough to think about, and I started wondering what a fish must feel like when it gets caught. I think it has a lot to do with the personality of the fish. A carp, for instance - being the sorry excuse for a fish that it is - will pretty much just let you reel him in. On the other hand, a redbreast - even a small one - ounce for ounce will fight as hard as any fish there is. I decided that getting caught must be a very frightening thing to a fish, the way it pulls one way and another, and tries to wrap your line around a snag, the way it jumps and tries to throw the lure, and even flops around once you've got it in the boat. A carp must just faint. Then I started to think about what a fish must feel like when it gets away, or when it's not big enough to be a keeper

Dr. Charlie Burry, Jr.

and gets released. It sometimes just floats there close to the surface for a few seconds, getting the water going through its gills again, and then it's gone like a flash. Bass tournaments have a catch and release rule. The competitors try to keep their fish alive through the official weigh-in - in fact, they're penalized a certain number of ounces for each dead fish - and then the fish are released back into the lake. It's a sporting philosophy that, if you wanted to put a little religious twist to it, could be described as very forgiving. Can you imagine what that must be like? To be caught and almost forever dead, and then have that life-giving oxygen start coming back into your blood again? To be almost in the hell of a deep fryer's boiling oil, but then instead feel fresh, cool water flowing through your gills again? To be caught and released - a very forgiving philosophy indeed.

Can you see that big, old Kodiak up here with me now? He's right behind me. He's about nine feet tall, and I can even smell him. There are times when I'd like to shoot him. But then I would be . . . a man without a conscience. Think about that concept, not having a conscience . . . not being bothered by the least bit of apprehension or guilt or regret about anything we've ever done or would consider doing. That's the psyche of a cold-blooded killer, an assassin, a mass-murderer - someone who would do anything and stop at nothing. So, when I think about my conscience from that point of view - considering the temptations of each day, my weaknesses, and my sinful life in general - I then realize that God, just as He does with everything, assigned that Kodiak to me for a purpose. And if that old bear is going to follow me and be there every time I turn around, I probably ought to try to make the best of the situation and get comfortable with him.

Thankfully, God gives us - in case you've got your own bear - some options to help that happen. Those options are in a book that includes the standards of right and wrong conduct, examples of the kind of people God wants us to be, parables from which we can learn, stories of inspiration and faith, and all kinds of suggestions about how to keep that bear off our backs if we so choose. But being human, we're not always going to make the right choices. And so God, in His infinite wisdom, gives us an option there, too. He's got His own catch and release rule, and it's called repentance. In Psalm 32:5, David said, "I acknowledged my sin to Thee, and my iniquity I did not hide; I said, 'I will confess my transgressions to the Lord'; and Thou didst forgive the guilt of my sin." Confessing our transgressions is a way to make the punishing weight of that bear a little lighter and make him smell a little better by washing him clean of all our guilt. Repentance - an option, along with our professed belief in Jesus Christ as the Son of God - is God's plan for our eternal salvation.

Repentance from sin, profession of faith, and eternal salvation . . . a very forgiving philosophy indeed. One that all believers will be thankful for on that ultimate day of judgment when, as Lewis Grizzard once said, "You always get caught."

18

Do You Know Any Last-Minute Shoppers?

From the time my family moved to Hartsville when I was eight years old until I finished high school, I always had a part-time job at my dad's dime store. He let me work when I needed money and wanted to work, and he also found hours for me when I didn't especially want to work - like during school holidays. A lot of my time during my Christmas school vacations was spent at the old Hartsville 5 & 10 behind the snack bar, in the stockroom, or bagging at the cash register for our checkout lady, Mrs. Corrie Moore.

One of my clearest memories of working at the dime store is of a man who came knocking on the glass doors a few minutes after we had closed one Christmas Eve. The holiday season in the retail business is long and difficult, and we were all tired and ready to go home. The last thing we wanted to hear was a late shopper knocking on the door even if it meant the prospect of one more sale. My dad went to the front of the store, explained to the man through the locked doors that the store was closed, and turned to walk back to the office. The man knocked again, more urgently, and explained that he hadn't bought a Christmas present for his little boy. The man pleaded desperately with my dad to let him in so his son wouldn't be disappointed the next morning. Perhaps thinking of his own children, my dad let the man in and asked what he had in mind. The man looked around quickly, then stopped at the jewelry counter and picked out a wristwatch for his son's Christmas gift.

The relieved father paid for the watch and thanked my dad again and again on his way out.

Anyone who has ever known the height of a child's expectations on Christmas morning can appreciate the sense of urgency that the man experienced in his search for an open store. And, anyone who has considered the prospect of a child's disappointment on this most wonderful of all days can share the relief that the man felt when he realized that his son's Christmas had been saved. He knew that instead of the everlasting regret of a child's empty Christmas, the day would be a joyous occasion after all. I have often wondered if the boy liked the watch and if he and his dad had a good day.

I also have wondered if the man was a Christian; if he had ever looked for, found, and accepted the greatest gift of all. I have wondered if the man ever shared the Christmas story with his son, and told him of Jesus' birth, and how God gave His only Son so that those who believe might have everlasting life. I have wondered if the man ever saw the prospect of God's offer of salvation with the same sense of importance and urgency with which he searched for a wristwatch that Christmas Eve.

Finally, I have wondered why it's so easy for us to forget to recognize and appreciate the real reason for celebrating Christmas. I have wondered what we might do on the day God calls us to our final resting place, and we suddenly realize that we haven't remembered His gift. And - on our way to our eternal home - we discover that the stores are closed.

19

Columbine

Following are comments that I made to Hartsville High School students, faculty, and staff over the public address system on April 26, 1999, about a week after the massacre at Columbine High School in Littleton, Colorado. Are the comments, twenty years later, still relevant today? Absolutely. Just watch the news.

Most people have been stunned, and then horrified, by what happened at Columbine High School in Colorado last week. We have watched the television reports, first of the panic and confusion of the attack, then the news confirming the deaths of twelve students and a coach, and the suicides of the attackers. We have seen interviews with witnesses and wounded victims, listened to tapes of the 911 calls, and Sunday we watched the first of the funerals and memorial services that have gone on all this week. As we have tried to take all this in, and understand it, the questions come. How could such a thing happen? Why would such a thing happen? Who would do such a thing? What is wrong with us, and can we do anything about it? While our hearts go out to the people of Littleton, Colorado, we are also troubled by other questions. It's happened before, so where will it happen next? Columbine seemed so far away, with all that was going on here last week - the Exit Exam, all the spring sports, and the prom. Our world here last week was springtime, and it snowed Wednesday in Littleton. Are we that far away and that different, or could it happen to us, here, at Hartsville High School? The answer is yes, it could happen anywhere.

The tragedy at Columbine High School will be investigated and analyzed in great detail to determine exactly how it happened. There will be tons of evidence and hundreds of pages of testimony. More important to those of us at Hartsville High School, is the question of why it happened. Blame is already being placed in many areas. We've heard that the entertainment industry is responsible because of the violence that is so much a part of music, movies, television, and video games: young people have become less sensitive to the reality of death and destruction because they see and hear so much of it as entertainment. Some are saying that the easy availability of guns is to blame. I watched an interview with a gun store owner who cheerfully discussed the features - semi-automatic action, ten-shot magazine, light and easy to carry, cost only $179.00 - of a gun just like one used in the Columbine massacre the previous day. Why would any average citizen, much less a high school student, need a gun like that? Why would anybody need to saw the barrel off a shotgun? Others are saying that the parents are responsible; they should have known that their sons were making bombs in their bedrooms and had been planning the attack for a year. I've heard that teachers and counselors were to blame; they didn't see the warning signs (which seem so obvious now) and offer help to two troubled teenagers. Some are saying that the popularity of the goth culture - wearing all black all the time, playing games like Doom and Dungeons & Dragons, Satan worship, and the fascination with death - is to blame. People who know anything at all about World War II and the Holocaust must blame the sick mind of anyone who could idolize Adolph Hitler, one of the most horrific murderers in history. One of the preachers at the funeral of Rachel Scott - a junior at Columbine - was saying how we need to get prayer back in our schools. As a counselor, I've learned that part of being a teenager is just not seeing the long-term, sometimes permanent, consequences of decisions made during the confusing time of

Dr. Charlie Burry, Jr.

life called adolescence. I think all of these things were factors in the death and destruction that exploded at Columbine High School last Tuesday. All these things, like them or not, are part of our society and culture today.

But the catalyst for what happened at Columbine High School can't be found on a CD or in a video game, or in the gun case of a pawn shop, or in the day planner of two working parents, or in a biography of Adolph Hitler. My opinion is that the thing that caused that school to blow sky high last week was a simple, terrible human attitude called hate. The Trenchcoat Mafia and the other groups, or cliques, of Columbine students had been caught for years in a vicious cycle of harassment and hatred just because they were different from one another and weren't willing to tolerate those differences. Please clearly understand two points. First, I am not in any way trying to justify what Eric Harris and Dylan Klebold did. The measure of revenge they took on their classmates was far in excess of anything that had ever been done to them. Nothing can excuse that kind of action. No amount of being threatened, bullied, or picked on can justify turning a high school library into a war zone. However, I am saying that if respect for fellow human beings - on the part all the social groups at Columbine - was more a part of student life and the school climate, I just don't believe this would have happened. Secondly, please don't interpret this as criticism of Columbine High School. To say that they brought this on themselves would be terribly insensitive and inaccurate. Coach Dave Sanders didn't bring it on himself; he just helped young people for the last twenty-six years of his life. All one student did to die was to profess her belief in God to one of the killers right before he shot her. Columbine High School students are no different from thousands of other high school students all across our country and here in Darlington County.

I think these are the questions we should be asking ourselves. What makes us so insecure as human beings that we have to pick on others to feel better about ourselves? What makes us so convinced that our music or lifestyle or the way we dress is so right that we look down our noses at people who are in some way different from us? Why can't we be man or woman enough to talk out differences instead of fighting? Why can't we just let some things slide instead of making a big deal out of a minor difference of opinion? What makes being popular so important to us that we'll ridicule people who aren't in our group? What makes us think we can force people to respect us instead of earning it by respecting them? What kind of attitude makes us want to cause someone who is troubled or hurting to feel even worse? What makes us think that prejudice is a stronger character trait than tolerance?

Can't we all just offer respect to one another? And if we can't bring ourselves to that point, can't we just tolerate one another? Columbine High School or Hartsville High School - we are all the same. We shouldn't need metal detectors and police officers on campus to keep us safe from each other. We shouldn't need some expensive government study on school violence to tell us what human decency is. We just need to follow one simple rule . . . the Golden Rule. Members of the Hartsville High School family, just treat others the way you would like to be treated. I'd like to ask each of you, if you aren't doing that now, to give it a try. It could solve a lot of problems, and help a lot of people feel better. And, it just might help prevent another Columbine.

20

9/11/01

Following are comments that I made to Hartsville High School students, faculty and staff via a video presentation on September 17, 2001, about a week after the attacks on the World Trade Center and the Pentagon. The battle against terrorism continues to rage worldwide today.

On April 20, 1999, we all reacted with horror when two teenagers turned Columbine High School in Littleton, Colorado, into a war zone. This past Tuesday - September 11, 2001 - another holocaust of even more unimaginable proportions played out before our very eyes on live television from New York City, Washington, DC, and the rural Pennsylvania countryside. Thousands of citizens of the United States - working men and women beginning an ordinary day - were murdered by a group of terrorists in a manner so savage that the replays, even though we've seen them dozens of times by now, still almost take our breath away. The weapons used by the terrorists included hundreds more innocent men, women, and children who suddenly and inexplicably found themselves riding in a giant bomb of an airplane, knowing that they were bound for an instant, fiery death. Other casualties were hundreds of heroic firefighters and police officers, rushing in without regard for their own safety to help the victims, only to become victims themselves as one hundred and ten stories of concrete, glass, and steel came crashing down upon them. All these people - mothers, fathers, grandparents, sons, daughters, husbands, wives - gone from their families and friends forever in a matter of minutes, dying at the hands of madmen so terribly misguided by their religion and politics that they were willing to die themselves in order to accomplish their mission from hell.

What sense can be made from all this? How could this possibly happen; how could someone do this to the United States? How could people have such hatred in their hearts? How could a just and loving God allow such a thing? Are we safe now, or can it happen again? What should be done about it - are we going to go to war? And once we finally work our way through the shock and sorrow and grief, what lessons should be learned from this? Much of this is so hard to understand and accept, and there is so much that we may never understand. The book of Proverbs tells us not to lean on our own understanding but to trust in the Lord. That's all that some people in New York, Washington, Pennsylvania, and maybe some of us have right now.

A couple of books that I've read recently are by Tom Brokaw - entitled *The Greatest Generation* and *The Greatest Generation Speaks*. These books describe, sometimes very vividly and other times very emotionally, what Americans who are in their seventies and eighties now, probably some of your grandparents, did to save our country's freedom - and the freedom of the world - during World War II. One of the purposes of Mr. Brokaw's books, other than recognizing and honoring those great Americans, is to try to help those of us whose freedom has never been threatened to understand what it cost. One of the points is that the freedom we take so much for granted today didn't come cheaply. Another of the points is that the reason patriotism is so lame with today's young people is that we've never had an event in our lives that actually threatened the freedom that our forefathers fought and died for. Well, I hope you realize that last Tuesday we had that event. Someone, for the first time since Pearl Harbor, attacked our country and has threatened our freedom. And if you don't understand that,

Dr. Charlie Burry, Jr.

maybe you ought to go up to New York for a few days and help remove some bodies from what used to be the World Trade Center.

Most people believe very strongly that our country must take some kind of military action against the people who are responsible for the terrorism. President Bush has said, "We are at war." The FBI and other government agencies have committed huge resources to track down the terrorists and their supporters. Anger and the desire for vengeance of an equally horrible nature to be visited upon those responsible is a natural human reaction. And in today's world, the act of punishing our enemies to a degree that such a thing is not likely to happen again is probably necessary for the protection and safety of our country. The terrorists must be shown that they are messing with the mightiest military force on earth, one they cannot intimidate or frighten, cannot defeat, cannot escape, and cannot outlast. In most people's minds, justice will come in the form of swift, sure, and deadly attacks against those who attacked us. The consequences and repercussions of such actions, only God knows. President Bush also has told us that "all Americans should be ready to sacrifice."

What happened last Tuesday was a tragedy the like of which our country has never before seen. But I think there could be a worse tragedy to come of this, and that would be that if the primary lesson learned from September 11th is that revenge is the only answer in a situation like this. A counterattack, one that will teach those agents of the devil himself a lesson - while no doubt justified and well-deserved - won't get at the root of the problem. The root of the problem is the lack of understanding and tolerance that people of differing political, economic, and religious beliefs have for one another. The root of the problem is that the value of and respect for human life can somehow be disregarded in the interest of politics and economics, with religion somehow dragged along as a justification. On the other hand, the solution to the problem lies in a compassionate effort to understand our fellow men. The solution to the problem lies in the tolerance of differences and respect for the rights and feelings of others, no matter what race, or nationality, or religion. The solution to the problem lies in obeying God's instructions to "love one another as thyself."

There are those who would say, and maybe rightly so, that such an attitude is just not realistic in today's world. Already we have heard about scam artists preying on the misfortunes of those suffering in New York. There are those who would say that such an idealistic attitude would leave us defenseless and open to attack from the madmen who are still at large today, probably even in our own country. Maybe that's right. So, what can we do, as members of the Hartsville High School family? If such an attitude of compassion and caring and love is not practical or possible on the world stage, is it possible here on a smaller scale in Hartsville, at our school?

I think that it is. I think that one thing that all of us, as citizens of Hartsville High School, could do to honor those who died last week is to become a more caring and compassionate and tolerant community of people ourselves. I think those rescue workers, who are fighting so hard right now to find survivors in the ruins of those two skyscrapers, would take a break for a minute and smile with relief if they knew that the huge pile of rubble that they're working in became the reason that there would never be another unkind word, or fight, or theft, or act of vandalism at Hartsville High School. I think all those thousands of new souls in Heaven would smile down on us if they knew that their earthly deaths had somehow caused us to become a more caring and compassionate people, dedicated to getting along more cooperatively, respectfully, and peacefully among ourselves. If that kind of thing could happen at Hartsville High School, maybe it could happen in some other places, too.

21

It's a Small World

"It's A Small World" is a devotion that I gave to the Board of Deacons at Hartsville First Baptist Church on September 8, 2002.

Our Scripture tonight is 1 John 4:12: "If we love one another, God lives in us and his love is made complete in us."

The daughter of a co-worker of mine at Hartsville High School is spending the fall term of her senior year in college studying in Australia. It's been interesting hearing about her travel and experiences while she's been on foreign study half way around the world. For one thing, it took her twenty-three hours of flying time to get there - and I thought jets were pretty fast. Another thing that I never quite have gotten a handle on is this International Dateline thing - in Australia, today is already tomorrow. These far-away elements that make our world seem so big have been especially fascinating for a guy who hopes to visit Europe one day - when they build a bridge across the Atlantic Ocean.

As we approach September 11, 2002, we are all reminded that there are some world issues that aren't so far away any more. We can still close our eyes and see the holocaust that played out on live television a year ago from New York City, Washington, DC, and the rural Pennsylvania countryside. So, as we near the first anniversary of another day that - like December 7, 1941 - will live in infamy, what does a person like myself say in a devotion about world peace and our response to terrorism? And more than that, reference that subject to appropriate Scripture? As I was sitting in front of my computer and scouring a concordance, it suddenly dawned on me that I was making it all too hard - that trying to analyze and relate the factors and relationships affecting world peace was going at things from entirely the wrong perspective. I realized that the Scripture that I needed - 1 John 4:12 - and the idea to tie all the complicated issues related to world peace together was right in a fifth and sixth grade Sunday school book that we'd used earlier this year.

The ideas that Carolyn Winburn and I tried to help those eleven and twelve-year-old children to understand last spring are simple and pure. We talked about God's love and how when people truly have God's love in their hearts - instead of things like selfishness and greed, prejudice and intolerance, and jealousy and vengeance - that gets to the core of and solves a whole lot of seemingly complicated issues. The catch to dealing with things in such a manner is that our big old world - even here in Hartsville - is not simple and pure and that such an idealistic attitude regrettably leaves us vulnerable.

Given those circumstances, do we adopt an attitude of survival of the fittest and just protect our own interests? Will that change the world? If Jesus and His disciples had operated that way, would we be here tonight as Christians? Jesus and His disciples believed that they could change the world, and they did. God has commissioned us to do the same thing. Our church mission statement says that's what we're about here. Think about it this way. Each of us operates in our own worlds - our church, our families and friends, our work or our schools, and our communities. With God's love in our hearts, we can change each of those worlds for the better, and - this is the key - the great potential that exists in this concept is that all our worlds are related. Some of your children go to school in my world. I do business in some of your worlds. We enjoy sports, recreation, and entertainment in some of the same worlds. Other parts of my world include my brother, who lives near

Baltimore. I occasionally IM with an old coaching buddy who lives in Michigan. One of my best friends from high school lives - and I still don't understand why - in Boise, Idaho. I recently made contact with a college fraternity brother whom I hadn't heard from in twenty-nine years; he's a guidance counselor in an Atlanta high school, and one of the first things he told me about his wonderful family was that they have a fifteen-minute devotion every weekday morning. We have opportunities every day to weave our worlds together in a blanket of God's love and peace. As that happens, that blanket covers a little more, and it warms and comforts a few more people in the world.

So tonight, instead of a decidedly non-worldly person foolishly attempting a September 11th commentary on the complexities of world peace, I'll just ask you this simple question: How many of us have ever made the statement, "Well, my goodness, it sure is a small world"? Looking at it that way - with God living in us, and His love made complete in us - maybe we can make it a better one, too.

22

Unanswered Prayers

"Unanswered Prayers" is a devotion that I first gave on February 12, 1996, at a meeting of the Board of Deacons of Hartsville First Baptist Church. I used it again, modified somewhat, when I delivered the message for the Baccalaureate Service at Hartsville First Baptist Church on May 31, 1998. It's about a turning point that occurred in my coaching career in 1985, and it's important to understand that I needed eleven years of hindsight and perspective before I was able to write this. I've mailed a copy of this message to a number of my good friends and colleagues over the years when they faced circumstances similar to what mine were, now thirty-five years ago, hoping that it would be helpful to them.

I'm uneasy, to say the least, about talking to you this morning. First of all, public speaking is not one of my favorite activities or something that I'm accustomed to doing. This reminds me of when I was a nine-year-old little league baseball player. I had to bat against a big, twelve-year-old, right-handed, side-arm, fast-balling pitcher on the Hal's Esso team. His nickname was Wild Bill, and I was so scared that my knees shook. They're shaking about the same way right now. You also should understand that I had to get the permission of my two daughters to do this. I told them to relax, that it could be worse. At least I'm not singing.

I've been attempting to convince myself since the day I told Russ and Bob that I'd do this that I have some credibility speaking from this pulpit. I think about the wonderful men of

God, beginning with Dr. Sanders, whom I've heard preach from this spot. I see a group of people, many of whom I grew up respecting as pillars of First Baptist Church, who have provided a Christian example for me since I was a boy. I also see people closer to my own age whose Christian commitment I've admired and respected for quite a while as being much deeper than my own. There's even one of my former players who has been much more positively influenced by being married to my sister than playing basketball for me. And here I am, talking to you. God does work in mysterious ways.

Most importantly, I see a group of young people - including one of my own daughters - who probably see me at Hartsville High School more often than I'd like to admit in a far less than perfect light. This troubles me because I don't want them, or you, to see me speaking from this pulpit as a hypocrite. I was honored three years ago when I was elected to the Board of Deacons, but I also felt very unworthy, much the same way as I do this morning. One of the people that I talked with about my feelings was one of my high school coaches, a former deacon in this church, and now a deacon in Aubrey Floyd's church in Pamplico. I told him, "Coach, I do this and I do that, and I don't do this - I'm just not a good enough Christian." He said, "Charlie, you don't understand. You don't have to be perfect, just try your best to live like God wants you to. You just have to do the best you can do." So, here I am before you this morning, a long shot from being an ideal Christian. Perhaps my greatest sin is not always trying my best. God's purpose for me right now, though, is to tell you about an experience in my life that you might learn from.

I enjoy listening to country music, and some of you may think that's my greatest sin. I started enjoying that kind of music when I was in college and Charley Pride was singing *Kiss an Angel Good Morning*. As I listened more, I also learned to appreciate the music of earlier stars like Hank Williams, Sr., and Patsy Cline. One reason that I listen to country music is that I believe there's occasionally some good, solid philosophy of life in the lyrics. It can be more than just lost loves, mama, trains, pick-up trucks, prison, and gettin' drunk. At times it's as simplistic as Mary Chapin-Carpenter, who by the way is an Ivy League graduate, when she sings, "Sometimes you're the windshield, sometimes you're the bug." Other times it has a little more substance.

Several years ago, a song by Garth Brooks came out about a guy who had gone to a high school reunion and football game. That night he saw his old high school sweetheart for the first time in twenty or twenty-five years. This was the girl that, while he'd been in high school, he'd prayed over and over again that he'd somehow marry one day. While attending that football game with his wife and children, whom he loved far more deeply than anything he could have prayed for twenty-five years before, his thinking changed. He realized that, as the song goes, "Some of God's greatest gifts are unanswered prayers." This morning, I'm going to tell you about one of my unanswered prayers. Graduates, this story actually began when I was about your age, with plans, hopes, and dreams just like the ones you have today.

The most influential men in my life, other than my father, have been my coaches, teachers at school and Sunday school, guidance counselors, and scoutmasters. Men like Cliff Malpass, Tim Watson, Paul Chapman, Hubert Twitty, Ray Petty, Bucky Goudelock, and J. T. Alford. I knew when I graduated from Hartsville High School and went to Furman University in the fall of 1969 that I wanted to be like them. I wanted to be to other boys what those men were, and still are, to me.

I pursued that goal, and in the summer of 1978, I was named head basketball coach at my high school alma mater and came back to live in my hometown. My dream had come true, my picture was in the paper, and I was following in the footsteps of the men I'd admired most in my life. Seven years later - after winning the first boys' basketball AAAA region championship in school history, but also coaching our teams to six losing records, including the two most recent seasons - I was sitting in my principal's office. He and my superintendent were telling me that they weren't sure they could renew my assignment as head basketball coach for the next school year and that I should consider resigning that position. In all honesty, after six losing seasons in seven years, I probably should have been replaced regardless of the circumstances. My response to them was that I would not quit - that my coaches had taught me never to quit - and I asked for one more year to coach. One of the bedrocks of my coaching philosophy was, and is "Tough times don't last, tough people do." I still believed that I could turn it around, and I told my principal that if we didn't have a winning season the next year, my resignation would be on his desk the morning after the season was over. I was trying to cut a desperate deal, and I went home and prayed to God for one more chance to save my job and career as a basketball coach. I prayed for a month, more fervently than I have ever prayed for anything in my life, that God would make my principal, my superintendent, and the school board give me one more season to save my dream.

My prayers went unanswered. I stayed tough, more on principle than common sense, and told them that they'd have to fire me before I'd quit. Well, they did. One of the last things I told my players was that God had a reason for what He was doing and that I'd see it one day, but I don't think I really believed that at the time. I applied for basketball jobs in Kershaw County, Oconee County, and several other places in between, and prayed for one of those positions. I realize now that there are more important things in this world than ball games and coaching, but at the time I felt like I was dying. I would have taken my wife and daughter just about anywhere to be able to continue my career as a basketball coach. My prayers still went unanswered.

I returned to Hartsville High School the next year as a social studies teacher and junior high assistant football coach. I didn't know who or what I was. My whole self-image and professional identity for twelve years had been that of a basketball coach, and now that was gone. I grew a beard to try to disguise the shame and lack of purpose that I felt. That December there were things printed in the newspaper that heightened the anguish that I felt. I would slip into the gym late at night, sometimes after midnight, to torture and punish myself working out in the weight room. I avoided public places as much as possible because of my humiliation. There were many Sundays when I sat in that back corner of the sanctuary away from my family, listening to Bill West with tears in my eyes, and struggling with my faith. On the night Hartsville's next basketball season opened with a new coach, I stood at the kitchen window of our house looking toward the gym three blocks away and cried because God hadn't answered my prayers.

I don't mean to make more out of this than I should. One of the contradictory things about coaching high school sports is that the monetary compensation in those one-year assignments is almost minuscule compared to the amount of time and effort one puts in. I was never in any danger of losing my teaching position or being able to support my family. As long as I was willing to swallow my pride and return to Hartsville High School as a teacher, not coaching basketball would only cost me about $2000 a year. I've never fought in a war, or suffered a serious health problem, or worried about where my next meal was coming from. So, I know some of you are thinking, "Shoot, this guy doesn't know what hard times are." And you're right. I'd lost a lot of ballgames, but never a wife, or a child, or a brother or a sister, or until eighteen months ago, a parent. God tried to help me put things in perspective on the day I was officially fired. One of my boyhood friends was burying his father that afternoon, and I walked out the door of Hartsville High School after getting the final news from my principal and looked across the street at Magnolia Cemetery at the funeral. I stopped for a minute and thought about how my friend's father had gone camping with us in Boy Scouts and pitched batting practice to us, and then I got in my truck feeling sorry for myself. God tried to straighten me out again when I got home. That was the day that Beth rode her bicycle without training wheels for the first time. I watched her for a few minutes, forced a smile to acknowledge her accomplishment, and then I went in the house feeling sorry for myself. So again, I don't mean to get this out of proportion with what is really important in life. I understand a lot more about that now. I'm also telling you that it's a hard thing to come back home among family, former teammates, and life-long friends to coach at your alma mater - to fulfill a dream - and instead be a failure.

All this happened thirteen years ago when you graduates were in kindergarten, and I know now from that experience that some of God's greatest gifts are unanswered prayers. I didn't realize until I got away from basketball what an effect my intensity toward the game was having on my health, and that the one more year I'd prayed so hard for - whether we won or lost - might have killed me. I know now what a poor job I was doing as a husband and a father, and how much happier my family is today without basketball. I know how much happier I am professionally as a guidance counselor than I was as a classroom teacher. I know how my doctoral program has allowed me to grow professionally and provide greater financial security for my family. I know there's a lot less pressure making suggestions as an assistant coach rather than decisions as a head coach.

And most of all, I know I've been able to grow enough spiritually to have the opportunity to serve the Lord with a greater commitment than ever before. All of these blessings that my family and I have today are things that I don't believe would have happened if God had answered my prayers the way I wanted Him to in the spring of 1985. God took me away from a situation that was bad for me physically, emotionally, and spiritually and did something good for me that I was too hard-headed and self-centered to do for myself. Those unanswered prayers that I thought were the end of my world in 1985 have turned out to be some of the best things that have ever happened to me.

God has a reason for everything He does, and the way to reach an understanding of this concept is through faith that His way is best for us. The next time that God seems to be ignoring our prayers, maybe we should think again about what we're praying for and, instead, just pray for guidance and acceptance of His will. It's then, through faith, that we may realize that He's been answering us after all in ways that we've been too blind to see, or that for some reason we just aren't supposed to understand yet. Graduates, I hope all of your dreams come true. But if that doesn't always happen - and it won't - and when God doesn't seem to be answering your prayers the way you want Him to - and He won't - keep working, never quit, and have faith. Because, like the country music song says, "Some of God's greatest gifts are unanswered prayers."

23

The Velveteen Rabbit Tattoo

My daughters, Beth and Caye, have tattoos on the inside of their wrists. I had some misgivings about that development when I first noticed them, but gradually changed my mind upon closer examination and a little more thought. Beth's tattoo is, "O Ye of Little Faith" and is a reminder for her to have more faith in God's plan for her life, especially during difficult times. I'm fine with that. Caye's tattoo is "It Is Well" and serves as a similar reminder to her from the hymn *It Is Well with My Soul*. That hymn was sung at both my parents' funerals. I was okay with that one, too. Although a tattoo is a little more permanent than a rubber band reminder (see chapter 14), the fact that both were spiritually based gave me some peace, and I actually decided that they were pretty cool. So cool that I began thinking about getting a tattoo myself. I didn't know what I wanted it to be, though. I knew I wouldn't have to live with mine as long as they would, but I didn't want to make a mistake. I kept thinking.

It was Christmas morning 2016, and our family was following our tradition of opening presents in the den while listening to Christmas music. We'd been at it a while when Caye brought two presents, each wrapped exactly alike, to Beth and me with instructions that we were to open them at the same time. We did that, and pulled out two throw pillows. They were exactly alike, and as I turned mine over, I found an embroidered phrase in cursive handwriting. It took a moment for what it was to register with me, and then I dissolved into tears. Once I collected myself, I knew what my tattoo would be.

On Wednesday, December 28, 2016 - the one hundred and ninth day of my sixty-sixth year - I got a tattoo. It is on the inside of my right forearm and is, "Real isn't how you are made, it's a thing that happens to you." That is a quote from *The Velveteen Rabbit* by Margery Williams that my father used in a letter that he wrote to my daughter Beth in 1992 when she turned thirteen years old. The tattoo is copied from that letter, and it is in my dad's own handwriting.

In the letter, my dad is telling Beth about a Sunday School lesson that he taught on the day she was born in which he used a conversation between two toys in a child's playroom - the Velveteen Rabbit and the Skin Horse - as an analogy to illustrate how people are saved by God's love through Jesus Christ. The old and wise Skin Horse explains to the brand-new Velveteen Rabbit how toys become real as the result of a child's love in this way:

It doesn't happen all at once. You become. It takes a long time. That's why it doesn't often happen to those who break easily, or have sharp edges, or who have to be carefully kept. Generally, by the time you are Real, most of your hair has been loved off, and your eyes drop out, and you get loose in the joints and very shabby. But these things don't matter at all, because once you are Real you can't be ugly, except to people who don't understand.

In the story, the Velveteen Rabbit eventually became real because a child loved him for a long, long time.

In the thirty-one months since I got the tattoo, there has not been a single moment - even the time that I got raised eyebrows and a questioning look from my superintendent - when I wasn't happy that I had it done. When I look at my arm now, I'm reminded of my dad's love for his family, and I think of the love that I have for my own family. I think of an old guy, a little loose in the joints and with most of his hair gone, who got himself a Real tattoo. And, I think, "Maybe I've become."

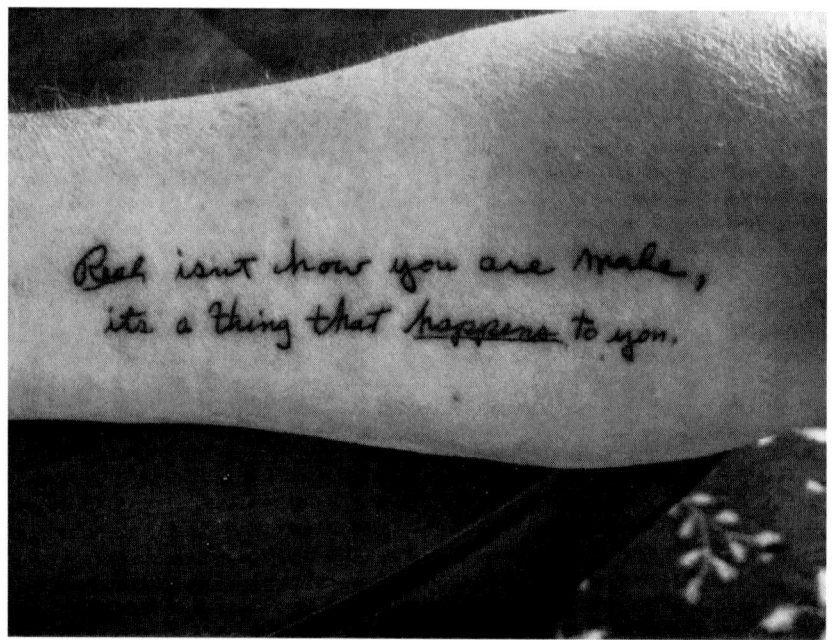

The Velveteen Rabbit Tattoo

Dr. Charlie Burry, Jr.

24

The Last Lesson

"The Last Lesson" is a devotion that I gave to the Board of Deacons at Hartsville First Baptist Church on January 13, 1997. I later used it as my message to the First Baptist congregation on Fathers' Day, June 15, 2003.

A little less than a year ago, in February, I stood before you and discussed the virtues and deeper meanings of country music. I also talked about how some of God's greatest gifts occasionally come disguised as unanswered prayers. And as a means of putting some difficult times that I have had in my coaching career and my life into proper perspective, I mentioned in that devotion that I had lost a lot of ball games, but never a parent, a spouse, a brother or a sister, or a child. That has changed now since my father's death in October. Lately, the Loom of Time has woven some of the darker threads into the tapestry of my life.

I learned a great deal from my dad in forty-five years. He taught me how to ride a bicycle, hit a baseball, and fish with a spinning reel. He gave me my first job when I was eight years old, selling popcorn on Saturdays in front of the Hartsville 5 & 10 and letting me keep a penny for every bag I sold. He showed me how to shave, polish my Sunday shoes, and tie a necktie. He taught me how to drive in a million trips around the dirt road that we lived on, then called Miller Road Circle, in a straight-drive, green and white, 1957 Metropolitan. He went with me the summer before my junior year in college when I bought my first car. He showed me how to use his woodworking tools, and now I can make furniture for my own house, although not with the skill that he did. He taught me to be patient and to listen to what other people had to say. And he taught me - sometimes with the backside of a big hairbrush - to tell the truth, to do things right, to not make excuses when I was wrong, and to finish what I started. My dad showed me how to live. And, in the two weeks leading up to October 25, 1996, through his Christian witness that was just as natural to him as life itself, he taught me one last lesson. My dad showed me how to die.

Part of our scripture for tonight is the 23rd Psalm:

The Lord is my shepherd; I shall not want. He maketh me to lie down in green pastures: He leadeth me beside the still waters. He restoreth my soul: He leadeth me in the paths of righteousness for His name's sake. Yea, though I walk through the valley of the shadow of death, I will fear no evil: for Thou art with me; Thy rod and Thy staff they comfort me. Thou preparest a table before me in the presence of mine enemies: Thou anointest my head with oil; my cup runneth over. Surely goodness and mercy shall follow me all the days of my life: and I will dwell in the house of the Lord forever.

Sometimes when I'm faced with difficult situations - like tonight - I think of the 23rd Psalm. It is a source of comfort and courage for me, and I think in the last year of my dad's life, it might have been for him, too.

I will forever treasure the last face-to-face conversation that I had with my dad. That's when the last lesson began. We were in his room at Byerly Hospital in Hartsville on the day before he was transferred to Richland Memorial Hospital in Columbia. We talked about how God had blessed our family by bringing us to Hartsville: a place where he could make a good living for his family - although I do remember some of the song lyrics that he sang around the house in those early years were from Tennessee Ernie Ford's cover of "Sixteen tons and what do I get? Another day older and deeper in debt." I know he was thankful for being in a place where he could realize his dream of having his own business on the main street in a small town, where he and my mom could raise three children in a good environment, and where he could return some positive contributions to the community that has been so good to us. He told me how fortunate he felt to have lived seventy-two years, to have made a decision like he made in 1959 when we came to Hartsville, and to, in his own words, "not have one regret." He talked about how wonderful the fiftieth wedding anniversary drop-in in September had been and how honored and humbled he'd been - and how much fun he'd had - at the Rotary Club's *Charlie Burry Day* just a couple of weeks earlier. He joked that those two things were, again in his words, "kind of like being able to go to your own funeral - being able to sit there and listen to people say all those nice things about you." We also talked seriously about the recent health problems he'd had, and realizing what he might be facing again for the second time in eleven months, my dad then told me that he was not afraid to die. He certainly had not resigned himself to that, but he had come to terms with that possibility, and was at peace with it. I allowed as how I admired that attitude but reminded him that God just might not be quite through with him yet here on earth and told him that I loved him. I didn't realize until I started writing this how much the course of that last conversation, and the situation in which it occurred, paralleled the 23rd Psalm.

I also didn't really expect that in less than two weeks, my dad would show me, even more clearly, the courage and faith with which he'd been speaking:

Yea, though I walk through the valley of the shadow of death, I will fear no evil: for Thou art with me; Thy rod and Thy staff they comfort me. . . . Surely goodness and mercy shall follow me all the days of my life, and I will dwell in the house of the Lord forever.

My dad had begun to teach me one last lesson. My dad would be showing me how to die.

We believe that a blood clot in a lung precipitated my dad's final illness. As our family gathered that Friday night and in the early hours of Saturday morning, the doctors and nurses informed us of his gravely critical condition and gave us very little hope for any kind of recovery. We spent the weekend expecting word of his death every time the doors to the Intensive Care Unit opened. But God wasn't quite ready for him and, instead, on Sunday he miraculously rallied. His condition remained extremely critical, however, and we still had little cause for optimism. In the early hours of Tuesday morning before his death on Friday, my brother, Brent, and I were staying in Pop's room. Emily was spending the night in Hartsville for the first time in several days, taking care of her three-month-old daughter, Carly. Our mom was not with us, having gone to our cousin Nancy's house for a few hours of sleep. At about 3:00 AM, Brent and I began to notice a slow but sure change in our dad's condition. We weren't - and still aren't - sure what was happening medically, but he may have been having another stroke. We did believe that he was about to die, and we called our mom to hurry back to the hospital, which she did. ". . . Yea, though I walk through the valley of the shadow of death, I will fear no evil: for Thou art with me; Thy rod and Thy staff they comfort me. . . ." The last lesson was about to be completed.

As a distant look came to my dad's eyes, and his breathing slowed and became shallow, and his hands turned cooler, a peaceful, holy comfort came down upon the four of us, and my dad began to smile. I felt the presence of God wrapped around me, holding me, as I have felt it few times in my life. Although my dad actually lived for three more days, I believe with all my heart that he was seeing the light in the open door of the house of the Lord that night, and he knew that he was heading up the walk. And he was so pleased to see God there in the door with open arms that he couldn't help but smile. ". . . Thou art with me; Thy rod and Thy staff they comfort me. . . ." My dad was providing one last Christian witness, and as I put my hand in his hand, he seemed to be saying to me, as he'd said so many times before in my forty-five years, "Son, this is how to do it."

As with many of the lessons my dad taught me, I didn't catch on right away. How could a man face death with a smile? You see, there's no pretense when you're dying. My dad was courageous, but I think it was more than that. My dad knew he was going to Heaven to see his parents and brother and sister again, but I think it was more than just the anticipation of that. My dad was in some physical pain, but I think it was more than just relief. My dad was a man of great Christian faith, but I think there was more to it than that. Where did he get the inner peace and strength to face death with a smile? What else was my dad trying to teach me about dying?

As I have thought about it more, I have realized that in the last two weeks of his life, while teaching me how to die, my dad was actually teaching me something else. I think you'll understand, too, if you'll listen to Philippians 4:7-13:

And the peace of God, which passeth all understanding, shall keep your hearts and minds through Christ Jesus. Finally, brethren, whatsoever things are true, whatsoever things are honest, whatsoever things are just, whatsoever things are pure, whatsoever things are lovely, whatsoever things are of good report; if there be any virtue, and if there be any praise, think on these things. Those things, which ye have both learned, and received, and heard, and seen in me, do: and the God of peace shall be with you. . . . [and then] I can do all things through Christ which strengtheneth me.

Even die.

So, the lesson follows this sequence: God, through His son, Jesus Christ, teaches men how to live. And Godly men try to teach their sons how to live. And when we walk through life according to God's will, in the paths of righteousness . . . doing whatsoever things we have learned, and received, and heard, and seen in the life of our Savior, Jesus Christ, . . . we are building the foundation for the inner peace and strength that it takes to face all the trials and tribulations of life, and, ultimately, death. And finally, we are granted the comfort with which 1 Corinthians:15 concludes:

. . . then shall be brought to pass the saying that is written, Death is swallowed up in victory. O death, where is thy sting? O grave, where is thy victory? . . . But thanks be to God, which giveth us the victory through our Lord Jesus Christ.

My dad was, and will continue to be, my example of inner peace and strength - those characteristics founded on a strong faith in God, those characteristics to which he was a Christian witness all his life, until he took his last victorious breath. God teaches men to live by those characteristics - the Bible is full of those kinds of lessons. And then, Godly men try to teach their sons how to live. So now we understand that my last lesson - our last lesson - in the two weeks leading up to October 25, 1996, when my dad was teaching me how to die, was actually a little more than that. My dad, in showing me how to die, was really teaching me one last lesson . . . about how to live.

25

What Color Were His Eyes?

"What Color Were His Eyes?" is a devotion that I gave to the Board of Deacons at Hartsville First Baptist Church on February 9, 1998. It is a timeless lesson about what is important in life.

Our Scripture tonight comes from Ecclesiastes 2:4-11:

I enlarged my works: I built houses for myself, I planted vineyards for myself. I made gardens and parks for myself, and I planted in them all kinds of fruit trees; I made ponds of water for myself from which to irrigate a forest of growing trees. I bought male and female slaves, and I had homeborn slaves. Also, I possessed flocks and herds larger than all who preceded me in Jerusalem. Also, I collected for myself silver and gold, and the treasure of kings and provinces. I provided for myself male and female singers and the pleasures of men - many concubines. Then I became great and increased more than all who preceded me in Jerusalem. My wisdom also stood by me. And all that my eyes desired I did not refuse them. I did not withhold my heart from any pleasure, for my heart was pleased because of all my labor and this was my reward for all my labor. Thus, I considered all my activities which my hands had done and the labor which I had exerted, and behold all was vanity and striving after the wind and there was no profit under the sun.

It was about eight o'clock on the Monday before Thanksgiving, and I had just gotten home from football practice. It had been cold that afternoon, and I had peeled off several layers of clothes and was in the kitchen reheating my supper in the microwave. I still had my mind on Easley's football team. I knew that they had a Shrine Bowl tailback, a fullback who was probably even better, and a tremendous offensive line. And, as if their talent didn't present enough problems, we knew that having to travel nearly four hours there to the game would make winning an even more difficult task. There were still several hours of watching videotape and breaking down scouting reports ahead of me that night, working alone in my study. But, eighteen-hour work days were okay. We were one game away from the opportunity to go to Williams-Brice Stadium and play for the state championship.

Debby was helping Caye, our sixth-grader, with her homework in the den. Her science assignment had something to do with genetic family traits. The assignment required the students to list the genetic traits of family members: brothers and sisters, parents, and grandparents. I wasn't really paying a lot of attention, but I recall hearing them talking about height, and hair color, and so forth. And then I heard Caye call into the kitchen, "Daddy, what color were Granddaddy's eyes?"

As her question registered in my mind, I began to panic. What color were my father's eyes? Within a few moments, the panic engulfed me, and my mind raced as the full realization came upon me. What color were my father's eyes? I couldn't remember! The man into whose eyes I had looked thousands of times because he taught me to look a man in the eye when you talked to him - and I couldn't remember what color his were. The man whose eyes I had desperately searched during his last days for some sign of life or recognition - and I couldn't remember what color they were. The man whose memory I cherish beyond measure, and I couldn't remember the color of his eyes. What was wrong with me? I remembered that when Byrnes' coaches put #1 and #12 in an inverted slot offensive set, that #1 always ran a short route and #12 always ran a deep route. And I knew that when Easley's offensive formation was

East Left Split Right, they always ran 47XXP and threw to the tight end. But I couldn't remember the color of my father's eyes. What kind of son was I? As my panic changed to incredible despair and guilt, I went into the living room, slumped down on the couch, stared out the window at my mom's house, and dissolved into a complete emotional wreck. I was devastated.

In the days since that night, I have thought quite a bit about what it all meant. This is how I've sorted it out. On the one hand, I've realized - again - how difficult it is to properly prioritize things in a world that on most days just seems to whirl uncontrollably around us. Every minute seems filled with telephone calls, conferences, meetings, commitments, deadlines, some kind of crisis, and a thousand other things that just can't wait. We become so immersed in our work or our daily activities that many times it seems as though that's all we do and all we are. That project has got to be completed, that parent has got to be called, that student or teacher has got to be seen, and we've got to win. And nobody else can do it. Our priorities are such that, as it says in Ecclesiastes, "our hearts are only pleased by our labors and the rewards of our labors." And when that becomes the case, we forget - and neglect - the most important things in our lives: our God and our families. We are football coaches, and guidance counselors, and television zombies, and couch potatoes, and college basketball junkies, and Internet surfers . . . instead of husbands, and fathers, and sons, and brothers, and children of God. But every now and then God finds a way to remind us that all those seemingly higher priorities are "vanity and striving after the wind and there is no profit under the sun." Sometimes we need to be smacked in the face, and that's what He was doing to me one November night when He had my eleven-year-old daughter knock me to my knees with that question.

On the other hand, I have also realized that I am not the kind of person who goes around noticing the color of people's eyes. I even looked at my driver's license to see what color my own eyes were, discovered that they don't put that information on driver's licenses anymore, and had to go look in the mirror. You may be going through some of the same thought processes now that I did that night. But if I were you, I wouldn't be overly concerned with doing that. After thinking about it more, I've decided that eye-color is probably not such a high priority piece of knowledge, except possibly for a school project. Although Caye's question initiated some painfully productive soul-searching, I have - for the most part anyway - quit beating myself up so much over what happened that night.

But, don't miss my point. I'm sharing this story with you because its symbolism is the way God made me stop and think about some things that should be most important to me - the things that should be the highest priorities in my life. What kind of lasting effect will this have on me? Well, I'm going to try harder to slow down and notice - and spend time enjoying - God's precious gifts and the true blessings of life. Next year, it will have been forty years since Dr. Sanders baptized me into the membership of First Baptist Church. I can still go into the fifth and sixth grade Sunday School class that I help teach, look at the portrait of Miss Jo Erwin on the wall, and remember how she and Mrs. Quick, and Bucky Goudelock (who was a young man then), and so many others taught me. In a year-and-a-half, Debby and I will celebrate our twenty-fifth wedding anniversary; be assured that coaches' wives have to be very special people. Beth graduates from high school in June and will go away to college next year, but I remember Debby bringing her to our basketball games in a wicker basket when she was barely two months old. Caye, our baby, starts junior high next fall, but I remember the first night she slept at home in a cradle that my dad made of cherry wood that was almost as beautiful as

Dr. Charlie Burry, Jr.

she was. Brent and I still play practical jokes on Emily, but she doesn't cry when her big brothers pick on her like she used to. I can still look out the front windows of our house and see my mom working in her yard almost every day, and we eat supper with her every Sunday night. I'll always remember how thrilled she was when we were on a trip three years ago to Chapel Hill for her birthday, and she got to meet and shake hands with Dean Smith. When I walk through the den in our house, I can stop and run my hands over the bookshelves that my dad lovingly crafted for us in the weeks before Christmas of 1983 . . . and remember watching him work.

The things I've just mentioned are the true blessings in my life. Those are God's special gifts that I need to take more time to enjoy. Those are the things that I need to be sure to remember. I know, if you'll take the time, that you can think of the same kinds of blessings in your own life.

And by the way, Debby told me later that night . . . his eyes were blue.

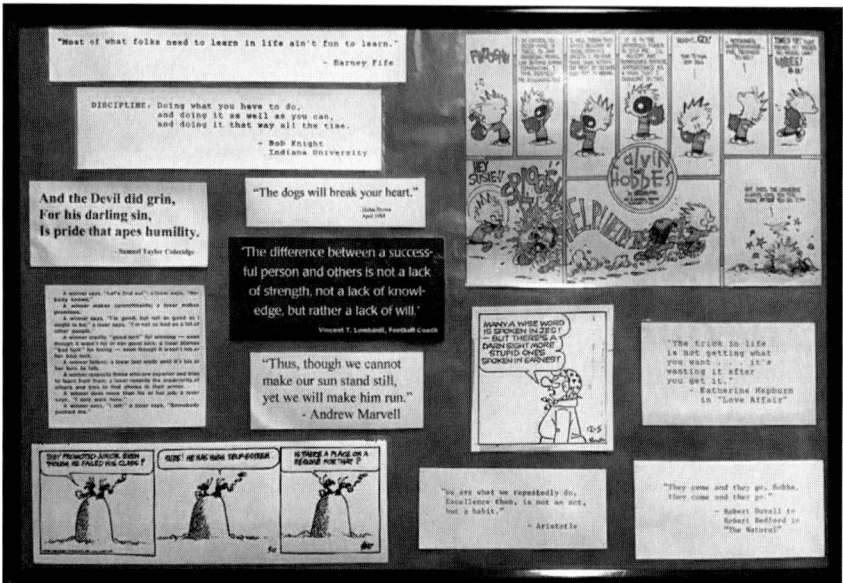

Quote Lessons

I've been a quote collector for nearly all of my adult life. I used them for self-motivation and inspiration when I needed a reminder or a kick in the pants, and I used them with the teams that I coached when I was trying to motivate my players. As principal, I occasionally used quotes as encouragement or to make a point with our faculty and staff. I continue to use them to try to understand life. For many years, both when I was a guidance counselor and principal, I kept a quote wall in my office on which dozens of my favorites were displayed. I'd sometimes notice students and their parents, as well as teachers, who were visiting my office absorbed in reading the quotes. Occasionally, we'd have a conversation about one of them, either at my suggestion or because one of them had caught someone's interest.

Quotes, I think, are like short parables in that when the context is supplied, they teach lessons or illustrate a point of view. If there's some humor or sarcasm hidden in one, that makes it a little more effective or memorable. The best quotes are those that, the instant you read them, provide an "Aha!" moment that helps you see something from a different perspective. This section includes some of my favorites, and I've added commentary to explain what each one means to me.

26

Life's Basic Problem

"Life's basic problem is that you live it looking forward, and understand it looking backward."

- Soren Kierkegaard

I was talking with one of my daughters recently and was telling her that while I didn't wish for many do-overs in my life, one that I would like to have would be my time as a student at Furman University. Please understand that my years at Furman were some of the happiest of my life. It was, and still is, a wonderful institution of higher learning. I graduated from an academically prestigious school, played on the freshman basketball team, enjoyed fraternity life and intramural sports, and met some of the best friends of my life - including the girl who would become my wife. I was, however - at best - just an average student at Furman, and I failed to take advantage of the many academic opportunities and relationships with wonderful professors that were available to me. I just got by and now, with the benefit of hindsight and some maturity that I was lacking at that point in my life, I wish that I'd done better. Academically, I fell victim to life's basic problem.

My problem in this particular area of my life began in high school when I was - without really trying - a well above-average student. I made high grades, except in math, and hardly ever studied. As a result, I never learned how to study. The manner in which I handled the college application process illustrates my attitude toward academics at the time. I had applications to Furman, Davidson, and Wake Forest, but submitted only one of them - to Furman - because that application was the easiest to complete. The others asked for a list of books that I'd read recently and had essay questions. The list of books was a problem because *Sports Illustrated* magazine didn't count, and the essay questions were way too much trouble to answer.

As a result, I arrived at Furman with a rude awakening in store for me. To make matters worse, when confronted with those academic challenges, I didn't respond well at all. I became intimidated rather than attempting to rise to the occasion, and my strategy became that of just trying to fly under the radar of my professors. For the most part, I was able to do that, and my grades reflected it. While I never failed a course at Furman, I also never made an A. I made mostly C's, and every B that I managed was usually accompanied by a D. Looking back at that time with the perspective I have now, I'm amazed that my parents - especially my dad - even let me stay there. And, my daughters - while reading this - are for the first time in their lives becoming aware that they were far better students at Furman than their dad was. One graduated Magna Cum Laude, and the other was a Cum Laude graduate. I graduated Thank the Laude.

A nice postscript to this story is that in my master's degree program at Francis Marion and my doctoral program at USC, my grades improved dramatically. I finally learned how to study, and I rarely made a grade below an A. I think there's something about paying for your education out of your own pocket that helps to bring about such an epiphany.

So, what's the life lesson here, given that we can't change the fact that we live life looking forward and understand it looking backward? I think one lesson should be - while we can't use hindsight to change any part of our past - we can certainly use the benefit of understanding the past as we look forward with greater perspective. We may wince occasionally in looking at the past, but hindsight also helps us to see the future more clearly. And maybe a further lesson should be - at least in our younger years - we should check the rearview mirror more carefully.

Dr. Charlie Burry, Jr.

27

Which Way Are You Going to Do It, Mister?

"This is the right way to do it. Which way are you going to do it, mister?"

- Vince Lombardi

In late January or early February of each year, the winning team in the Super Bowl is awarded the Vince Lombardi Trophy. Vince Lombardi is an iconic figure in the history of the National Football League, and he is best known as the head coach of the Green Bay Packers from 1959 through 1967. He led the Packers to five NFL championships in seven years, including the first two Super Bowls in 1966 and 1967. The Packers were my favorite professional football team as I was growing up, and I greatly admired Coach Lombardi, as well as players like Bart Starr, Jim Taylor, and Ray Nitschke. Vince Lombardi is considered by many to be the greatest coach in NFL history, and his unrelenting demand for perfect execution by his teams was the trademark of his coaching style. I certainly never played for Vince Lombardi or even saw him in person, but during eleven of the fourteen years that I was principal of Hartsville High School, my superintendent was Dr. Rainey Knight, who always challenged her team of principals in the same manner.

In the spring of 2004, Dr. Knight recommended to the Darlington County Board of Education that I be appointed as the new principal of Hartsville High School. That I am indebted to her is an understatement, to say the least. She gave me a chance to contribute to Hartsville High School and the Hartsville community in a manner that became the most rewarding experience of my career. She was my boss, mentor, colleague, and friend. She helped me through some crisis situations, professionally and personally. Her support and guidance as superintendent were crucial factors in the success of The Red Fox Renaissance. There was never any doubt in my mind that she had my back, as long as I was right. And with Dr. Knight, there could be no doubt about what was right and the right way to do it.

Rainey Knight is one of the most intelligent people I've ever been around. She made it her business to have an in-depth, hands-on knowledge of every aspect of running a school district, and did so in a practical manner that was clearly understood. Her knowledge of curriculum and instruction at all levels was thorough, as was her expertise in personnel and legal issues. Another of her strengths was in the area of finance, and she was able to get the Darlington County School District through a severe, prolonged budget crisis while making capital improvements. She made DCSD a model of financial efficiency and stability and raised fiscal responsibility to a new level. In any of these areas, if she asked you a question, you knew that there was a good chance that she already had the answer. You also knew that your answer had better be right.

Her passion for the job and her work ethic were exceptional. She worked tirelessly and set the same standard for everyone who worked for her. It didn't matter how much time you spent at school or working at home, it was not going to exceed what she put into the job. She demanded commitment, but you knew that she was in there with you, working at least as hard as you did. With a political background in her family, she was also a savvy negotiator. I believe that she enjoyed a good fight from time to time, too, and she didn't mind using a few choice words to emphasize her points.

Rainey Knight did her job the right way, and she helped to make me the successful principal that I was. The culture that she developed in our school district was that of a winner. She made us that way with her own unrelenting demand for excellence, which was the trademark of her administrative style. I can see her in my mind's eye now, standing in the front of the room at a principals' meeting where - no matter what the topic of discussion was - the lesson and challenge would be "This is the right way to do it. Which way are you going to do it, mister?"

28

An Ounce of Presumption

"An ounce of presumption is worth a pound of manure."

- Shelby (paraphrased) in *Steel Magnolias*

I've often said that my personality was not well-suited for the job of being a high school principal. I like to do one thing at a time, and having to multi-task aggravated me. I want things to happen according to the day's agenda without a hiccup. My open-door policy was a necessity for being the accessible administrator that I wanted to be, but obviously was the source of countless interruptions. Preparation and organization are my strengths, and I did not enjoy winging it. In other words, everything that I disliked about random, unexpected things interfering with what I'd planned to accomplish during a particular time frame is exactly how a high school principal's day happens. I quickly learned that presuming things were going to happen as expected was an unrealistic and frustrating way to operate, and that doing so greatly increased the peril of stepping in a pile of it.

What I've just described to you about the manner in which I approached my job is the reason my truck was parked outside the administration building at Hartsville High School most Sunday afternoons. While I knew that the job was unpredictable, I wanted to be sure that I was well-prepared for what was already on the calendar for the week ahead. I figured that if I had those things under control, that I'd be better able to respond effectively to what wasn't expected. By extension, I also wanted our assistant principals to be aware of and prepared for what was going to be required of them. We wanted to serve our students, their parents, our faculty and staff, and the community in an exemplary fashion, and being well-organized increased our chances of meeting that responsibility.

I applied the same line of thinking with preparation for our commencement exercises. Graduation is the highlight of the school year, and the spotlight is bright. It is the culminating event that, more than anything else, about two hundred and fifty seniors and their families look forward to all year. As principal, I wanted that ceremony to be perfect for everyone, and especially our graduates. The logistics for the event are detailed and, to some degree, fairly complex. We did mental, and sometimes actual physical, walk-throughs of every piece of the plan several times during the weeks and days before the ceremony. We tried to make the information and instructions for graduates, their family members, and guests as clear as possible. The information was disseminated by mail, by phone, on social media, and in person. The seniors were required to attend a practice the morning of graduation day in order to participate in the ceremony that night. The lineup of graduates was checked again and again. The person who was to announce the graduates' names during the ceremony practiced correctly pronouncing all the names. Graduates were allotted a certain number of tickets, we made it clear that lost tickets would not be replaced, and we had a plan for identifying counterfeit tickets at the door. We had typed copies, in a three-ring notebook on the podium, of everything that every person who had a speaking role on the program had to say, and I kept an extra copy of my remarks in my hand. Our policy was that there would be no cheering for the graduates as their names were called or other disruptions that would detract from the dignity of the ceremony. We had a means to enforce that expectation, and had to resort to corrective measures only twice in eight years.

While other graduation ceremonies - high school and college - often deteriorated into an undignified atmosphere, Hartsville High School's graduation was - and continues to be - a model of respect and dignity that the graduates deserve. The lesson is that we had a good formula, there was not an ounce of presumption that was a part of it, and we came out smelling like a rose every time.

29

Prepare the Child for the Road

> "Prepare the child for the road, not the road for the child."

- Source Unknown

I believe that it's a common characteristic of being a parent to want your children to grow up better than you did as far as having material things is concerned. For the offspring of adults who lived through the Great Depression of the 1920s and 1930s, in most cases that probably just amounted to easier access to the basic necessities of life. Those of us who are Baby Boomers - children of the 1950s - came to expect a little more. When I was a senior in high school in 1969, which was the only year that I was allowed to drive to school, my ride was a 1957 Metropolitan. I hitch-hiked back and forth to Greenville during the first two years I was at Furman, and it wasn't until my junior year that I finally had a stereo in my dorm room. Fast forward to my years as principal, when I would walk through the student parking lot at Hartsville High School and see nicer vehicles than those that our teachers were driving. Ninth graders are given new cars for their birthdays. Today, I see newlyweds who expect to have the same kind of house and furniture when they're twenty-five years old as their parents have after having worked for thirty years. While it's perfectly natural for parents to want their children to have a smoother road than what they experienced during their own childhoods, I believe we've reached a tipping point in that line of thinking at which better is too much. Our young people need to understand and appreciate having to travel a road that's a little longer and a bit rougher as far as material possessions are concerned.

The parenting style of which I've been speaking has also become evident in the disciplining of children. I can't tell you the number of times that I've heard folks my age and even younger say something like "When I was young, if I got in trouble at school, I was in worse trouble when I got home." Sadly, that level of parental support for schools and teachers is rarely seen anymore. It's much more common for parents to make excuses for their children in an effort to get them out of a difficult situation, rather than require that they own up to being wrong, accept the responsibility, and suffer the consequences. The young person is being taught that you don't have to be held accountable for making a mistake, and that is a life lesson which has serious long-term implications. I recall one instance when I was conferencing with a student and his mother. We reached a point at which I knew the young man was being untruthful, his mom knew he was being untruthful, and he knew that we knew he was being untruthful. Yet the mother still didn't have the courage to force the issue, and she continued to make excuses for him. When they walked out of my office, there was no doubt in my mind about who was running that household and that it would not be long before they made a return visit.

More extreme cases of this style of parenting would occur when the teacher or school policy was blamed for the child being in trouble. This was when the parent would decide that the best defense was a good offense and would allege that the teacher was incompetent, unqualified, unfair, immoral, prejudiced, or any other sinful characteristic that they could invent. Another common defense was "I know my son/daughter, and he/she would never do anything like that." It was all I

Dr. Charlie Burry, Jr.

could do to keep from rolling my eyes when I heard that one. And, probably the worst lesson of all is that the child is sitting there listening to the parent make excuses. I don't mean to imply that teachers are always right because they're human, and everyone makes a mistake occasionally. What I am saying, though, is that when you've got conflicting information from a mature, responsible professional on one side and a teenager who is in some serious trouble on the other side, the teacher's version of the story is likely to be closer to the truth.

Life is a bumpy road sometimes, and we as parents and professional educators aren't doing our jobs if we don't allow our children to learn that lesson. While it's hard to watch your children suffer consequences or fail at something, it gives them valuable experience. Sometimes the best lessons in life are the hardest and most painful ones. Those are the lessons that will prepare the child for the road.

30

I Lost It

> "We have not passed that subtle line between childhood and adulthood until we move from the passive voice to the active voice - that is, until we stop saying 'It got lost,' and say, 'I lost it.'"
>
> - Sidney J. Harris

My parents started teaching me about accountability at a very young age. While my mom seldom deferred judgment or consequences to my dad when I misbehaved, I usually faced a more strenuous inquisition when he got home from work. Part of my upbringing was that I had a few daily and weekly chores to perform, and that was before I even knew what an allowance was. The chores were expectations, plain and simple. When I was about six years old, one of my daily chores was to feed our pet rabbit, Whiskers. It was a simple task that took no more than about five minutes, except on the one day of the week when his cage had to be cleaned. On one of the cage-cleaning days, my mom asked me about mid-afternoon if I'd fed Whiskers yet. I assured her that I had, even though I hadn't been near the rabbit cage that day. I've never been a very good liar, and it only took my mom a quick visit to the rabbit cage to confirm her suspicions that I hadn't fed Whiskers and that I'd also lied about doing it. She quickly and forcefully rectified the immediate situation, and the clock started ticking until my dad would get home from work.

Another part of this story is that my dad was the manager of the local Kress store at the time. I visited his store occasionally, usually spending most of my time in the toy department. The boys in my neighborhood used to play army quite a bit, and our weapons were simulated hand guns and dirt clod grenades. The arms race escalated when one of us was able to find an old broomstick to use as a rifle. There was a toy army rifle at my dad's store that I'd had my heart set on for quite some time, as acquiring such a weapon would likely result in an immediate promotion in rank among my playmates. I wanted that rifle so badly I could taste it.

So, my dad arrived home on the evening of Whiskergate, and it was time for me to face the music. Standard interrogation procedure was for me to sit on his knees facing him, and his opening statement was usually something like "Well, don't sit there like a knot on a log. Tell me what happened." The rest of the conversation that evening went something like this:

Me: "Whiskers didn't get fed."

Daddy: "Why didn't Whiskers get fed?"

Me: "Nobody fed him."

Daddy: "What do you mean, nobody fed him?"

Me: Silence.

Daddy: "Who's supposed to feed the rabbit?"

Me: "Me, I guess."

Daddy: "What do you mean, I guess?"

Me: Silence.

Daddy: "It's your job to feed the rabbit, and you didn't do it, right?"

Me: "Yes, sir."

Daddy: "And then you lied and told your mother that you did, right?"

Me (with tears in my eyes): "Yes, sir."

Daddy: "So tell me what you did wrong."

Me: "I didn't feed Whiskers and then told mama a story that I did."

Daddy: "Go out to my car. There's an army rifle in the back seat. Bring it in the house."

Me (wide-eyed): "Huh?"

Daddy: "You heard me, boy. Go out to my car and bring that army rifle in here."

I followed my dad's instructions, thinking that somehow a miracle had occurred. I came back in the house, carrying that rifle with sweaty hands and caressing the polished wooden stock like a baby, and after a minute or two the conversation picked back up here:

Daddy: "Now, go put that rifle back in my car."

Me (more wide-eyed): "Huh? Why?"

Daddy: "So I can take it back to the store in the morning."

Me (with more tears in my eyes): "Yes, sir."

You've guessed by now that the army rifle never made it back to the Burry house to become a part of my playtime arsenal. I also figured out later that my mom and dad collaborated a little bit sometime that afternoon before he headed home from work. You can also see that my dad's line of questioning made me move - as Sidney J. Harris said - from the passive voice to the active voice. While I was still a long way from becoming an adult, I learned a formative lesson and grew up a little bit that day.

31

Most of What We Need to Learn in Life Ain't Fun to Learn

"Most of what we need to learn in life ain't fun to learn."

- Barney Fife

I spent a good bit of time, beginning when I was about eight years old, working in my dad's dime store - the Hartsville 5 & 10. My first real job was on Saturdays when my dad would roll the popcorn machine out onto the sidewalk in front of the store, and I'd sell popcorn all day for ten cents a bag. I got to keep a penny for every bag that I sold, and on a good Saturday I'd make two or three dollars. While that was pretty good money for an eight-year-old boy in 1959, I can't say that I enjoyed spending my Saturdays at the store. But it taught me the value of a dollar which, at the time, was a hundred bags of popcorn.

A year or two after that, we started selling fireworks in the store during the Christmas holidays and leading up to New Year's Day. My dad bought the inventory and turned the fireworks counter over to me. I was being paid by the hour by that time - fifty cents an hour, if I'm not mistaken, or about four dollars a day. One afternoon, I had a good customer and made a big sale of ten dollars and forty cents. The customer handed me a twenty-dollar bill and - trying to be helpful - also gave me a quarter, a dime, and a nickel to cover the forty cents. All I had to do was give him a ten-dollar bill as change. I did that, and then carefully counted out and handed him another nine dollars and sixty cents. He apparently decided at that point to help himself instead of me, applied the finders/keepers-losers/weepers theory to the transaction, and left. I sensed that something wasn't right, but it wasn't until I started matching up the money in my shoebox with what I knew I'd sold that I realized the man got more than ten dollars' worth of fireworks for eighty cents. If you're quicker at math than I was when I was ten years old, you've figured out by now that I worked the next two and a half days at the Hartsville 5 & 10 fireworks counter for free. I learned to be more careful making change from that experience, but it sure wasn't fun. I still think about that lesson today when I hand cashiers at fast-food restaurants $10.35 to cover a $7.35 sale, and it totally confuses them. Been there, done that.

Over a period of years at the dime store, I was promoted to the stock room. My job there was to open and unpack boxes of freight, check the merchandise against the invoices, affix adhesive price stickers to the items, and carry them out to the sales floor to be put on the counters and shelves. I used a box-cutter razor to open the cardboard cartons, and one of the first things my dad told me was to be very careful when cutting a box open so as to not cut into whatever merchandise was inside the box. Well, I opened a carton of breadboxes one afternoon, and I wasn't careful enough. The breadboxes were metal, and the lids were painted red. When I put the box-cutter down and opened the carton, I realized that I'd cut a razor mark into the paint right across the middle of three breadbox lids. Needless to say, my pay envelope was considerably thinner that week, and I was the proud owner of three slightly damaged breadboxes. I don't remember what I did with those breadboxes, but I can't recall having much fun with them. I still think about that lesson today when I open a box from Amazon that's been delivered to our house.

Dr. Charlie Burry, Jr.

Most of my memories of the Hartsville 5 & 10 are good ones. That store provided a livelihood for our family for many years and paid for my college education. My dad employed wonderful people who worked hard, and were honest, dependable, and loyal. Many of them became like family to us. I learned both the necessity and value of having a job and that all honest work is noble whether you're managing a store or sweeping a floor. My dad's long, hard hours for six days a week were an example of a work ethic that I carried with me throughout my career in public education. But there were also some lessons that I learned about popcorn, fireworks, and breadboxes that ain't fun to remember.

32

We Are What We Repeatedly Do

"We are what we repeatedly do. Excellence, then, is not an act, but a habit."

- Will Durant

Student report cards in the Darlington County School District, and statewide in South Carolina, are generated from a software program. The standard information is primarily grades and attendance, but while I was principal of Hartsville High School, we created a customized template on which to print the report cards. The template included the school name, our mission statement, the Red Fox Pledge of Honor, the grading scale, frequently used school telephone numbers, and a list of important upcoming school events. Also, at the top of the template was a Will Durant quote that I mistakenly attributed for years to Aristotle: "We are what we repeatedly do. Excellence, then, is not an act, but a habit." Aristotle actually said, "These virtues are formed in a man by his doing the actions." Regardless of who said exactly what, it's good philosophy.

One of the Darlington County School District's basic beliefs is that every child can learn. Consistent with that belief, at Hartsville High School we encouraged our students to do their best and to fulfill their maximum potential, whatever that might be. Even in the world of a standard grading scale where 90 is an A, 80 is a B, and so forth, my belief was that excellence had different criteria for every person. Our goal when I was principal was that Hartsville High School would be "A Place of Hope and

Possibility" for every student. Following that philosophy of daily encouragement, my position was that if a student was fulfilling his/her potential, then that level of achievement met that particular individual's criteria for excellence. Realizing that this philosophy is pretty subjective, I also think that allowing students who have coasted to an A with little or no effort to believe that they have done excellent work is giving them a false sense of what excellence really is. On the other hand, I think that students who have worked as hard as they possibly can to achieve their full potential of a C deserve to feel a legitimate sense of excellence. In either case, students know - deep down - whether or not their work has been excellent. Finally, understand that I am not advocating for participation trophies. I used to keep a cartoon on my wall about a mother who noticed that her son got a report card grade of A for Self-Image, and the father asked if there was a place for that on a job application. At some point in life, everyone has a showdown with reality. That's when Durant's quote becomes truly meaningful.

In getting to the real meaning of the quote for every student, it was important to have the above discussion about the definition of excellence. As for the real meaning of the quote, Durant is telling us that excellence - if we achieve it - is who we are; and, more importantly, who we are is the result of a process. In neither case is excellence a single act. In athletics at the highest level, one indication of excellence as induction into a Hall of Fame, but a baseball player isn't elected to Cooperstown as a result of hitting one home run or even leading the league in home runs for one year. That standard of excellence is achieved through a combination of talent and dedication to a sport over a long period of time. That person became an excellent player because of years of habitual hard work and repeatedly doing things the right way, every day. It was a process. In academics, one indication of excellence at the highest level is being named as a Rhodes Scholar. But a person doesn't become a Rhodes Scholar by scoring well on a standardized test or by making the Dean's List a few times. That standard of excellence is achieved through a combination of intellectual ability and diligence in the classroom, library, and research lab over a long period of time. That person became an excellent student because of years of habitual hard work and repeatedly doing things the right way, every day. It was a process.

In the showdown with reality, most of us are not going to become Hall of Fame athletes or Rhodes Scholars. Most of us are going to lead average lives and, hopefully, be good people. Will Durant and Aristotle are simply teaching and encouraging us to become the best we can be and to achieve that level of excellence in our individual lives by habitually doing things - to the best of our abilities - the right way, every day.

33

Blessed Are Those Who Can Laugh at Themselves

> "Blessed are those who can laugh at themselves, for they shall forever be amused."

- James Carlos Blake

We take life far too seriously sometimes, but having a good sense of humor can help us put things in the proper perspective. Laughter over a good joke is often the best medicine when circumstances in our lives seem bleak. Sometimes we laugh to keep from crying. We need to be able to laugh with others but also to have enough self-confidence to laugh at ourselves. We've got to be comfortable enough with our own self-images to be able to enjoy it when we see ourselves as others do, whether we're the victim of a practical joke or when we've done something embarrassing. It's healthy to be able to laugh at ourselves.

It helped Phyllis Griggs to be able to laugh at herself when someone posted a picture on Facebook of her putting gas in her vehicle after she'd run out in the parking lot in front of Hartsville High School. It helped Jimmy White to be able to laugh at himself when someone planted an autographed Polaroid photo of a scantily-clad woman in his dirty clothes bag at a coaches' clinic, and his wife found it when he got home. It helped Pat Hewitt to be able to laugh at herself when someone smeared Vaseline cream on the toilet seat in the restroom next to her office, and she almost slid off onto the floor when she sat down (there were no actual eyewitnesses to this event). It helped Dean and Leigh Boyd to be able to laugh at themselves when someone who'd been house sitting for them one summer surprised them by leaving a female mannequin dressed in one of Leigh's nightgowns in their bed and another one, unclad, in their bathtub.

And, then, there's the Bill Laimbeer story.

I've been a Boston Celtics fan since the days of Bob Cousy and Bill Russell. My interest has waned somewhat recently, but in the 1980s - the Larry Bird years - I was rabid. It was on my bucket list to see a game in the old Boston Garden at North Station before it was demolished in favor of the new TD Garden. In January 1992, Beth Bass - who worked for Converse shoe company at the time and was recently inducted into the Women's Basketball Hall of Fame - made my dream come true by arranging a trip to Boston for me and a good friend. Hal Baldwin and I flew to Boston on a Friday morning, ate lunch at Cheers (location of the television show) and then shot baskets on the parquet floor while touring the Garden that afternoon, and saw the Celtics play the Phoenix Suns that night. We went sightseeing all day Saturday, ate lobster at our hotel that night, and saw the Celtics play the Detroit Pistons on Sunday afternoon. Being a long-time Celtics fan, I harbored great dislike for the Pistons - known as the "Bad Boys" - and in particular their six-foot ten-inch center, Bill Laimbeer. I thought that he was the dirtiest player in the National Basketball Association, and it infuriated me when he took a cheap shot at Larry Bird, Kevin McHale, or Robert Parrish. That's the background for the story.

Hal and I were eating dinner in the restaurant of our hotel on Saturday night when it occurred to me that if the game was at noon on Sunday, the Pistons must already be in town. I went on a half-serious rant about finding out where the Pistons were staying that night and looking up Bill Laimbeer to give him a piece of my mind. I calmed down some, we finished our meal, and went out into the hotel lobby. There, standing at the elevators, were the Detroit Pistons. Isaiah Thomas, John Salley, Rick Mahorn, Joe Dumars, and the whole team was there . . . except Bill Laimbeer. We watched open-mouthed as players that we'd seen only on television boarded the elevators, and then I went on another rant about what a good thing it was that Laimbeer wasn't there, that I'd have cursed him up one side and down the other. Hal and I then went over to the hotel gift shop. I was standing at the magazine rack, looking down at the bottom shelf, when a pair of brown shoes - at least size eighteen - walked up and stopped right beside me. I looked up, and then up some more, and there - standing not two feet away from me - was Bill Laimbeer, all six-foot ten-inches of him. I gulped, looked back down, and then took a glance over my shoulder to find Hal. He was in the corner of the gift shop, laughing so hard that he could hardly stand up. I eased away from Mr. Laimbeer and slipped out of the shop with my tail between my legs. It was truly one of the funniest things that has ever happened to me in my life.

At the game the next day, we had seats two rows from the court, and when I got ready to heckle Bill Laimbeer, Hal looked at me and said, "You just keep your mouth shut. You had your chance last night." All I could do was laugh at myself, and Hal and I are still greatly amused - to say the least - every time we tell that story.

Hal Baldwin and Charlie Burry

Dr. Charlie Burry, Jr.

34

Don't Fight the Rabbits

"Don't fight the rabbits. Because, boys, if you fight the rabbits, the elephants are going to kill you."

- Bob Knight

My first year as principal of Hartsville High School was by far the most difficult of my forty-five-year career in public education. When I assumed those responsibilities on July 1, 2004, I had been at the school for twenty-six years as a teacher, guidance counselor, and coach. I thought that I knew a lot about the school, and in many respects, I did. It didn't take me long to realize how much I didn't know. There were days if someone had called and offered me a job driving a truck cross country, it would have taken me about two seconds to throw my Hartsville High School keys on my office desk and walk out the door. I tried not to let it show - I don't think I did, at least at school - but it was truly a daily emotional and spiritual struggle.

Thankfully, I inherited an experienced and capable team of assistant principals - Bob Abbott, Reggie Alford, Candy Holcombe, and William McCall. Although I had never been even an assistant principal, they were receptive to my being promoted from my job in the counseling department into a position as their supervisor. They accepted the new administrative team structure, and I never had cause to question their loyalty or work ethic. We had a two-day retreat at Lake Robinson in July to hash out organizational issues and administrative team responsibilities, and one of the first things that I told them was what they were going to hear most from me was "What do you think?" I did ask that question quite a bit during that first year and throughout my tenure as principal. However, one of my big problems - especially in the early years of my principalship - was that I did a poor job delegating responsibility. I fought too many rabbits.

What Coach Bob Knight was telling his Indiana University basketball team about fighting rabbits was that they shouldn't let small things bother them. He was saying that if they worried too much about little things, that the bigger problems in basketball and life - the elephants - would overwhelm them. I'd read this quote in the January 26, 1981, issue of *Sports Illustrated* in an article by Frank Deford about Bob Knight entitled *The Rabbit Hunter*. I even put it on my quote wall, but I did a poor job of relating it to the world of school administration. I had a good team of rabbit hunters, and they fought some really big rabbits for me on a daily basis - as well as an occasional grizzly bear - but I spent too much time in the briar patch with them. I nearly let the rabbits drive me crazy during that first year, and that made my job of handling the elephants much more difficult. And believe me, there were plenty of those big guys, too.

Another way to look at Coach Knight's lesson is that you have to choose your battles. You have to be able to figure out which of them are the keys to winning the war. Some of the battles, in the grand scheme of things, are just not worth the time and effort. I learned that working out a compromise over a minor issue with a disgruntled parent at the school level, even though I might not be entirely comfortable with it, was more efficient in terms of time and effort than having the situation taken to the district office, the school board, or a local television station where it most assuredly would become an elephant. I also learned that if I disagreed with my superintendent over an issue, most of the time the smart thing to do was just let that rabbit run and do my job, knowing that I wasn't going to win many of those battles anyway. Another effective strategy is to intentionally lose a battle occasionally in the interest of better relationships. A person doesn't have to be wrong to apologize.

There are two dangers involved in fighting rabbits. One is that rabbits can multiply very quickly, and if you don't get to the root of the problem and deal with mama rabbit and daddy rabbit, then suddenly you'll have a bunch of baby rabbits hopping around your feet. The second lesson that I learned about fighting the rabbits is that sometimes an elephant can show up disguised as a rabbit. You see, they both have big ears, and some problems when brought to your attention aren't what they might seem to be initially, either intentionally or unintentionally. If you aren't perceptive enough to sense that or gauge the potential for such a development, then you might find yourself being squished into a corner by something that came in the door looking like an innocent little bunny.

So, as Bob Knight said, "Don't fight the rabbits, boys." Actually, another lesson that I learned over the years is that it's best to make friends with the rabbits. That way, when the elephants show up, at least you've got them outnumbered.

35

The First Law of Holes

"The First Law of Holes: When you're in one, stop digging."

- The Washington Post

During the last few years that I was principal of Hartsville High School, I had an outstanding team of assistant principals - Von Cranford, James Ford, William Lenard, and Corey Lewis. Among their many duties and responsibilities, one issue - unfortunately - was student discipline. They did an excellent job keeping most of those issues from coming across my desk, until - either due to the frequency of the problems or the severity of a situation with a student - I conducted what we called an In-House Hearing. Such a hearing was the last stop on the line before an expulsion hearing with the school district hearing officer. The In-House Hearing required the presence of the student's parent, and while the consequences were usually pretty severe, I always tried to make it a teachable moment for the student and - if necessary - the parent, too. As a result, one thing that we often discussed was "The First Law of Holes."

One fairly common reason that a discipline situation would come to my attention was that a student who had become involved in a relatively minor problem turned it into a major offense by his reaction to the initial situation. A teacher might address a student about some inappropriate behavior, and instead of acknowledging responsibility for the problem, the student would cause the situation to escalate by becoming verbally abusive toward the teacher. A student observed to be in violation of the cell phone policy would, when a teacher - as per his/her responsibility - attempted to confiscate the device, refuse to surrender the device. A student who had accumulated multiple after-school detention assignments would refuse or forget to attend, even after several reminders, leaving the school administration no other choice but to resort to a more punitive tactic. In each case, the students - instead of easily making their way out of relatively shallow holes - chose to dig themselves into deeper holes from which a way out was much more difficult. So, the teachable moment in the student's In-House Hearing would be a discussion of The First Law of Holes, which is "When you find yourself in one, stop digging."

As an illustration, I would use the story (fictional, of course) of my being stopped for speeding on I-20 even though I was in a line of vehicles that were all going at least eighty-five miles per hour, and some were going even faster than I was. I would attempt to get the student to understand that when the Highway Patrol officer came to the window of my truck and asked for my license, registration, and proof of insurance, that moment was not the time to argue about how fast everyone else was going or to question the reason that I was the only one of many speeders who was stopped. I would offer the suggestion to the student that at that moment, it was time for me to do precisely as the officer requested and to do so in a most respectful manner. I would further suggest that if I believed the officer to be wrong, my best chance of successfully arguing the point would be in traffic court and not on the side of a busy interstate highway. I would finally suggest that the student learn to apply that scenario (fictional, of course) to other situations and to avoid further violations of The First Law of Holes.

Another aspect of the First Law of Holes is that some people, upon finding themselves in a small hole, attempt to tunnel out. By that I mean their choice to deny responsibility, rather than facing a direct confrontation, would involve being untruthful about the matter of concern. One problem with attempting to blindly dig oneself out of a situation is that you don't know exactly where you're going to come up, and that you could well emerge dirty, and being no better off - or in a worse place - than you were when you started digging. I'm reminded while writing this of the cartoon that showed an escaped prisoner who had tunneled his way outside the prison wall into the hole beneath an outhouse and the messy outcome of that mistake. A further complication of an attempt to deceptively tunnel one's way out of trouble is that one untruth often leads to another. In that case, the strategy often leads to an entire network of falsely constructed tunnels, none of which is adequately supported by a timber of truth. Such an underground complex of falsehoods is subject to a total collapse with one misplaced lie, resulting in everyone who has become involved being buried alive with consequences.

The lesson that I've learned in my life about the First Law of Holes is found in its simply stated truth - further excavation is not a good idea. If you use dynamite, you're just going to blow yourself up, and the truth is always the best way out - even if you think you have a golden shovel.

36

If It's Your Job to Eat a Frog

"If it's your job to eat a frog, it's best to do it first thing in the morning. And if it's your job to eat two frogs, it's best to eat the biggest one first."

- Mark Twain

We all have to eat a frog from time to time. Some folks, unfortunately, are faced with such a task on a daily basis. Other people, thankfully, are only required to do so occasionally. Every once in a while, if it's a really bad day, we must eat two. It can be in your chosen profession, or it can be in your personal life. No matter how many times we change jobs, and regardless of what improvements we might make in our personal lives, frog is going to show up on the day's menu every once in a while. And, I'm not talking about frog legs, either. I'm talking about when a dog tries to eat a frog, and the dog ends up foaming at the mouth.

So, acknowledging Mark Twain's witticism, if you've got something distasteful to do, why put it off? Why ruin the whole day thinking about it? You know that frog is not going to jump off your plate onto someone else's. You know that there's no nice person who is going to come along and say, "Yum, let me eat that frog for you." You know that frog is not going to magically turn into a piece of chocolate cake. Why not go ahead, get it over with, and forget about it? My personal outlook is that putting things off just added stress to my life. That frog was always in the back of my mind, and I couldn't relax until I'd taken my medicine.

Maintaining a level of physical fitness, at least for an older guy like me, is not something that is particularly enjoyable. When I was working, I took care of my exercise routine first thing in the morning because I knew that there probably would be no time for it later in the day. Now that I'm retired, I'm still at the YMCA at 6:00 AM so that I can finish my workout and move on to more pleasant things, like breakfast and reading the newspaper. Speaking of not-so-enjoyable things, growing up I was taught to always clean my plate, and that sometimes meant eating food that I didn't like. Even today - while we don't have meals that I don't like at our house, and I certainly don't order anything in a restaurant that I don't like - I always eat my least favorite item first and save the best until last.

During the time that I was principal of Hartsville High School, if I had a choice, I always tried to schedule meetings that I knew might be difficult or unpleasant for early in the day. If I had a telephone call or an email for which a response was probably going to be troublesome, I tried to get that item checked off my to-do list as soon as possible. I didn't want the anticipation of having to do something unpleasant to be on my mind any longer than necessary. I wanted to go ahead and get that frog off my plate. I had a similar philosophy when I knew that I had two amphibious entrees on my menu for the day. I wanted to deal with the big problem first, knowing that if I could manage to get that one down, I'd be more confident about swallowing the smaller guy even if I was starting to feel a little bloated. Also, if circumstances required that the second frog be put in the refrigerator until the next day, I wanted it to be the small one.

Mark Twain's frog metaphor is obviously a lesson about procrastination, which - over a period of time - opens the door

Dr. Charlie Burry, Jr.

for an accumulation of frogs, both big and small. If you don't wash dishes regularly, they get piled up in the sink. If you don't eat the right foods, you have high cholesterol. If you don't change the oil in your car, the engine doesn't run well. If you don't study, you make poor grades. If you don't pay attention to the people you love, relationships suffer. It might not be a problem occasionally to put off eating your frog until the afternoon or even the next day. If you do it too often, though, your boss is going to walk in one day and see that washtub full of frogs that it was your job to eat, and you'll be swimming for your life in some swampy water.

37

You Got Some 'Splainin' to Do, Lucy

"You got some 'splainin' to do, Lucy."

- Ricky Ricardo on the *I Love Lucy Show*

My tenure as principal of Hartsville High School was probably the most rewarding time of my career. We were able to make some changes at the programmatic level that truly made the school better for students, faculty and staff, and the community. The most enjoyable part of my career, however, was the seventeen years that I spent in the school counseling department. I still tell people that I had the best job in the school - helping students while not being tied to a teaching schedule, and being able to continue coaching as well. As with any job, though, one of the things that made it most enjoyable was the relationships with my colleagues. I was blessed to work with some wonderful people - Debbie Berry, Janell Britt, Barbara Dampier, Shirley Freeman, Sandra Gaskins, Hibby Jeffords, Juanita McFarland, Vicki Norment, Ray Petty, Dierdra Robinson, and Tim Scott.

And then there was Paula Terry, who was in the guidance department when I became a counselor, and later transitioned to an administrative position as Hartsville High School's first Ninth Grade Academy Coordinator. I got to know Paula and her husband, Steve, in 1978 when I came back to Hartsville High School as the boys' basketball coach, and he was the men's basketball coach at Coker College. I'd go over to their house on College Avenue, and Steve and I would sit in their living room and draw up basketball plays. The friendship between the Burrys and the Terrys deepened over time as our families grew, our jobs changed, and relationships evolved. Over the years, Paula became my closest colleague in the counseling department, a trusted member of my kitchen cabinet while I was principal, and a dear friend. We seemed to share a similar sense of humor, and laughter was an enjoyable part of our relationship, professionally and personally.

A ready sense of humor is an important part of working in a high school setting. As you might imagine, there are some difficult and stressful situations with which to deal, and the occasional infusion of a little laughter at an appropriate time helps to ease the tension. To that end, Paula and I developed a repartee drawn from the old television shows I Love Lucy and The Andy Griffith Show. Paula was Lucy Ricardo, and - mimicking her husband, Ricky - I would sometimes look at her and say, "You got some 'splainin' to do, Lucy." I was Barney Fife, and - imitating Sheriff Taylor - Paula would occasionally shake her head and say to me, "You beat all, Barney." We'd then move on to the problem at hand, refreshed by a quick smile or laugh to help us put things in perspective, and we would soon get the issue resolved or get things back on track.

The life lesson from "You got some 'splainin' to do, Lucy" goes beyond a quick laugh, though. The quip had a deeper meaning of trust that was also saying, "I understand the situation, and it couldn't be helped." The joking remark carried a message of reassurance that was verifying "I don't know how this happened, but we're going to work together to get it fixed." The wisecrack conveyed a message of support that counseled, "This is a mess right now, but it could have happened to anybody." Or, "You got some "splainin' to do, Lucy" could have been my own confession that slyly admitted, "This is really my fault, but I don't know how in the world you could let me do something like this." What was meant, sensed, and understood went far beyond Ricky's words. The real message of trust, respect, support, and honesty was easily received and deeply valued.

The lesson is that relationships with a foundation of respect and affection are stronger with humor as a component. The chemistry of the team is enhanced when its members can laugh at and with one another. Practical jokes and funny stories are enjoyed more. Misguided trespasses are more quickly forgiven and forgotten. Memories are fuller and richer. Goodbyes are harder, yet easier. And finally, cherished friendships last forever when "You got some 'splainin' to do, Lucy."

Paula Terry

Dr. Charlie Burry, Jr.

38

The Trick in Life

"The trick in life is not getting what you want, it's wanting it after you get it."

- Katherine Hepburn in *Love Affair*

During the first two years of our marriage, Debby and I lived in Florence, South Carolina, where I taught at the South Carolina School for Boys, and Debby worked as a registered nurse at Bruce Hospital. My main hobby at that time was fishing, but I did some small-game hunting, too, mostly shooting doves, and hunting squirrels and rabbits. I owned a 12-gauge pump shotgun, but for quite some time, my eye had been on a .22 caliber lever-action rifle that I'd seen in a hardware store downtown. It was a beautiful gun. As Christmas 1974 approached - our first as a married couple - Debby and I made our Santa wish lists known to each other. At the top of my list, of course, was that .22 rifle. I gave my bride of four months an exact description of the rifle, the name, location, and phone number of the hardware store, and the cost. I left no chance that there would be any confusion on Santa's part when he left presents under the Christmas tree.

Christmas morning arrived, and I was as excited as a little child. We put some Christmas music on the stereo, sipped coffee and ate sausage casserole, and began to open presents. I didn't see anything that looked like it could be a .22 rifle, but I figured that Debby had it hidden away for the grand finale. As things began to wind down, though, some doubt started to creep into my mind. Maybe she didn't get it. Maybe when she went to the store, the rifle had been sold. As we prepared to drive to Hartsville about mid-morning for Christmas at my parents' house, I was not a happy boy. But then my spirits were renewed when I thought, "She took it to Hartsville, and she's going to surprise me there!" However, Christmas at the Burry's house in Hartsville - as far as I was concerned - was sadly uneventful. There was still no rifle among the shirts, ties, and socks that I was collecting. After more coffee and sausage casserole, we headed on to Columbia for lunch and Christmas with Debby's parents and family. I was in full pout mode by that time, and Debby knew it. The trip to Columbia was made in mostly silence. We arrived at the Sturgeon's house, and I put on my happy face for my new in-laws. Lunch was delicious, as usual, and was followed by more opening of presents. I added a couple of pairs of khaki pants to my sock collection, faking a pleasant mood the whole time. Finally, after the last presents had been opened and the last pictures were taken, Debby walked into the room with one more present - a beautifully wrapped box with a big bow on it that was just the right size to hold a .22 rifle. As she handed my last present to me, I realized that everyone was watching me.

And then it dawned on me that everybody in both families, all day long, had been in on Debby's plan to fool me. As I removed my beautiful rifle from the box, I had two emotions. One was embarrassment for acting like I was about five years old for most of the day, and the other was happiness in getting just what I wanted from Santa. Pretty immature on both counts.

But the trick in life, as Katherine Hepburn said, is not just getting what you want. I've probably shot target practice with that rifle half a dozen times during the last forty-five years, and I've been hunting with it about the same number of times. It's place of honor now is under my side of the bed, ready in case of an intruder, and I get it out to dust it off about once a year. You see, after I got it, I didn't want it very much. And to make matters worse, I've got a closet full of things that I was once burning up to have - a compound bow, a shotgun, a .38 caliber pistol, a drone, a unicycle, a kayak, a set of golf clubs, and a whole collection of hats - that I hardly look at anymore. I should have a yard sale or open a sporting goods store.

So, what's the lesson here? How do you know what you really want? How do you make sure that you're still going to want something after you get it? Or, is Hepburn's quote just a cynical, inescapable truth about life? And then the real kicker - does the quote just pertain to material things, or can it apply to personal relationships as well? Most everybody has a garage or an attic full of junk that, at least once, brought us great enjoyment. Therefore, I think that we can put most material things into that category, except for those with true sentimental value. That's when we head toward the real context of Hepburn's quote - that she's talking about personal relationships. So, what makes a personal relationship valuable, and what makes it last? In order to avoid writing an entire psychological treatise here, I think it boils down to genuine, unconditional love - a pretty complicated issue in and of itself. But when you figure out why you truly love someone in that manner - or why you don't - that's when you'll know if you're always going to want that person. And also, if that person is always going to want you.

39

Where Do You Find Peace?

"I've learned from this odyssey that peace is not the absence of troubles, trials, and torment but calm in the midst of them."

- Don Meyer

During the 2003-2004 school year while I was working as a full-time guidance counselor and coach, I also partnered with Madge Zemp in a part-time private counseling practice. I met all of the criteria and passed all of the exams to obtain my certification as a Licensed Professional Counselor and was looking at the possibility of moving into a full-time LPC practice when I retired from public education. Madge and I shared office space in the upstairs portion of a small house on West Carolina Avenue. After several months of only moderate success with my LPC practice and never feeling entirely comfortable with it, I decided to back out of that venture. I wanted to get that piece off my plate and slow down a little bit. I remember telling someone that I just wanted some peace in my life. Six months later, in the irony of all ironies, I became principal of Hartsville High School - so much for any peace in my life.

On July 1, 2004, I began an odyssey that would prove to be the most difficult year of my professional career, a year in which I probably could have benefited from some counseling myself. The troubles, trials, and torment began in the summer, when every salesman and vendor in South Carolina came out of the woodwork to try to sell something to the new principal.

On the first day of school for students, I became aware of a gang presence on campus that had to be subdued. That fall, two of my decisions involving student discipline were finally upheld after being appealed all the way to the school board. It seemingly took forever to convince our students to conform to the new student identification card policy. Our school began months of preparation for our five-year Southern Association of Colleges and Schools evaluation in March that would determine our future accreditation. In October, just before basketball practice was to officially begin, the coach for our varsity boys' team resigned. In December, we had a huge altercation in the parking lot after a basketball game that made front page, above-the-fold headlines of the *Hartsville Messenger*. In March, I made an exceptionally difficult change in the leadership of our football program that would cost me one of the best friendships of my life. In April and May, I hired a new football coach, a new boys' varsity basketball coach, and a new athletics director. There were countless professional development meetings, locally and statewide, for first-year principals throughout the year that required my attendance. In looking back just recently at my desk calendar for that year, I was unable to find an entry for peace anywhere, and there certainly was not an absence of difficulties.

My problem that year, and actually for a number of years - as Coach Meyer said - was that I was looking for peace in the wrong place. I was not going to find it noted in my desk calendar, and I was not going to accidentally encounter it in my daily routine. I couldn't find peace at school in the late afternoon or early evening when everyone else had left for the day, and it wouldn't even come to me at home. While my outward demeanor may have projected the image of a leader who was cool, calm, and collected, my inward state of mind was about as far from being peaceful as it could get. The one tell-tale sign, our administrative team said, was that they could see when I was upset because I'd slowly rub my hand back and forth across my head. Or, if I was really upset, I'd rub both hands. I must have rubbed a lot of hair off during that first year.

To follow Coach Meyer's advice, I needed to recognize and accept the fact that as long as I was a high school principal, there were always going to be troubles, trials, and torment. I also needed to recognize that I had control, not outwardly over the difficulties, but inwardly over how I responded to those challenges and how I allowed them to affect me. I needed to realize that many times, after about twenty-four hours, I could laugh - or at least smile - about some things that had me chewing Tums as fast as I could the day before. Perspective can teach us valuable lessons, one being - if we can look at a situation this way now, then why were we all upset about it earlier? The lesson in this case is the same as when we seek shelter from the rain and lightning of a thunderstorm - that while the difficulties and crisis situations of the day storm all around us, we can always find peace in a quiet, calm place inside.

40

You Got to Know When to Walk Away

> "You got to know when to hold 'em, know when to fold 'em, know when to walk away, know when to run."
>
> - Bobby Bare and Kenny Rogers in *The Gambler*

I didn't change jobs very much during my forty-five-year career in public education. I worked at only three schools - the South Carolina School for Boys for three years, Gilbert High School for two years, and Hartsville High School for forty years. I was a classroom teacher and coach for fourteen years, a guidance counselor and coach for seventeen years, and a principal for fourteen years. While I did consider other job opportunities a few times, I actually pulled the trigger on moving from one job to another only four times in my career before making the decision to retire in June 2018. On each of those occasions, and a handful of others when I didn't make a change, I tried to approach the situation in an analytical manner - coaching with my head. I made lists of pros and cons, and assigned values to each consideration, and ended up with a total number of points for each option that would give me a clear answer. I also paid attention to my gut feeling about the situation - call it instinct, intuition, hunch, or whatever - coaching with my heart, which gave me a much more nebulous answer. It was when the two answers differed that the struggle between hold 'em and fold 'em took over my thoughts and dreams. Poker players always look for some sort of sign - a "tell" - from their opponents about what kind of hand they have. Sometimes life gives you a tell, too. Following are two examples.

Lon Armstrong and I coached together at Gilbert High School during the 1977-78 school year. Lon was an excellent coach and a fine man, and we became very good friends. He taught me how to chew tobacco, and I taught him how to fish. In the spring of 1978, we were both considering other job opportunities, though - Lon was talking with Mid-Carolina High School about their football position, and I had applied for the basketball job at Hartsville High School. Lon had been at Mid-Carolina before, prior to spending a year at Hannah-Pamplico High School and then being at Gilbert for a year, and he wanted to go back. I'd only been at Gilbert for two years, but Hartsville was my alma mater and my hometown, and it would be a move from a Class A school to a Class AAAA school. Lon and I were both conflicted, though, because the GHS students were great kids, and Gilbert was a wonderful community of people. Also, Gilbert High School was under the very capable leadership of Bob Whitehead, who was an outstanding administrator and an even better man. So, Lon and I had been talking quite a bit about our futures. One night, we were returning home from a meeting of schools that were in a newly realigned conference that was going to include Gilbert High School the next year. Lon was driving, and we were talking, chewing and spitting, and listening to the radio when a song we'd never heard before entitled *The Gambler* came on. The version we heard that night was sung by Bobby Bare before Kenny Rogers made it a big hit a few months later. But when Lon and I heard the lyrics, "You got to know when to hold 'em, know when to fold 'em, know when to walk away, know when to run," we looked at each other and knew what we were going to do if we had the opportunities. Life had given us a tell. Lon went back to Mid-Carolina, and I moved to Hartsville.

Thirty-nine years later and going into my fourteenth year as principal of Hartsville High School, I was beginning to think about retirement. I was tired from working sixty-plus hour weeks and being under the 24-7 pressure of ultimately being responsible for everything that happened that had anything to do with Hartsville High School, no matter when or where it occurred. School safety had been on my mind quite a bit, and every morning on my way to school I prayed that it would not be my school in the national news that day. On the other hand, I had an outstanding administrative team in place - Von Cranford, James Ford, William Lenard, and Corey Lewis were our assistant principals; Brian Howell was our IB Programme coordinator; and Phyllis Griggs was our athletics director. They were the ones who were actually running the school at the administrative level, and they kept a number of problems off my desk. The school was doing well academically, our fine arts programs were flourishing, our athletic teams were winning championships while our athletes were earning scholarships, and we were getting wonderful community support. Our students had bought into the idea that if we were going to have a great school, they were going to be the ones to make it that way, and our school climate was the best it had been since I had become principal. On one hand, things were going great, yet on the other hand, I was thinking about leaving. I was conflicted, and I was looking for a tell.

In February, I noticed a couple of things that caused me to make an appointment with my doctor, Rob Elder. I had some bloodwork done on a Monday morning, and when the results came back, Rob advised me to make an appointment with a gastroenterologist in Florence. I saw Dr. Veeral Oza on Thursday, we talked about possible concerns, and he made another appointment for me to see him again on Monday. He cautioned me that if I began to feel disoriented over the weekend to call him. That caused me some mild concern. The next day about the middle of the morning, Dr. Oza's partner, Dr. Davinderbir Pannu, called me at school to tell me that he wanted me admitted to the hospital immediately and that I should come to McLeod Hospital in Florence as quickly as possible. That raised my level of concern considerably, as well as that of my wife. Upon being admitted, I learned that my liver enzyme numbers were exceptionally high, but the doctors were unable to determine the cause. I was told if those numbers did not soon come down drastically, that - worst case scenario - I'd be transported to the Medical University of South Carolina (MUSC) in Charleston as a potential candidate for a liver transplant. I had not only seen my tell, but it had hit me right between the eyes.

I spent six days in McLeod Hospital where I had a liver biopsy done, and then went to Charleston to see Dr. Heather Simpson, who is a liver specialist at MUSC. The diagnosis from Dr. Simpson was autoimmune hepatitis. That's when, for no known reason, the white blood cells in the body attack the liver. Thankfully, although I'll have the disease for the rest of my life, it can be managed well with medication, and my long-term prognosis is excellent. I returned to work the following week, weakened considerably from my hospital stay and with a distinctly yellow skin tone. I was thankful to be getting better, and thankful to be back at school, but I began to think much more seriously about retirement. There's no doubt that my illness was the tipping point in my final decision to step down. There was no denying that I had my tell.

I walked out of Hartsville High School as principal for the final time on June 15, 2018. As I am writing this, I still miss being principal immensely. I miss the students, my colleagues, and some of the best friends of my life. I miss the extra-curricular activities, and I miss interacting with the community. I miss making a difference in the lives of young people. All things considered, though, I believe that I retired at the right time. You've got to know when to hold 'em, know when to fold 'em, and I think God was telling me when to walk away.

Lessons Between the Lines

Being totally honest about my career choice, I will have to admit that I chose teaching in order to become a coach. I can also tell you that the best coaches that I have known are, before anything else, great teachers. Coaching at its essence is teaching a young person how to play a sport and teaching a group of young people how to play as a team. I think that is why great athletes sometimes don't become great coaches. The game comes naturally to great athletes, and they may not have to work as hard at mastering the fundamentals and learning the intricacies of a sport. They just do something that comes naturally to them really well and may not understand how or why they did it. Average players who have to scratch and claw for everything they get are forced to learn those things through long hours of practice, and as students of the game themselves, they may be better able to teach the fundamentals of a sport to others.

Another issue in the sometime convoluted relationship between academics and athletics is the concept of the student/athlete. Particularly in big-time college sports, the term student/athlete is regarded facetiously as academics and athletics are often strange bedfellows. In fact, sometimes they don't even sleep in the same house. However, during my time as a guidance counselor and coach, I believed academics and athletics to be a good marriage and promoted it as such. I tried to help our student/athletes to understand that if they had the work ethic to succeed in a sport, the same self-discipline and diligence could be applied to their school work. Ironically, athletics is often the front porch of a school and attracts more passionate community interest and support than academic achievements.

Finally, in terms of life lessons, many positive character traits are better taught and learned in the arena of athletics than anywhere else. The physical nature of sports, the competition, and the camaraderie inherent in the concept of a team raises the stakes when learning and internalizing the qualities of dependability, responsibility, accountability, toughness, and loyalty. Striving as a team member for a common goal against difficult circumstances forges those character traits into better people, spouses, parents, and citizens.

Following are stories of some life lessons learned between the lines during my thirty-one-year coaching career.

41

You Can't Fire Me! I Quit!

One of the big lessons - maybe the biggest lesson - mastered by successful leaders of organizations is to surround themselves with good people. Sometimes it takes a while for that lesson in administration to manifest itself in reality, but one of the key moves that I was able to make during the spring of my first year as principal of Hartsville High School was when I separated the athletics director's position from all coaching duties and hired Phyllis Griggs for that job. An athletic department as large as ours required the full-time attention of an administrator with no coaching responsibilities, and an added benefit was assuring everyone that there would be fair and unbiased treatment regarding the support that each of our fourteen sports received. Phyllis had prior experience coaching four sports and possessed a high level of administrative and organizational skill. She and I were also very much on the same philosophical page about the role that an athletic program should have relative to the mission of the school and in impacting the school culture. Her integrity was unquestioned. The final selling point as far as selecting her for the job was her love for Hartsville High School and our community, as well as her deep passion for Red Fox athletics. She approached her job as athletics director with the same intensity with which she coached her teams, and there was no doubt among our faculty, coaching staff, and our student/athletes about who was in charge of our athletic department.

I was intense about my position as well, and as a result - when we occasionally had differing opinions about how something should be done - Phyllis and I would have some pretty heated discussions behind closed doors. I'm fairly sure that she secretly enjoyed talking to me in a manner that no one else at Hartsville High School dared to chance, and I was fine with that because of our mutual respect and loyalty to each other. Occasionally, when I would intentionally instigate that type of exchange during a faculty meeting, she'd just laugh when others would say to her afterward, "I can't believe you talked to him like that!" I sometimes jokingly described our relationship by saying that I would fire Phyllis a couple of times a week, she'd quit about twice a week, and the other day we got along fine. In reality, we had many rewarding and reflective talks about high school athletics, the welfare of our student/athletes, school administration, as well as life issues on road trips to ball games and South Carolina High School League meetings in Columbia. Those talks deepened our relationship, both professionally and personally, and when our mothers passed away a little more than a year apart, we talked a lot about them on those trips. As athletics director, Phyllis Griggs not only became a valued and trusted member of our administrative team, but one of the best friends of my life.

What our school and the community got out of the lesson was an athletics director who worked tirelessly to provide our coaches and teams with the administrative, organizational, and financial support that they needed to be successful. Her long-standing connections with the Hartsville community revived the support from local business and industry that has also been a key to the success of our athletic program. That success was evidenced by numerous region and state championships won by our teams, as well as a number of sportsmanship awards won by our school. Phyllis was recognized several times as Region 6-AAA Athletics Director of the Year, once as the South Carolina AAA Athletics Director of the Year, and in 2018 she was awarded the South Carolina Athletic Administrators

Association's Distinguished Service Award. The Hartsville High School athletic program became known as a class act throughout South Carolina, and that was a reflection of her leadership. Athletics - justifiably or not - is often the front porch to the image of a school in a community, and the success of our sports program under the leadership of Phyllis Griggs was a key to The Red Fox Renaissance.

Ironically, and maybe fittingly, Phyllis and I both retired at the end of the 2017-18 school year. Obviously, we don't see each other as much now as when we were working, but we still enjoy an occasional lunch downtown, a cookout at The Retreat in her backyard, or a visit with each other at a Red Fox athletic event. Although the circumstances of our relationship have changed, this aspect of the lesson endures - she remains one of my dearest and closest friends. I won't fire her, and she won't quit.

Charlie Burry and Phyllis Griggs

42

Be Yourself

"Be yourself" is advice that is generally intended to be of some comfort and encouragement to someone who is about to encounter a stressful situation. It's a phrase that is meant to tell people that they should be confident in themselves and their abilities. But, if we think about it more than just superficially, what does it really mean to be yourself? The converse of that statement would be to suggest that a person be someone else. We all have people in our lives that we respect, admire, and hope to emulate, or be like, in some manner. I've mentioned a few of those people in my life in the first section of this book. So, in our life-long journey toward self-realization and fulfillment, how do we decide who we really are? Should I be Charlie Burry or Tim Watson? Or, a tougher question yet - for me, anyway - was, should I be Charlie Burry, Jr., or Charlie Burry, Sr?

Part of answering this question is understanding that we can adopt admirable qualities from different people who have influenced us. If we admire someone's persistence, we can become more persistent. If we appreciate someone else's compassion, we can become more compassionate. If we value another person's loyalty as a friend, we can become a more loyal friend. If we like the way someone does his job, we can blend some of those characteristics into the manner in which we do our work. The trick is in not attempting to be someone's clone, but to blend pieces of different qualities that we'd like to emulate into whatever fits the total person that is our own unique identity. In the long run, you've got to be you, not someone else.

I think that answering that question and realizing who we are is also a journey of personal discovery. We learn that we have certain talents and abilities - things that we do well, and other things that we don't do so well. I have some athletic ability, but I can't carry a tune in a bucket. I've been told that I write pretty well, but I have no aptitude for playing cards, and I probably couldn't solve a Rubics Cube in a year. I did relatively well in English and social studies and not as well in math and science. So, as you learn what you do well, you gain confidence in those abilities. Over time, we also learn things about our personalities. Some people are shy, and others are the life of the party. Some people are leaders, and some people are followers. There are procrastinators in life, and there are people who are five minutes early for everything. Flying by the seat of your pants is how some of us roll, and others have a list or a chart for everything. So, as we learn about our own personalities, we become comfortable in our own skin. I think these two things - discovering one's talents and learning to like one's personality - are most important to realize and accept in the journey to knowing oneself. Everyone, as a child of God, has value. You may have heard before that "God don't make no junk." Remember that about yourself, no matter what you hear from anyone else.

The importance of being yourself was pointed out to me early in my coaching career, but I was too immature to understand it at the time. I took my basketball teams to summer camp for several years at The Citadel in Charleston, South Carolina, where Les Robinson was the head coach. Coach Robinson later went on to be the head coach at East Tennessee State University and also at his alma mater, North Carolina State University. He retired from coaching and became athletic director at NC State and concluded his career with a return to The Citadel as athletic director. Les Robinson was a great coach and athletic director and is an even better human being. I don't know that there is anyone more well-liked in college basketball than Les Robinson, and he probably has a story about everyone he ever met. One of the benefits of taking my team to summer camp at The Citadel for me was being a part of the late-night staff meetings with other coaches when we could relax with a cold beverage after a long, hot day and listen to those stories. One night, Coach Robinson and I began talking about a mutual acquaintance who was no longer coaching, and I made the statement that I didn't think he was himself at a previous position. That was really just an offhand comment by a young coach who didn't know what he was talking about, but at that point Coach Robinson looked me in the eye and told me, "You said a mouthful there." Fast forward about forty years to a night when I was watching the SEC Storied documentary about Pete Maravich on television. Pete's dad, Press Maravich, was his coach at LSU and was a close friend of Coach Robinson. Press Maravich's coaching career at LSU, despite his son becoming college basketball's all-time leading scorer, was only mildly successful. Part of the documentary was an interview with Coach Robinson to ask his take on the Maravich years at LSU. Coach Robinson had kept some old hand-written letters from his friend and was commenting on those when he said about Press Maravich, "I don't think he was himself at LSU." That comment sent my mind racing back to that hot summer night at The Citadel when I'd heard Coach Robinson emphasize the same thought to me. As I processed that, I decided if being yourself had been so much a part of Coach Robinson's philosophy for that long during his remarkable career, it must be pretty important. If I'd been smart enough to understand what he was trying to tell me that night long ago - that I should be myself and not try to be someone or something else - my own basketball coaching career might have been a little more successful.

So, why is being yourself important? I think that it's the key to the personal satisfaction and psychological well-being which comes with being true to oneself. And that comfort level results in a person doing a job optimally well and fulfilling one's potential. No one ever becomes completely comfortable trying to be someone else, whether one does it well or not so well. It took me some time to realize this, especially when I moved back to Hartsville at the age of twenty-seven to teach and coach at my alma mater. I was coming home to a place where my father was a highly respected and well-known businessman and citizen. And, as blessed as I was to have the parents that I did, being Charlie Burry, Jr., and trying to live up to the standard that my dad set in every part of his life was a hard thing to do. I understood that he was a merchant and I was an educator and our worlds were different, but it took me a while to realize that I could only consider myself a success if I walked in my own shoes instead of trying to fill his. His were way too big for me, and I became a lot more comfortable, successful, and happier when I finally found a pair that fit me - and I could be myself.

43

What I Learned from Getting Fired

The first thing I learned in 1985 when I was fired from my basketball job at Hartsville High School is you have to win, even in high school. Having a team culture that contributes positively to the school is important. Having players who are good citizens at school and in the community garners support for the program. At some point, however, the community and the school administration can no longer support a program that consistently produces losing records. During my forty years at Hartsville High School, I experienced this athletic truism on both sides of the principal's desk. Either way, it hurts, and you never get over it.

In a previous chapter about *Listening to Old People*, I talked about the value of experience. There have been many times that I've wished that I'd known in the early part of my coaching career what I know now. I'm fairly certain that we'd have won more games and that my players probably would have enjoyed playing for me a lot more. My career as a head coach began at Gilbert High School in 1976. I was moving past a previous coaching experience in which, in hindsight, I thought we'd have had more success if our coaching staff had chosen to exercise more control over some issues within and surrounding our team. I learned that lesson too well. When I became a head coach, I was determined to control everything. I made up my mind that if my teams didn't win, it wasn't going to be anybody's fault but my own. And it was.

In the late 1970s, basketball was a much different game than it is today. One of the main differences is that there was no three-point shot. Another major difference was that pattern or continuity offenses were much more popular and prevalent during that era. In theory, a pattern or continuity offense not only runs a set play, but it also runs that play continuously - over and over again - until what the coach deems to be a good shot presents itself. The cuts, picks, and passes are precise and always within that disciplined pattern. Good shots are created as a result of that pattern, and it is an offensive philosophy that allows individual players very little freedom. It is also a system that limits creativity and actually restricts - other than the pre-scribed options - the use of individual talent. It's not very popular today among fans, players, or coaches. Also, with the shot clock as part of the game now, it's not even practical. But, in 1976, I was sold on it.

I remember a post-game conversation with an opposing coach when he said, "Charlie, your guys run that offense like robots." I took that to mean that we were a disciplined team, which was important to me, and that he was paying me a compliment. I should have been smarter. I also recall a brief conversation that I had with Coach Dean Smith one Sunday morning in Chapel Hill. My mom was a huge Tarheel fan, and I'd taken her and my dad to see UNC play Wake Forest during the weekend of her 70th birthday. The game was on Saturday night, and we'd come back to the Smith Center the next morning to visit the Memorabilia Room when we happened to run into Coach Smith in the parking lot. He was very cordial to my parents, and then he asked me what kind of work I did. I told him that I was a high school guidance counselor and football coach, but that I used to coach basketball. He asked me which sport I liked best, and I said, "Basketball, but I think my personality is better suited to football." He then asked, "Why is that?" My answer was something like "Because I think you have more control in football." Coach Smith's response to that was a slightly quizzical smile and the rhetorical question "Oh, really?" I hadn't gotten any smarter.

I know now that basketball, when a team plays at an optimal level, requires a delicate balance between an organized, fundamentally sound structure and the freedom to allow players to maximize their talent and creativity. I also know that players, especially today, find that kind of system of play more enjoyable. Fans enjoy that style of play because its more exciting. There's probably more room for debate about what a good shot is - at least among coaches - but with the skill level of today's players (see Steph Curry), almost anything goes. As I've thought about that conversation with Coach Smith over the years, I think that he was trying to get me to re-evaluate my concept of control. I think what he was trying to get me to understand was - at least in his opinion - teaching basketball players the concept of control within an optimally functioning, but more loosely structured system actually requires a more refined type of control than simply teaching a football player to run to a specific hole, block a certain gap, or even react to a particular defensive stunt or coverage (although football today has evolved into more reading and reacting as a play develops). Anyway, I've finally gotten a little smarter, and if I was coaching basketball today, I'd let my players play the game.

As a principal, I adopted a similar philosophy about teaching. It didn't take me long as a principal to figure out that just like good players can make you a pretty good coach - if you'll let them play - good teachers can make you a pretty good principal - if you'll let them teach. While we had curriculum standards that we had to follow, there were a lot of ways to skin that cat. I used to jokingly tell prospective teachers during job interviews that I didn't care if students were swinging on the light fixtures when I walked in their classrooms, as long as I saw teaching and learning happening. Because of that philosophy,

I think our teachers enjoyed working at Hartsville High School. We required them to be professionals, but I let them teach. As a result, most of them fulfilled their potentials as teachers, they were happier professionally and personally, and our students learned to the best of their abilities.

So, what did I learn from getting fired? First, as former UCLA and Hall-of-Fame basketball coach John Wooden said, "Never mistake activity for achievement." In other words, results are what counts. And second, when you've got good players, you gotta let 'em play. And, when you've got good teachers, let 'em teach.

Dr. Charlie Burry, Jr.

44

Some Days, Even My Lucky Underpants Don't Help

"Some days, even my lucky underpants don't help."

- Calvin and Hobbes

While I was coaching at Hartsville High School, I was interviewed by a member of the school newspaper staff for an article that she was writing about superstitions. Her first question was "Are you superstitious?" My answer was something like "Why, certainly not. However, I do have certain ritualistic things that I do - especially on game days - that serve to put me in a more comfortable and confident state of mind." You see, part of being superstitious is never admitting that you're superstitious. That would be bad luck.

Athletic activity is an area of our lives that is rife with certain rituals, especially I think, for coaches. The most common axiom in athletics - confirmed by Crash Davis in the movie *Bull Durham* - is "Never screw with a winning streak." We were fortunate to win quite a bit during my time as a Red Fox varsity assistant football coach so that led to a lot of repetitive behavior. On each Thursday night before a Friday game, the varsity coaches and our wives always ate supper at The Beacon restaurant in Hartsville. The Beacon had a Red Fox Room with walls covered with Hartsville High School athletic pictures and memorabilia, and that room was reserved for us on Thursday nights during football season. We sat at the same tables in the same chairs, and - as long as we'd won the week before - I ordered the same entrée from the menu. We won fourteen games in a row in both the 1992 and 1993 seasons, and while The Beacon had a great fried chicken recipe, I got pretty tired of eating it. Anything for the team, though. But remember, all this did not involve superstition, only rituals that put me in a more comfortable and confident state of mind.

Game day attire was also subject to ritual. Head Coach Lewis Lineberger kept a record of the team uniform color combinations - pants and jerseys - that we'd worn for each game of the season going back for twenty-one years. If we had lost to another team in recent years, that losing uniform color combination was never repeated against that team. However, there was one exception that took precedence over all other available data. For a big game, the Red Foxes were going with a solid color combination, occasionally red pants and red jerseys, but most often - especially if it was a really big game - all black. Personally, I had one pair of socks and boxer shorts that were designated for game day. Thankfully, in football there is a week between games, so my socks and underwear did get washed and were clean for every game. I can't speak for the other coaches on the staff, though. I chewed tobacco during my days as a football coach, and I'll have to admit that habit probably was due more to enjoyment than anything else. But, at the conclusion of pre-game warmups as the team headed back to the locker room for last-minute reminders and Coach Lineberger's motivational speech, I always spit my chew out at the same spot on the hash mark of the forty-yard line closest to the locker room. That ritual always put me in a more comfortable and confident state of mind, and that's when I knew we were ready.

Some of my ritualistic behavior followed me into the Hartsville High School principal's office in 2004. I certainly didn't forget football when I stopped coaching, and I always knew that a Red Fox victory was assured if Janice Davis brought the principal half of a BLT sandwich from the Carolina Lunch restaurant on Friday morning - a ritual that put me in a more comfortable and confident state of mind. Also, my desk was made of wood, and I knocked on it quite a bit, especially during the first year - just to feel more comfortable. As I entered my office each morning, I would - in this exact order - flip on the wall light switch, turn on the other floor lamps and the lamp on my credenza, put my briefcase on the floor beside my chair, turn on my computer and monitor, put my school ID around my neck, sit down, and knock on wood. Then, being in a more comfortable and confident state of mind, I was ready for the day. About an hour later at 8:05, I would make announcements that would include the day of the week and the date, saying for example, "Good morning, this is Monday, the tenth day of September 2018." However, I did change my script a couple of times each year to read, "Good morning, this is Friday, April thirteenth, 2018." I simply thought it would be a good idea for my morning ritual to not include the words, ". . . Friday, the thirteenth . . . ." During our Thursday afternoon administrative team meetings, every assistant principal was absolutely forbidden to utter the words, "You know, we haven't had a student fight in a long time." I learned early in my tenure that mentioning that, or sometimes just thinking it, absolutely guaranteed a fight within twenty-four hours and sometimes within minutes.

Being principal of Hartsville High School was the most rewarding experience of my career, but it was also a very difficult job. The lesson is that, despite my best ritualistic efforts to create a more comfortable and confident state of mind - due to reasons completely out of my control - occasionally I was going to have an absolutely terrible day. It was on those evenings, sitting at home in my recliner and contemplating every possible cause of the day's events that had brought me such consternation, I'd remember that I was wearing my favorite pair of boxer shorts. At that point, it was just time for me to wryly acknowledge the lesson that, "Some days, even my lucky underpants don't help."

45

What Did You Do on the Worst Day of Your Life?

I was watching a ball game on ESPN one night in late November 2007 and noticed a news item scroll across the bottom of the screen that read, "Ralph Beard, guilty in 1951 NCAA basketball point-shaving scandal, dies at age seventy-nine." That made me think.

Ralph Beard was an outstanding basketball player at the University of Kentucky from 1945 through 1949. He was one of famed Kentucky coach Adolph Rupp's *Fabulous Five* and was on teams that won NCAA national championships in 1948 and 1949. He was a three-time first team All-American at Kentucky. Beard was on the United States Olympic basketball team that won a gold medal in 1948. He was a second-round pick in the 1949 National Basketball Association draft and averaged 15.9 points and 4.4 assists per game over two years with the Indianapolis Olympians in the NBA. In 1985 Beard was inducted into the Kentucky Athletic Hall of Fame, and in 1995 his jersey number "12" was retired by the University of Kentucky. His success on the basketball court undoubtedly made him one of the elite players of his time. Yet when he died, the storyline on ESPN and the headlines in newspapers across the country didn't mention any of those accomplishments.

This is the reason. In October 1951, authorities charged Beard and two teammates with taking bribes as part of an NCAA point-shaving scandal that took place between 1947 and 1950. He pled guilty and admitted that he took seven hundred dollars from gamblers but denied ever shaving points in a game. As a result, Beard was banned for life from the NBA. While I don't know everything else that happened to him in the remaining fifty-six years of his time on earth, that was probably the worst experience of his life. He never played organized basketball again. He considered suicide. In a 2002 interview, he said, "Basketball was my life. It's what I lived for." Beard tried to make amends when he was invited back by the University of Kentucky to speak with their players about the dangers of sports gambling. Thousands of college basketball fans - especially in Kentucky - know about Beard's amazing career, yet millions more know only what they saw on television the night he died or in the newspaper headline the next day. And that made me think some more.

I believe if we had the opportunity to ask Ralph Beard what he did on the worst day of his life, he'd answer pretty quickly that it was when he took that seven hundred dollars. But how fair is that? A man who was one of the most celebrated figures in the storied history of Kentucky basketball, and that's how he's remembered? A former athlete who became a prosperous businessman in Louisville, and that's the lead line in his obituary? A man who lived for seventy-nine years and had a strong marriage for fifty-two years and a family, and that's what his family members see and hear when their husband and father died? How fair is that?

The answer is that this is one of the things about life that sometimes isn't fair, and that's the lesson that we need to learn from Ralph Beard. Too often in life, we tend to remember the bad instead of the good. The media reinforces this mindset by headlining the bad news. Just recently in Columbia, South Carolina, the trial of Timothy Jones for murdering his five children dominated the front page of *The State* newspaper for three weeks. Surely there were other good things that happened

Dr. Charlie Burry, Jr.

during that period of time, but the Jones trial was what people wanted to read. What sometimes was difficult for me to remember as principal of Hartsville High School was that about ninety percent of our discipline problems came from about ten percent of our students. As a football coach, I remember more about our state championship game losses than I do about our wins. And, while we all have feet of clay, people tend to look more at other people's feet than their own. That's human nature.

To help us have a more compassionate and forgiving perception of this issue, perhaps we should ask ourselves this question: What would it be like if all people were most remembered for the worst thing they ever did in their lives? To make it more personal, as well as more thought-provoking, maybe the question should be this: How would you like to be most remembered for the worst thing you ever did in your life? The answer to both of those questions is that we'd all probably look pretty bad. Perhaps those questions should enter into our decision-making process when it comes to life choices, especially those of the greatest importance. Would you want the consequences of a poor choice to be the next day's newspaper headlines or in your obituary? Would you want the repercussions of a bad decision to be the first thing that your family members think about when they see your name on caller ID or remember you on holidays? That might help us to dismiss the justification that we often use when we're ready to surrender to temptation. Beard, when he was only twenty-one years old, could clearly see that justification. His father had abandoned his family, and his mother worked as a cleaning lady. Growing up in those circumstances, seven hundred dollars probably looked like seven million. But if Beard had it to do over again, I'm pretty sure he would think differently about what he did on the worst day of his life. Will any of us have to learn this regrettable lesson in as painful a manner as Ralph Beard did?

46

Know What Play You're Going to Call

Athletics, whether you're playing or coaching, teaches many life lessons. If you're playing, you learn about physical and mental toughness, teamwork, discipline, sacrifice, and loyalty. When you're coaching, you learn about organization and preparation, the complexities of the game, how to teach, and how to motivate young people. In an educational setting, academics always comes first, but I can tell you that there are a lot of life lessons illustrated and learned through athletics that can't be taught any other way.

Part of my philosophy as a coach was that I always wanted my players to be prepared for whatever they might encounter in a game. Practice was teaching and rehearsing what we would need to do, individually and as a team, to be successful against our opponents. Practice repetitions would assure that we would be able to execute those same things under the stress of a game situation. As a coach, the preparation had a similar purpose. Strategically and personnel-wise, I wanted to our team to be able to take advantage of our strengths and exploit our opponent's weaknesses. That preparation extended to specific game situations. Generally, in football, it was field position, down and distance, score, time left in the game, a desired personnel match-up, and the anticipated alignment of our opponent. If you watch football on television these days, you'll notice the detailed play sheets carried by the offensive and defensive coordinators and the armbands worn by players with the codes needed to decipher the coach's signals from the sidelines. Some teams even go so far as to script the first series of offensive plays that they're going to call. All teams have, somewhere on their play sheets, a list of short-yardage plays that they believe will be successful in goal-line or fourth-down situations. Coaches carry an extra point card with every possible score differential to tell them whether to kick for the extra point after a touchdown or go for a two-point conversion. A coach is always prepared for crucial game situations and doesn't have to go through a long thought process under pressure to make a decision. A coach knows what play to call and signals it to the huddle. The players have run the play in practice, probably a number of times. Coaches and players are as prepared as they can possibly be for what they're going to do in that particular situation.

The idea of game preparation, planning ahead, and knowing what play you're going to call can easily be transferred to real life situations. When I was a guidance counselor, I had conversations with students, sometimes individually and other times in groups, about making good decisions - which is sometimes a difficult thing for teenagers to do. I would ask them to think about a time when they'd been in trouble or maybe even had gotten in a fight. I would then have them answer four questions, either verbally or sometimes in writing: (1) Where were you? (2) Who were you with? (3) Did you have a choice or a decision to make? (4) When it was all over, was it worth it? Usually - if the students were willing to admit it, at least to themselves - it would be obvious that if only one of those questions could have been answered in a different way, the trouble probably would have been avoided. If they'd been better prepared in any one of four ways, they could have called a better play. I would then go further into the situation in an attempt to help them understand that the best decisions are usually not made in the heat of the moment. I would ask them three more questions: (1) Was there peer pressure? (2) Were you embarrassed? (3) Were you hurt or angry? Usually, if any or all of those circumstances had been present, the students would be able to realize how their emotional states contributed to the problem. Hopefully, the students then would understand the value of preparing a mindset and a response in advance to resist peer pressure, to not allow an embarrassing situation to bother them, and to not allow pain or anger to determine a decision. Again, if they'd been better prepared to deal with these circumstances, they probably would have called a better play. By talking through these circumstances, students would usually understand four things about avoiding troublesome situations: (1) Be aware of your surroundings, and don't be in the wrong place at the wrong time. (2) Hang with good people, and you're more likely to make good decisions. (3) Anticipate what choices you're going to have and make your decisions ahead of time to minimize emotion. (4) Realize what the consequences of your actions might be, and decide if it's worth the price.

Emotion often has too much to do with decision making, especially with young people. A key to helping people manage emotion is to get them to understand that it is generally reactionary, and that they - regardless of the circumstances - always have control over how they react to something. I had countless students tell me over the years that someone made them mad. I tried, sometimes successfully, to get them to understand that no one could make them mad, but that they could allow themselves to get mad about something someone had said or done to them. They had to accept the fact that their emotional reaction to become angry was a choice that they made and a play that they themselves called. Finally, it is important to realize that by nature, some of the situations we've talked about are going to be first-quarter circumstances and some are going to be fourth-quarter circumstances. Plays are a lot easier to call in the first quarter when there's plenty of time left in the game, and you aren't down by a touchdown. The decisions are harder

Dr. Charlie Burry, Jr.

when the clock is winding down in the fourth quarter and the outcome is on the line. At that point in the game, when the crowd is on its feet and you can hardly hear yourself think, it's important to know what play you're going to call.

47

Just Call Some of Those Good Plays

Before Hartsville High School's Kelleytown Stadium was remodeled, the team locker rooms were underneath the concrete grandstands. As teams would enter and exit the field, players and coaches would come in very close proximity to the fans who were in that part of the stadium complex. Some of them purposely stationed themselves in that area in order to get a closer look at their Red Foxes. When teams were going onto the field to start the game, those fans often formed a tunnel of cheers and encouragement. When leaving the field after a win, the adulation of the crowd was even louder. If we had lost, everyone was subdued. If we were behind at halftime, we usually faced a gauntlet of pretty harsh commentary on our play. Red Fox fans take their football seriously, and their expectations are high. A lot of them think they know a lot about football, and some of them do.

I don't recall the year or the opponent, but at some point while I was on the varsity coaching staff, we'd played a first half in which our performance did not meet our expectations. We weren't behind by much on the scoreboard, but no one from the Hartsville camp was pleased. As we were going to the locker room and making our way past our unhappy fans, I was walking directly behind Coach Lineberger. It was then that an elderly woman, dressed all in red to support her beloved Foxes, leaned over the fence, shook her fist at Coach Lineberger, and screamed, "Just call some of those good plays!" Although he didn't acknowledge her, he must have heard her because she was only about two feet away when she offered her advice.

Just a minute later, the coaching staff had gathered outside the door of the locker room to discuss the first half and what we needed to do better or differently in the second half. As was his practice, Coach Lineberger sought advice from each of his assistant coaches. When he asked for my suggestions, I said, "Well, shoot, just call some of those good plays." We came from behind and won that night, probably due more to improved execution by our players than better play calling by the coaching staff. That began a ritual that lasted for the remainder of my coaching career and throughout my tenure as principal. I would always shake hands with Coach Lineberger or Coach Calabrese sometime during pre-game warmups and say, "Call some of those good plays tonight." They always did.

So, what message was I trying to send, and what is the life lesson behind this ritual tongue-in-cheek advice to our football coaches to call some of those good plays? The immediate message simply was an affirmation of my confidence in our team's preparation to play a good game, and another way of saying, "I know you're ready. Good luck, tonight." The lesson for the moment was that you must have enough faith in your abilities and preparation to remain calm during pressure situations and call a good game. That lesson learned, in a broader sense, has to be evident to the people you're supervising so that they'll believe enough in the plan to make it work. The more far-reaching impact of the lesson is that you've got to know that you have a good business plan that will get the results you're after, and you have to be confident enough to stay the course during the challenging times. In the one game that I was telling you about, I don't think Coach Lineberger called plays any differently in the second half than he did in the first, and that was a reflection of the philosophy of our program over the years. We were confident in our system because it had proven to be successful. I'm sure that the lady who gave us halftime advice thought that he called some of the "good plays" she'd suggested in the second half because we came back and won. That happened because the same plays that don't look so good when they're poorly executed look a lot better when good players make them work. A business plan is more successful and profitable when capable employees do their jobs well. In both cases, you've got to have confidence in their abilities, too.

Understand, too, that there's a big difference between being comfortably confident in a philosophy and being too short-sighted or stubborn to see when change is necessary. There's a level of self-assurance that's necessary to believe that you can fix something that's wrong by deviating from the plan instead of simply freezing in the moment, refusing to change over the long haul, or not having enough courage to make a tough decision. There's also a level of confidence needed to make adjustments in the plan to compensate for the unexpected. What do you do when your quarterback gets hurt or your supplier goes out of business? Being confident enough to be adaptable and flexible in the moment is important, too.

Finally, an overarching lesson is to remain above the criticism and second-guessing. When you're in a leadership role, especially one that's in the public eye quite a bit, you need some thick skin. A lot of folks are going to think they know how to do your job better than you and won't hesitate to let you know about it. That comes with the territory. It's during those times especially when you'll need to have enough confidence in yourself and your team to "just call some of those good plays."

48

When Did You Become a Quitter?

Dr. Reggie High is a retired member of the University of Tennessee educational studies faculty. I knew him in the 1968-69 school year as Coach High when he was a social studies teacher, assistant varsity football coach, and tennis coach at Hartsville High School. I learned an important life lesson from Coach High that year, and following is a letter that I wrote to him at the University of Tennessee - thirty years later - thanking him for that lesson. When he received the letter, he graciously made a telephone call to me, and we had a wonderful conversation catching up.

> Dear Coach High,
>
> I doubt seriously that you remember me, and I hope you don't mind me addressing you as "Coach" - that's the only way I ever knew you. I graduated from Hartsville High School in 1969, played basketball for Coach Tim Watson, and played on the tennis team that you coached that year. One of my deepest regrets is that I didn't play football for you, Coach Wright, Coach Jones, Coach Daye, and Booster. I'm now in my twenty-sixth year of coaching and my twenty-first year at Hartsville High School. This is my twelfth year as a guidance counselor after teaching social studies for nine years. I came back to Hartsville as the head boys' varsity basketball coach and an assistant junior varsity football coach in 1978. I don't coach basketball anymore, but I've coached offensive and defensive backs on the varsity football staff for the last twelve years.

It seems more and more these days that we spend so much time talking to our players about character issues - attitude, dependability, persistence, and not being a quitter. We draw on our own experiences as players - things that helped to form our philosophy of athletics and coaching - and try to relate those to our own players. As I've thought about some of those things over the years, I've thought of you. No doubt it will amaze you that something you said to me in the spring of 1969, as a tennis coach no less, was one of the watershed events in my personal and professional life. I've run into Coach Wright a few times over the years, and Booster is still here in town but I'd never kept up with you or found out where you'd gone.

Well, I was talking to Madge Zemp this morning at a Career Fair that our guidance department was sponsoring (Madge and I share an office where we do part-time private counseling), and she said, "I was talking to Reggie High the other day and . . . ." It was loud in the cafeteria, and I wasn't sure I'd heard her correctly, and I exclaimed, "You were talking to who?!?" When she repeated your name, I couldn't believe it, that the name of someone I've wanted to get in touch with for years had just come up in a casual conversation. Madge promised to get me your address, so here I am tonight, writing this letter - finally thanking you for what you did for me thirty years ago.

You might recall that our tennis team that year was a real powerhouse, so good that Ken (Frog) Hughes and I alternated playing #1 and #2 singles all year. About half way through the season, I'd been playing #1 for a couple of weeks, and Ken challenged me. We played the afternoon before a match against Darlington the next day. I won the first set and was leading 5-2 in the second set, and

Dr. Charlie Burry, Jr.

inexplicably fell completely apart. Frog won the second set 7-5 and was leading 3-0 in the third when I just couldn't stand it anymore (if you remember anything about me, it might be my temper). I stormed off the court and told Frog that he could have the match. You stopped me and said, "When did you become a quitter?" I replied, "Just then, I guess," and got in my dad's green and white 1957 Metropolitan and drove off. The next morning at school I came to you first thing and apologized, and asked if you'd let me stay on the team. You agreed to keep me, and I played #2 against Darlington that day, and for the rest of the year. I was so ashamed of what I'd done that afternoon at practice, and I can hear you and see you in my mind right now, just as clear as if it were yesterday, saying, "When did you become a quitter?"

Coach High, I want you to know that I've never quit another thing. And when I'm tempted, I go back to that spring day in 1969 at the Prestwood Country Club tennis courts and I can hear you say, "When did you become a quitter?" I had a pretty undistinguished career as a basketball coach here, although we did win one region championship, and was fired from that position in 1985. My principal and superintendent offered to allow me to resign, but I told them I wouldn't do that, that they'd have to fire me, because my coaches had taught me never to quit. My principles might have gotten the best of my common sense at the time, but I have a clearer conscience today because of that. More importantly, though, is that I teach my players never to quit. And more importantly than that, I've tried to teach my two daughters never to quit. Maybe I've been too severe with my attitude about this from time to time - they say that discretion can be the better part of valor - but I believe it's better to err on the side of persistence than to be the other way. I think our young people need that now more than ever, in all parts of their lives.

Anyway, to end all this rambling, I thought you might enjoy knowing that part of your coaching philosophy - that it's not all right to quit - is still being passed on to Hartsville football players. And with your background being primarily football, I imagine you've gotten a real kick out of knowing that something you said - to a tennis player for Heaven's sake - turned out to be really, really important to that young boy. I'll always be grateful for that.

I doubt I'll be in Knoxville anytime soon, but if you ever make it back to Hartsville, I'd be honored to buy you dinner at The Beacon.

Sincerely,

Charlie Burry

Ken Hughes and Charlie Burry

Dr. Charlie Burry, Jr.

49

The Phantom Fox

An important lesson that can be learned from athletics is to always continue to believe that you can win and to never quit. At Hartsville High School, Red Fox athletes know that if they have that belief, a lucky break can come at the most unexpected time to change the outcome of a game. They know that if they continue to play hard while never looking over their shoulders for help, while still believing that no matter how dire the circumstances seem, they still have a chance. They understand that sometimes you have to make your own breaks. At Hartsville High School, those breaks happen when The Phantom Fox appears.

So, where is the proof of this mysterious, unseen spirit that shows up to help Red Foxes win in miraculous ways?

The Phantom Fox was there in 1981 when Hartsville scored on the last play of the game, as time ran out, to beat Airport 7-0 for the Division II-AAAA State Championship.

The Phantom Fox was there in 1987 when, after Goose Creek scored with less than a minute left in the game, the Red Foxes kicked a field goal as time ran out to beat them 24-22.

The Phantom Fox was there in the second round of the playoffs in 1988 when Hartsville beat Lancaster 9-7 after the Bruins fumbled on the Red Fox four-yard line with four minutes left in the game.

The Phantom Fox was there again in 1988 when the Red Foxes were behind 14-6 with two minutes left in the game, recovered a Berkeley fumble, scored with less than a minute left to tie the game, and went on to beat them 21-14 in overtime to win the Lower State Championship.

The Phantom Fox was there in the first round of the play-offs in 1991 when Hartsville scored on a fourth-down twenty-eight-yard pass with fifty-six seconds left in the game to beat Lancaster 14-9.

The Phantom Fox was there in 1992 in an epic battle between two 10-0 teams when a Red Fox player got a finger on a Wildcat extra-point kick, and Hartsville beat Dillon 7-6 to stay undefeated.

The Phantom Fox was there in 1994 when Hartsville's 155-pound quarterback ran a sneak over the 170-pound Red Fox center and scored with twenty-six seconds left in the game to beat Dillon 9-3.

The Phantom Fox was there in 2003 when a Wilson player was returning a punt down the sideline with no Hartsville player within fifteen yards of him, and he tripped and fell down on the Red Fox twenty-yard line. Wilson never scored on that possession, and Hartsville won 14-7.

The Phantom Fox was there in 2012 when Hartsville trailed the entire game against Strom Thurmond before making two huge plays at the very end of the game to win the Lower State Championship 20-10.

The Phantom Fox was there in 2014 when Marlboro County appeared to have won 20-17 but was penalized for roughing the kicker on a missed field goal attempt in the second over-time, and the Red Foxes went on to win 23-20, preserving a perfect season and capturing the AAA Lower State Championship.

The Phantom Fox was there in 2019 at Brookland-Cayce when, after trailing by two touchdowns for nearly the entire game, the Red Foxes scored twice in the fourth quarter - including a two-point conversion making the score 22-21 with just over

Dr. Charlie Burry, Jr.

two minutes left in the game - to advance to the AAAA Lower State Championship game.

The Phantom Fox is there - in all sports - when Red Foxes play as hard as they can play and when they believe in their hearts and minds and souls that they can win. Red Foxes also know that if they don't believe, he doesn't show up. The good thing about the Phantom Fox is that belief and attitude are things that we can always choose to control. We can choose to never blink, no matter what happens. We can choose to never give in, no matter what the score or the count is. We can choose to always believe, no matter what the circumstances are. The Phantom Fox is always there watching, looking into your hearts and souls, and he's ready to teach you that lesson . . . if you believe.

50

The Ghost of Might-Have-Been

Give one hundred percent. Leave everything on the field. Have no regrets. All of these phrases are used by coaches to encourage their teams and players to put forth their best efforts and do everything they possibly can to win. There are two parts to winning that go hand-in-hand, and one is futile without the other. One - execution during the actual competition - is in the short term, and its importance is underscored by the immediacy and urgency of the game situation. The second - preparation during the days, weeks and months prior to actually meeting an opponent - holds the real key to doing one's best and giving oneself an opportunity to be successful. Muhammed Ali once said, "The fight is won in the gym and on the road, long before I dance under those lights." I ran across the following poem a number of years ago and used it when I was coaching in an attempt to motivate our players to prepare to do their best when they got under those Friday night lights:

> Mr. Meant-To has a friend,
> And his name is Didn't-Do.
> Have you ever chanced to meet them?
> Have they ever called on you?
> These two friends live together,
> In the house of Didn't-Win.
> And I'm told that house is haunted,
> By the Ghost of Might-Have-Been.

These two friends and teammates didn't give one hundred percent in their preparation to play the game or the season. They couldn't leave everything they had on the field because they didn't give everything they had during workouts, film sessions, and practice. Their negative attitudes reinforced each other and were potentially contagious. As a result, they might be haunted by regret. I say might be because if Johnny Meant-To and Jimmy Didn't-Do hadn't cared enough to prepare to the best of their ability, then they might also not care enough to suffer regret. When I was coaching and our team lost a game, I always watched our players' reactions to the loss. While I didn't expect teenagers to be emotionally overwrought about losing a ball game, I did believe that if a player didn't show signs of being a little bit bothered by losing, then he probably didn't have much to lose in terms of his investment in preparing for the game. To suffer some degree of regrettable loss, people have to fail at something into which they've invested some effort.

I always wondered how effective this poem was in motivating young people because I think that its words become more meaningful as time passes. With perspective aided by some years of maturity, I believe that we all realize that we could have invested more and done better, at least in some areas of our lives (see *Life's Basic Problem*). Former players often come back to talk with current players to try to help them understand how it feels to take their jerseys off for the last time and have no more games to play. We don't want to be haunted by regret, but we can learn from it. And there is the true lesson from this poem.

Participation in athletics, particularly a team sport, teaches life lessons. It teaches us how to win and how to lose and why those things happen. It teaches us that there's accountability waiting when we don't do things right and that there are rewards for embracing the positive attributes of attitude, work ethic, and dependability. Learning the lessons about responsibility, honesty, and loyalty that make someone a pretty good high school football teammate also make him a good person, husband, father, employee, and citizen as an adult. Those are the areas of a person's life in which it would be truly regrettable to live in a house haunted by the Ghost of Might-Have-Been.

51

Courage Doesn't Always Roar

> "Courage doesn't always roar. Sometimes courage is just that quiet voice at the end of the day saying, 'I will try again tomorrow.'"
>
> - Mary Anne Radmacher

Courage has different voices. When we're physically afraid, but do what we have to do anyway, courage roars in the face of fear. When we're dealing with temptation, but do the right thing anyway, courage speaks with clear conviction. When we lack confidence and are hesitant to speak our minds, the voice of courage is one of calm reassurance. When we're discouraged but summon the persistence to try again tomorrow, courage quietly whispers words of resolve in our ears. Some of my favorite stories about athletics are about young men who had the quiet courage to try again tomorrow.

I saw some exceptionally gifted athletes during my time at Hartsville High School. However, whether they fulfilled their potential and became great players or not depended on their attitudes, how coachable they were, and their work ethic. So, understand that there's a difference between being a great athlete in terms of God-given talent and using that talent to become a great player in terms of performance. It was exciting to see someone who had truly exceptional talent and who also had an exceptional attitude and work ethic. Those guys didn't come along very often. On the other hand, it was disappointing to see great athletic potential go unfulfilled because attitude and work ethic were questionable - either on the field or in the classroom, or both. However, it was most rewarding to see a few whose athletic abilities were average at best, but whose truly exceptional attitudes lifted them far beyond what their potential appeared to be. The guys with that type of work ethic didn't come along very often, either. You see, those borderline-talent athletes had an added ingredient in their psychological makeup - they had exceptional courage, too. More often than not, they met with frustration on the field, but they didn't quit. They had the quiet courage, at the end of a day when progress had been slow and hard to see, to still say, "I will try again tomorrow." I'm going to tell you about two young men who had quiet courage - one was a heavyweight wrestler and the other was a flyweight flanker.

One of those quietly courageous young men played football for Hartsville High School a number of years ago. In order to get better at football, he also participated on our wrestling team. When he wrestled as a ninth and tenth grader, he wasn't very good. In fact, I'm not sure that he ever won a match. He had to wrestle as a heavyweight because he was big, but his strength hadn't begun to catch up with his size. He was wrestling opponents who were older and stronger than he was, and he frequently got pinned - sometimes less than a minute into a match. I watched that happen a number of times, and I hurt for him because it had to be frustrating and probably embarrassing as well. He always came back to try again the next time, though, and his teammates and coaches continued to encourage him. By the time he was a junior, he'd gotten stronger and had also gotten better technically as a wrestler, and he started to win some matches. During his senior year, he was still facing opponents who were bigger and stronger than he was, but he wrestled smart and was tenacious, and I watched him win a number of matches against wrestlers whom he had no business beating. The progress of Andrew Privette as a high school wrestler over the years is one of the best examples of the reward of hard work that I witnessed in my career. Andrew is now an attorney in Hartsville and has a wonderful family. I'd hate to have to wrestle against him in court.

Another of those quietly courageous young men was also a football player but one who was small in stature. Mainly because of his size, he played wide receiver and was a defensive back. He played strong safety, not because he was strong, but because he didn't have the speed to play the other positions in the defensive backfield. When he went in the game on offense, if our opponent had scouted us well, they would know that we were probably going to run the ball on that play. Practices were brutal for him because he got knocked around so much. He always got up and came back for more, though, and his teammates respected him for that. He worked hard in the weight room and was always asking what he could do to get better. He was smart, and although he knew the likelihood of him playing a lot was low, he knew his responsibilities on offense and defense as well as our starters did. Our football team didn't have a very good year when this young man was a senior, and he took every loss hard. But Vay Shire became a winner in everyone's eyes that spring when he secured an appointment to the United States Naval Academy. He graduated in 2003 and served six years as a surface warfare officer. Vay now has a highly successful career in management consulting in Raleigh, North Carolina, and also has a wonderful family. I'll bet he coaches his clients well.

I can't recall hearing Andrew Privette or Vay Shire roar much while they were in high school, but they were always ready to listen to that quiet voice of courage and try again tomorrow. The lesson is that as a result, tomorrow is now here, and we can be inspired by two of the best success stories that I know.

52

Situation Excellent

"Hard pressed on my right. My center is yielding. Impossible to maneuver. Situation excellent. I am attacking."

- Ferdinand Foch at the Battle of the Marne

In 1997, during my eleventh year as a varsity assistant football coach at Hartsville High School, we had a very good football team. After a loss in the second game of the season to an outstanding Northwestern High School team, we won twelve games in a row. The Red Foxes headed into the Division II-AAAA state championship game with a 13-1 record against Walterboro High School, whose record 11-3. On a personal note, it was the fifth time in eleven years that we'd played for a football state championship. We'd won in 1987 and 1988, but lost in 1992 and 1993. I was intent upon my own record in state championship games moving to 3-2 instead of 2-3. Another neat aspect personally was that one of the Walterboro assistant coaches was Kenny Schofield, whom I'd coached twenty years before when he was in the ninth and tenth grades at Gilbert High School. Kenny and I had a nice visit on the field before the game.

Momentum is a wonderful companion when it's on your side, and I don't know that I've ever been involved in a game where that was more evident than in the 1997 Hartsville-Walterboro game. The game started poorly for us when we had a punt blocked, leading to a Walterboro touchdown. The game continued in that fashion until Walterboro took possession of the ball right before halftime with a 21-0 lead. At that point, the Bulldogs ran the ball three straight times, seemingly content with a three-touchdown halftime advantage. But, as time wound down with the ball on our forty-four-yard line, Walterboro surprisingly attempted a Hail Mary pass into the end zone. We had it well-covered with our cornerback in good position, and our safety had it covered so well over the top that he actually overran the ball. However, the Walterboro receiver went up and made the catch, the Bulldogs kicked the extra point, and the two teams went to the locker rooms in decidedly different states of mind. Walterboro had all the momentum, and we had none - punctuated by a goose egg on our side of the scoreboard. It looked as though the Phantom Fox, like Elvis, had left the building.

Our locker room was a mixture of emotion, not much of it good - shock over the last play of the first half, disgust and anger with playing so poorly, and near disbelief that Hartsville could be on the wrong end of a 28-0 halftime score in a state championship game. I was particularly upset because I coached our defensive backs, and therefore I took ownership of Walterboro's last score. Strategically, our coaches decided to go with our Foxbone offense in the second half, which was a pretty unusual thing to do when facing a four-touchdown deficit. The Foxbone was more of a smash-mouth, grind-it-out offensive philosophy, usually with no more than one wide receiver, and I think the decision was simply indicative of our somber determination to somehow slowly get back in the game. Still, though, we were down 28-0.

At that point, just as Coach Lineberger was getting the attention of the entire team before heading back to the field for the second half, one of our assistant coaches - Carlisle Koonts - spoke up. His unforgettable words were these: "Y'all got to realize what an opportunity this is. We're down 28-0, and we have the chance to make the greatest comeback ever in the history of state championship football games! We can still win and make history!" I'll have to admit that my initial reaction was something like "Well, that's an interesting spin to put on things," but Mr. Momentum must have been listening to Coach Koonts, and he was ready to switch sides.

The second half was a complete reversal of the first, and with forty-four seconds left in the game, we scored to pull within one point, 28-27. I believe that all of our coaches had been thinking in the minutes leading up to that score, that - if we could get ourselves in that position - we were going to go for the win with a two-point conversion try instead of kicking an extra point for a tie score and have the game likely go to overtime. History shows that our two-point conversion attempt came up short, and Walterboro won by a final score of 28-27. It was a heartbreaking loss, for sure, but defeat always teaches lessons - sometimes better than winning. Our lesson from that game was to never give up and to never quit, no matter what the situation. The lesson that the Red Foxes learned from the 1997 Walterboro game was this: "Situation excellent. We are attacking."

53

You Never Know What's Comin' for You

"You never know what's comin' for you."

- Queenie in *The Curious Case of Benjamin Button*

The Curious Case of Benjamin Button is a 2008 movie starring Brad Pitt (Benjamin) and Cate Blanchett (Daisy) in which a baby is born with the appearance of an old man and ages in reverse through adulthood, adolescence, childhood, and back into infancy. Queenie, a woman who runs a boarding house, finds the elderly infant Benjamin abandoned on her doorstep and decides to raise him as her own. The movie follows Benjamin through the adventures of his life, including his relationship with Daisy, as he hopes that they will somehow come together - at least for a while - at the right juncture of their lives. The problem is that Benjamin and Daisy are progressing through the aging process in opposite directions. Queenie's loving and encouraging counsel to Benjamin at several points in his life is "You never know what's comin' for you." While our experiences in life may not be as adventurous as those of Benjamin Button, we, too - despite what may be discouraging current circumstances - should live with Queenie's eternal optimism that something good is coming for us.

Eleven years before Benjamin Button's birth, the Red Fox football team was having an excellent season. One of the strengths of our team was that we had three very good tailbacks, and any of the three probably could have started for many of the other teams we played that year. Our first-string guy was really outstanding, though, and he received the great majority of the carries. His backup, who was younger but an outstanding player as well, logged almost all of the remaining playing time. That left our third-string guy - who was a senior - on the sideline most of the time, despite being a pretty good player, too. He wasn't happy with that situation, and we had many conversations after practice about his dissatisfaction. He wanted to change positions to fullback, he wanted to play defense, and he wanted to quit the team. I encouraged him to continue to work hard, trying to help him understand that any of the other options would seal his fate as far as playing time was concerned. To his credit, his work ethic remained at a high level, as I continued to tell him that "You never know when your time might come."

In the semi-final playoff game - our fourteenth game of the season - our first-string tailback suffered a deep thigh bruise that put him out of the game. We still managed to win the game and advance, but we weren't sure that he'd recover quickly enough to play in the state championship game the next weekend. We thought we'd be fine with our second tail-back, though, until he became involved in a school situation that week that would prevent him from playing, too. So, within seventy-two hours - after fourteen weeks of personal frustra-tion - our third-string tailback became our starter for the state championship game at Williams-Brice Stadium in Columbia. As Queenie would tell Benjamin ten years later, "You never know what's comin' for you." That young man was ready, and I'd like to tell you that this story had a fairytale ending, but it didn't. He played well in the last game of his high school career, gained about seventy-five yards on a dozen or so carries, and helped our team to within two points of another state championship.

I haven't seen my former player in a very long time and don't even know where he is right now, but I believe he took something home from that state championship game that has been much more important to him over the years than a silver runner-up medal. I hope that he and his teammates learned - no matter how discouraging life might seem at times - to keep working, to stay positive, and to never quit. I hope that he and his teammates have remembered the life lesson that, as Queenie said, "You never know what's comin' for you."

54

How Tar Heel Basketball Makes You Feel

My mom was a huge fan of University of North Carolina athletics, particularly basketball - both the men's and the women's teams. Her loyalty originated in her hometown of Gastonia, North Carolina, and never wavered, even though she lived most of her life in South Carolina. She thought that Dean Smith walked on water and that Roy Williams was not far behind. The fact that she shared the same hometown with James Worthy, an All-American at UNC and NBA All-Star with the Los Angeles Lakers, heightened her Tar Heel fervor in the early 1980s. All of that was topped off when she became aware that Sylvia Hatchell, former long-time Hall of Fame coach of the Tar Heel women's program, was also a Gastonia native. Mom watched Tar Heel basketball religiously and wouldn't even answer her phone during a game. She usually sat right in front of the television in a Carolina blue and white wicker rocking chair, which was a gift from her children. She freely gave advice to the coaches, scolded the referees, and the closer the score got, the faster she rocked. One of the highlights of her life was when she, my dad, and I attended a UNC game in the Smith Center on the weekend of her seventieth birthday, and she was able to meet Dean Smith in person. Sylvia Hatchell topped it all, though.

The city of Myrtle Beach, South Carolina, has hosted a prestigious high school basketball tournament called The Beach Ball Classic during the Christmas season for many years. After a few years, a women's college double-header was included in the Beach Ball Classic as an added attraction, and UNC was a regular participant. Since Myrtle Beach is only about a two-hour drive from Hartsville and tickets were easy to purchase, I began taking my mom to the Myrtle Beach Convention Center to see the Tar Heels play in person. We would arrive at the game early so that we could get seats directly behind the UNC bench as close to my mom's beloved Tar Heels as we could be. I had gotten to know Sylvia Hatchell early in my basketball coaching career when she was the women's coach at Francis Marion College, prior to her going to the University of North Carolina. Part of her success as a coach is that - in addition to her knowledge of and skill at teaching the game - she is exceptionally loyal to her players and her school. She is also very amiable with colleagues, friends, and fans, always remembering a name and taking time to speak. Even though I do not know Sylvia well and did not see her often, when we arrived at the game each year, my mom and I would walk down to the court behind the UNC bench, and I'd manage to catch her eye. She'd walk over and speak to us, always talking to my mom more than she did to me. That suited me fine, because my mom was the main reason that we were there. Every year my mom at some point in their conversation would say to Sylvia, "You know, I'm from Gastonia, too."

One year we arrived at the game late, and there was no time for us to have our usual pre-game chat with Sylvia. I could tell that my mom was disappointed. After the game, we made our way down to the court and headed over to the UNC locker room. Sylvia was talking to the press, meeting and greeting friends, and we finally made our way close enough to her to speak. And then, as far as my mom was concerned, Coach Sylvia Hatchell clinched the biggest win of her career. She motioned for my mom to follow her, and she took my mom into the locker room. She introduced my mom to the team and asked if she'd like to speak to them. I was not in the locker room and didn't hear what my mom said to the team, and afterward my mom didn't remember what she'd said either, so there's no telling what her pep talk was like. But I do know that when my mom walked out of the UNC locker room, she was absolutely giddy and smiling from ear to ear. I don't think she got calmed down the whole way home.

I include that story in this book because I think there's a lesson for all of us in it. Sylvia Hatchell probably doesn't remember what she did after that game, but she gave my mom an experience that she never forgot and a story that she never grew tired of telling her friends. As the memory of that locker room visit faded a bit over the years, I think that the Maya Angelou quote, "People forget what you said, but they never forget how you made them feel," was proven to be true. Two minutes after my mom finished talking to the Tar Heels that afternoon, she was so excited that she couldn't remember what she or anyone else had said. But she never forgot how she felt coming out of that locker room. The big lesson for all of us, though, is that you don't have to be a famous, big-time basketball coach for the Angelou quote to apply. If you treat people well - the way you'd like to be treated - they don't forget it. Sylvia Hatchell won 1,023 games in her career, fifth most career wins of all women's college basketball coaches. She won an NCAA national championship in 1994, was elected to the Women's Basketball Hall of Fame in 2004, and in 2013 was elected to the Naismith Memorial Basketball Hall of Fame. But at the top of the list in Sylvia Hatchell's legacy, as far as our family is concerned, is the brief kindness that she showed to Wilma Burry one afternoon after a game in Myrtle Beach. My mom is gone now, but I won't ever forget how Sylvia Hatchell and the Tar Heels made her feel that day.

Wilma Burry

Red Fox
Renaissance Lessons

I officially moved into the principal's office at Hartsville High School on July 1, 2004. If you had told me six months earlier that was going to happen, I'd have told you that you were crazy. I never saw it coming. While I had been certified in secondary administration since 1976, I had never seriously considered becoming an administrator. I had what I considered to be the best job in the school as a guidance counselor and an assistant football coach. But when the principal's job became available that spring, I truly felt that I was being spiritually called to do it. At that time, Hartsville High School needed a leader who was familiar with the school and the community. I'd been back in Hartsville for twenty-six years at that point, and no one met that criteria better than me. I applied for the position, and the Darlington County School District Superintendent, Dr. Rainey Knight, took a chance on hiring a guy with zero administrative experience to lead a school with thirteen hundred students, ninety teachers, and one hundred and forty total employees.

My pitch during the application and interview process was a platform and a set of goals for the school that I called *The Red Fox Renaissance*. We had a good school at the time, but needed more focus organizationally and instructionally to become a great school again. That greatness eventually re-emerged as a result of the hard work and loyalty of many wonderfully talented teachers, excellent assistant principals, dedicated support personnel, strong district-level support, and rejuvenated backing from the community. The culture of an organization doesn't change overnight, however, and a great deal of patience was required to keep the faith during the

Dr. Charlie Burry, Jr.

first four or five years until some of the changes finally gained traction. Additionally, everyone had to understand that a renaissance is a long-term process and not a flash-in-the-pan occurrence. We had to make the conscious choice in everything we did to get better every day. We had to keep working at improving, and we did that for fourteen years. In the following chapters are some of the foundational philosophical ideas - and the story of one hugely significant development - that helped to bring The Red Fox Renaissance to fruition. While these principles are drawn from my experiences in leading Hartsville High School, I believe that the ideas in this section could well be applied to leadership in almost any secondary school setting.

55

Hartsville High School Is Going to Become a Great School Again

Here are the remarks that I made to the Hartsville High School faculty and staff on August 4, 2004, when I addressed the entire group for the first time as principal.

Hartsville High School is going to become a great school again. We have a good school now, but those of us who have been around here for a while remember when it was better. I remember when Hartsville High School was a beacon of academic achievement and was beyond a shadow of a doubt the flagship school in Darlington County and maybe in the whole Pee Dee area. I think those of us who were around in those times aren't really satisfied right now with the way things are, and that's why I'm so excited today about the opportunity we have. I don't mean to sound egotistical - those of you who know me well know that's not my character - but I believe Hartsville High School needs the kind of leadership that I can bring to the school. And I've discovered in the last few months that I needed the job, too. I'm re-energized, I'm doing interesting and challenging things, and I'm optimistic about Hartsville High School again. Most of all, I'm thankful that we've got a chance to make a positive difference in this place - for our students, for the community, and especially for you. I want it to become a school where you look forward to coming to work and enjoy it while you're here. If you're one of those people who can say at the drop of a hat how many years, months, and days, and maybe even hours you've got until retirement, I want you to begin experiencing the rewards of teaching again. If you're just starting your career in education, I want your experience here to reaffirm the reasons and the ideals that led you in that direction. I want Hartsville High to become a great school again for a lot of reasons, but especially for you. I want you to feel the optimism that I do. The most important reason though, is that if it's a great school for you, it will mean that there is great teaching and learning going on, and that's what we're all after. That's why we got into this business.

Now, let's come back down to earth. All of that is easier said than done, some of you are thinking - and you are exactly right. We didn't get in the shape we're in overnight, and we're not going to snap our fingers and suddenly be a great school again. It's going to take some changing of attitudes and some old habits, and it's going to take buying into some things that you might have some doubts about and maybe might not like or agree with. It's going to take persistence because there are going to be some tough times when it's going to be really hard to see any progress. Someone told me the other day that we are riding a wave of optimism, and I can't tell you how gratifying it is to hear that. But we've got some tough times coming, times when we're going to fall off that surfboard and come up gagging and spitting and snorting salt water, and times when we're in a dead calm sea in a scorching hot sun and the sharks are circling. My understanding that I wouldn't be able to please everybody has already been affirmed, and sometimes things have to get worse before they get better. We're not perfect, and we're going to make some mistakes. And when those things happen - and they will - you can't allow yourself to say, "Oh, well, same old Hartsville High," and slide back into that rut of pessimism. You've got to be tough and committed enough to allow yourself to have some faith. You see it in the athletic world all the time - if you don't believe in yourself and in your team, you aren't giving yourself a chance.

We also need to address another line of thinking. If you're one of those people who is saying right now, "Oh, I'll just mark time for a couple more years and play the string on out, and that won't hurt anything," let me tell you that that is not the kind of attitude and level of cooperation that I'm looking for. We're going to make some expectations very clear to our students, and I'm making this one very clear to you right now. This renaissance that we're talking about is going to take everybody believing that what we are doing is going to work, and everybody doing it. Notice I didn't say a good many of us, and I didn't say almost all of us - I said everybody. There are some things we're going to work on around here that require one hundred percent buy-in and cooperation - situations where if you aren't with us, then you're against us. We can't make the changes we need to make with only eighty percent of the faculty trying to make it work and the other twenty percent thinking that it's okay to let things slide. It's going to require some of you being more demanding and conscientious than you've ever been before.

On the teacher survey that you did for me last spring, your main area of concern was discipline. That was also a major concern in the surveys of students and parents. The foundation of addressing that concern is this: Hartsville High School is going to become a place where students respect teachers, where teachers respect students, where students respect each other, and where students have enough self-respect to do the right things with their schoolwork and the choices they make in their personal and social lives. Nothing we've been talking about will happen if students, parents, teachers, and administrators don't buy into the idea that we are all in this together and that respecting each other is the glue that holds that whole concept together. We are a team, and we are all working toward the same goal - to make Hartsville High School a better place for all of us. The new principal's philosophy will not be that there's

Dr. Charlie Burry, Jr.

a new sheriff in town, and he's coming in with both guns blazing. That's not my style, and it's not what will work here. And while you do need to establish some clear expectations and consequences regarding classroom management and student behavior, you've got to have some positive and cooperative relational things going on, too. I've known teachers who wrote ten discipline referrals a day and have known some others who might not write ten in a year. I know that there are a lot of factors that enter into that, but I've got to believe that a major factor is relationships and having the students know that you mean business, but that you care about them, too. What we're trying to accomplish here will be done a lot more easily and a whole lot less painfully if we go about it with a cooperative spirit that is founded on good relationships.

Our students have to begin doing the right things and making the right choices more often, not because of the threat of our discipline system - but because it's the right thing to do, and they want to help make their school a better place. When we talk to students about their behavior, their language, keeping the campus clean, or anything else - we would like for it to be something like "Come on, we're trying to make our school better, and you can do this to help," or, "Look now, that's not what we need to make our school better." Some of you are probably thinking right now that I've either lost my mind or have way too much guidance counselor in me. I know we're going to have some hardheads that there's only one way to reach, and we will not hesitate to use some punitive measures if that what it takes to make believers out of them. But we need to work hard at getting everybody on the same team.

Some of you have probably heard me use the phrase "fighting that classroom battle" in referring to teaching. Well, I'm not going to say that anymore, and we've got to try hard to not ever think of it that way. The teacher/student relationship cannot be adversarial. You know as well as I do that if it is adversarial, you've probably lost that student. What I'm trying to describe here is a very fine line that requires some people skills and some perception that in many cases may be far more important than your knowledge of the subject matter and your academic expertise. Don't misunderstand me. We're not going to tolerate disrespect and disruption of the learning environment, but remember that the best and most effective form of discipline is self-discipline. We will make our expectations clear and then work on establishing relationships so that most of our students will choose to discipline themselves. If each of you can win over just one student out of each of your classes, that's three hundred kids right there - think what a difference that would make in our school climate.

We can't make excuses. It's not productive. The point is that we have got to play the cards that are dealt us. We have no choice. We can't change the game or the rules, and we aren't going to fold. Rationalizing for low test scores and high suspension rates doesn't improve things one bit. What we've got to do is analyze the problem and figure out what to do about it. The sooner we recognize and accept that fact, the sooner we'll begin finding things that will help us solve our problems and become a better school. I don't intend to be in my office a whole lot during the school day. I am going to be out and about and visible, and everybody - especially the students - is going to know that I am intensely interested in improving what's going on in our classrooms and on our campus. We mean business, we are going to be intense about it, and I am telling you that Hartsville High School is going to become a better place for our students and for you. We are going to experience, slowly but surely, a revival of our school's spirit, pride, and academic achievement. Our students are going to be well-prepared for the future because you've been teaching and they've been learning every single day. Welcome from your new principal to a new school year, and welcome to a Red Fox Renaissance!

56

Philosophy of a Great School

The following principles are those which I regularly shared over the years with the Hartsville High School faculty and staff regarding the philosophical foundation of a great school.

Every successful organization needs a set of foundational beliefs as a framework for their practices, policies, and procedures. That's what a philosophy is. You've got to be able to say, in good times and bad, "This is what we believe in." It is what you believe to be the right way to do things, and it is what you base your decisions on, especially the tough ones. I think it is the responsibility of the leader of an organization - with plenty of input from the members - to establish and communicate that philosophy. You don't dream up your philosophy overnight: it is something that takes shape over a number of years as you're influenced by your life experiences, both personally and professionally. It also doesn't change quickly or drastically although it certainly should evolve some over the years. Evolve - I think that's a good word to describe how one's philosophy might adapt to changing times and influences in order to remain relevant. A lot of what follows actually comes from my coaching philosophy because being a principal is very much like being a head coach. The goal is to get all the members of the team - students, parents, faculty and staff, and community - working together in the most efficient way possible. And in order to do that, the team has to share, believe in, and actively support a core philosophy. Here we go.

Be well-organized. I learned a long time ago that even if intelligence is not one of your stronger characteristics, if you can be well-organized, you can at least give people the impression that you're fairly smart. So, with that thought in mind, we will be organized. We need to be organized with our day-to-day operations, we need to be organized with our school policies, and - most importantly - we need to be organized during emergency situations in which the safety of our students, faculty, and staff could be at risk. We will all work hard this year, and if we're going to put in that kind of effort, we need to be doing it efficiently and effectively. While everyone might not agree with the way we do things or with a particular decision, we are going to do those things for sound reasons and in an organized manner, and the expectation is that everyone will be on board the train. We are a team here, and teams are most successful - and collectively happier - when each member of the team does his/her job, and when everybody pulls in the same direction. Our organizational structure will give us a chance to do that.

Communicate clearly. It doesn't do much good to be well-organized if the structure isn't clearly communicated to the folks that you're trying to organize. I will do my best to keep you informed, to let you know when things are due, and when things are happening. I'll do the same with our students and the parents of our students. It would be most helpful if you would do the same for me and for each other. Hopefully, all of my communications will be with correct grammar, spelling, punctuation, and word usage. I would urge you to apply the same standard to all of your communications, especially those that go outside the school to the parents of our students and to the community. Finally, don't be in so much of a rush that you pass on opportunities to communicate face-to-face. Sometimes a lot of meaning and tone can be lost and/or misconstrued in an email, or even in a voicemail. Finally, a recommendation that

I sometimes have trouble following myself is this: don't press "Send" when you're mad.

Set high expectations. We will set high expectations at Hartsville High School, and we will give our students the means, the instruction, and the opportunity to achieve the expectation and the belief that every child can learn. All people are more comfortable when they know what is expected of them, and that is particularly true with teenagers in the classroom and in the overall school setting. When expectations are clearly communicated to our students, that makes their compliance and cooperation simply a matter of choice. Then, if students choose not to meet expectations, they are at the same time choosing the consequences for their actions. I also will challenge our faculty from time to time, maybe even to the point of discomfort, but understand that the purpose is always to make our school better. However, know that these expectations are not intended to constrict or limit your creativity and initiative to develop new and better ways of doing things and grow professionally. We have a lot of really smart, imaginative people on our faculty and staff, and we want those abilities to multiply and foster improvement in our school.

Hold people accountable. It is not only important that we all have the same high expectations, but that we all consistently hold our students accountable for non-compliance. If you've got a policy and don't hold people accountable, it's nothing more than a suggestion. And if all we do is suggest that our students comply with school policies and act respectfully, a lot of them will have other suggestions of their own. Some of our students - because of their backgrounds - look for reasons to mistrust adults, and nothing breeds mistrust between a teacher and students more surely than the teacher holding them accountable for failing to meet expectations that were not clear, or that change from day to day, or that are imposed inconsistently from student to student. If you've been here any time at all, you've heard me say that I can explain the reason for any policy that we have here, but what I cannot explain to any student, parent, or district administrator is our teachers choosing to be intentionally inconsistent in holding our students accountable. Don't expect me, or any other HHS administrator, to defend you if you're doing that. Our students and their parents will see the unfairness of those situations much more quickly than they'll complain about the substance of a policy.

Seek continuous improvement. I was taught early in life by those who parented, taught, coached, and mentored me that "You either get better or worse every day. There is no middle ground." More recently, a quote attributed to professional football player J. J. Watt suggests the same thing: "Success isn't owned, it's leased. And the rent is due every day." Education, like most other businesses in today's world, is competitive and continuously changing. Our students are changing, as is the manner in which they optimally learn. New technologies for instructional purposes are in constant evolution. The bodies of information available in all fields are increasing exponentially. Education today faces the daunting task of preparing students for jobs that do not even currently exist. The challenge for educators - and particularly classroom teachers - is to find a balance between traditional and foundational principles of instruction and newly developed material and teaching strategies that make learning experiences relevant to twenty-first century students. Having said all that, it is obvious that educators continuously seeking improvement through professional development is a crucial component of having our students learn in an efficient and effective manner. The rent is due every day.

Ask yourself, "Is it good for our school?" With each year that goes by, I struggle more and more philosophically with this question. If it's good for a student, doesn't it have to be good for our school? If it's good for our school, doesn't it have to be good for a student? I wish it was that simple, but it is not, because those two things - what is good for the individual and what is good for the organization - are not always in agreement. When they are, then everybody is happy, and I don't toss and turn all night. The reality is, as an administrator, I am constantly faced with decisions in which what seems good and right for an individual is counterproductive to the mission of the school. I weigh, day after day, what I believe is best for the school against what - at least in the short term - is not what a student and his parents think is good, or fair, or understanding of their situation. As principal, I believe that my ultimate responsibility is to do what is best for the school. I've joked for the last several years that the words written on my tombstone will be "He didn't want to open a can of worms." I have to guard against making a decision that would compromise the mission of the school, and I have to be careful not to set a precedent that will cause a problem on down the road.

Put students first. Our students are the reason we're here. Educating them and preparing them for their futures is the primary focus - directly or indirectly - of everything that we do here. What more significant purpose could an occupation or organization have than impacting the futures of young people? Listen to this carefully: What you do and say in your classroom this year could shape - for better or for worse - the next sixty years of a young person's life. That is an awesome responsibility, and it is an incredible opportunity that only the profession of education holds. We've all had those people in our own lives. Wouldn't you like to be remembered that way? You've heard me say it before - while our teachers are the backbone of our organization, our students are the lifeblood and the heartbeat of this place; they give our school its character and its person- ality. And if that's the case, we want this to be a place of hope and possibility for them. We need to give them a good reason to want to come here. Can you imagine what kind of school this would be if every student felt positive about coming here every day? We have students who come here from all walks of life, and that's one of the challenges and benefits of public education. But regardless of what their life circumstances are, they all need us in some manner, whether they realize it - or will admit it - or not. At some point in time this year, every child here will need a champion. Be a champion for one of our students every day. Teach like a champion every day for all of your students. For every student who walks in the door of your classroom, make Hartsville High School a place of hope and possibility.

57

Preparing for the Future by Learning Every Day

Public schools are required to hold membership in an accrediting agency, and in the southeastern part of the United States that agency is the Southern Association of Colleges and Schools (SACS). During most of my forty-year career at Hartsville High School, accreditation was achieved through an extensive evaluation which occurred every ten years. The organization that now encompasses several regional accrediting agencies is known as AdvancEd. It just so happened that Hartsville High School's ten-year SACS evaluation coincided with my first year as principal, and I have never quite decided if that was a blessing or a curse. On the one hand, with all of the other challenges of being a first-year principal, the preparation for a SACS evaluation was the last thing I needed on my plate. On the other hand, having to go through that process forced our school to evaluate curriculum, instruction, and assessment and to articulate what was necessary to improve in those areas. All things considered, at least in hindsight, it was a good thing for our school to successfully navigate a SACS evaluation during the first year of my principalship. It helped us early on to establish some goals that helped us to become a great school again.

The evaluation process involved having a team of outside educators conduct a three or four-day visit to the school. During that visit - in addition to observing classes - the evaluation team interviewed administrators, faculty and staff members, students, parents of students, and members of the community. One of

Dr. Charlie Burry, Jr.

the key components of the SACS evaluation had to be the mission statement of the school. It needed to be a clear and concise pronouncement that everyone in the school - and I mean everyone - not only knew, but could articulate at the drop of a hat when asked. From the thought and discussion involved in crafting such a statement, "Preparing for the Future by Learning Every Day" was born. In my experience, I believe that mission statements are often too wordy and too complex in an effort to be all-encompassing. The mission statement of Hartsville High School - developed for our 2004-05 SACS evaluation - captured what we were all about in eight words, and it continued to serve us well for fourteen years. Near the conclusion of the early morning announcements, every day of the school year, our students heard these words: "We hope everyone in the Red Fox Family will have a good day, always treating others with kindness, compassion, and understanding, as we focus - with an attitude of hope and possibility - on our mission of Preparing for the Future by Learning Every Day." Whether it went in one ear and out the other or not, every person at Hartsville High School heard our mission statement every single day.

58

Becoming an International Baccalaureate World School

At the time that I became principal of Hartsville High School, our honors level curriculum culminated with a strong selection of Advanced Placement (AP) courses. These AP courses individually were very rigorous, and students had an opportunity to earn college credit in a subject area by meeting a certain standard on an end-of-course examination. While our AP selection of courses was strong and our students performed well on the AP exams, the perception in our community and school district was that the academic program at Hartsville High School lagged behind that of Mayo High School for Math, Science & Technology, which is another of the four high schools in Darlington County.

Mayo High School is a magnet school whose enrollment is limited in size, but is open to qualified students (those who score above the fortieth percentile on standardized testing) throughout the entire school district and is not limited by local attendance zones. The limit on Mayo's enrollment necessitated a lottery to select students who would be offered a spot at the school. The lottery selection was a highly publicized and tension-filled event, as students and their parents anxiously awaited the drawing of names that would determine their Mayo eligibility. While Mayo was and continues to be an outstanding school, the fact that students had to be winners in the Mayo lottery in order to attend helped considerably to create the public perception that its academic standing was far superior to that of Hartsville High School. That perception led to our school losing about 20-25 of our best students to Mayo every year. That annual loss of academic talent multiplied by four years was making a significant impact on Hartsville High School - one that I was acutely aware of as principal.

The lottery also put pressure on Darlington County School District board members from parents whose children were not offered an opportunity to attend Mayo. It was that public pressure for more magnet school opportunities which prompted two DCSD board members to pay me a visit one afternoon in the spring of 2005. Their question to me was "Dr. Burry, would you be interested in having a magnet school at Hartsville High School?" It took me about two seconds to answer in the affirmative. That began a process in which a committee of administrators, teachers, students, and community members investigated magnet school options that might fit Hartsville High School. The investigation ultimately resulted in our decision to apply for certification as an International Baccalaureate World School.

It was at that point that I made one of the best decisions of my entire tenure as principal when I asked Johnny Andrews about his interest in chairing the committee that would navigate our journey though the IB application procedure. At that time, Johnny - a friend of mine going back to our Boy Scout days - was a veteran social studies teacher who was held in high regard by his fellow faculty members, our administrative team, and his students. He also was - and still is - a member of Hartsville's City Council. To the great good fortune of Hartsville High School, Johnny accepted that challenging responsibility and led us successfully through the two-year IB application process that resulted in our becoming authorized as an International Baccalaureate World School in the spring of 2007. Johnny then transitioned into the role of IB Programme Coordinator on our administrative team and - with his tremendous organizational skills and attention to detail as well as his great passion for the job - led for nine years the further development of a program that experienced tremendous success. While Johnny's leadership and hard work were certainly key factors, the backbone of the program was our IB-trained teachers who provided exemplary instruction, support, and motivation for our students. Meeting the opportunities provided by the IB Programme were the talented and dedicated students who, while facing unprecedented challenges of academic rigor, chose to excel.

Achieving International Baccalaureate Programme status was probably the most significant academic development in the history of Hartsville High School. The program provided a huge boost to our school's academic prestige and stopped the bleeding in terms of losing our best students to Mayo. In selling the program, we constantly used the analogy of "a rising tide floats the whole ship higher" in regard to the program's impact on our school. It most assuredly had a positive impact and was a huge factor in the Red Fox Renaissance gaining an academic foothold and prospering at Hartsville High School and in our community. Most importantly, the IB Programme offers the students of Darlington County the opportunity for an education that meets world-class academic criteria and is the gold-standard for a college preparatory curriculum. There could not be a more well-deserved and rewarding legacy at Hartsville High School for Johnny Andrews.

James Ford, William Lenard, Johnny Andrews, Corey Lewis,
Phyllis Griggs, Charlie Burry, and Von Cranford

59

Relationships Based on Respect

We talked with our students a great deal about relationships based on respect, as that was a point of emphasis every year. We wanted them to have enough self-respect to make the right choices in their academic, personal, and social lives. We wanted them to respect each other, and for the way they treated and talked to each other to be based on understanding and tolerance. We wanted them to respect our teachers so that we could have good learning environments. We wanted our teachers to respect our students so that they'd want to come to a welcoming classroom environment and learn.

We talked with our teachers a lot about respect, too. I asked our teachers at one point to think for a minute about their time as a student and think of a teacher who had a really, really positive influence on their lives. I asked them to picture themselves as elementary, or high school, or college students, and to picture that teacher in their minds. I then asked them to think about why that teacher meant so much to them because I believed in almost every case, the affection and regard that they had for that teacher wasn't based on the subject matter that was taught. I knew my daughter, Caye, loved "Mama Rita" Shire, but it wasn't because of what she learned about the Amazon River in Global Studies. It was the relationship. I knew that when Shannon Johnson (former HHS student/athlete and Olympic Gold Medalist) talked about Pat Hewitt, she didn't say, "You know, it was that cross-over dribble that Coach Hewitt taught me in the ninth grade that has really made the difference in my life." It was the relationship. I knew that when

I got emails, cards, and letters from Danny Nicholson it wasn't because I taught him to jump stop on the free throw line on a three-on-two fast break. It was the relationship. I knew that when teachers ran into former students that they hadn't seen in a long time, they didn't talk about the Pythagorian Theorum or photosynthesis or Shakespeare. They asked them about their families, and their jobs, and how they're doing. It is all about relationships. Our teachers needed to teach the standards and the curriculum, but before all that they needed to be sure to teach the person first. They needed to be sure they were student-centered and not subject-centered - teach the course, but teach the person first. I loved my teachers Vada Gore and Lib Howle, but it wasn't because of what they taught me about conjugating verbs in eighth grade Latin class or the causes of the Revolutionary War. It was the relationships. At the end of the day, that's what matters most. I told our teachers that if we could foster those kinds of relationships based on mutual respect, that's when we would have a great school.

60

Glasser's Questions

At some point early in my tenure as principal, I was involved in a professional development session in which the topic was "Glasser's Questions." That workshop made a significant impact on my educational philosophy from an administrative point of view, and I included some of those ideas in remarks that I made to our faculty every year since. In his book *The Quality School Teacher*, William Glasser emphasizes that high-performing teachers demand high-quality work from their students. Glasser says that a prerequisite condition for quality work is for the students to know, trust, and like their teachers. This was consistent with our school's philosophy of "relationships based on respect" and the premise that the success of a school depends directly upon the relationships between the adults and students in the school. Glasser believed that in order to build the kind of relationships that promoted high-quality student work, a teacher must answer six questions:

Who am I?
What do I stand for?
What will I ask them to do?
What will I not ask them to do?
What will I do for them?
What will I not do for them?

Since that time, I suggested that our teachers use these questions and their own answers with each of their new classes at the beginning of a term. I believed that the answers to these questions would help to sow the seeds for mutually respectful relationships, as well as making a teacher's expectations very clear to students. As principal, I also believed that it was beneficial to provide that same kind of information about me and my philosophy of education to our faculty. As the instructional leader of the school, I would expect high-quality work from each of them, just as they would expect that kind of work from their students.

Finally, when I was interviewing teaching candidates for our faculty, one of the most important questions I asked was for the person to explain his or her thinking on the importance of the teacher-student relationship to the teaching-learning process. What I was looking for were clues as to how the candidate might answer Glasser's Questions. By that point in the interview, the candidates probably had a pretty good idea about what I wanted to hear, but the manner in which they articulated the answer usually gave me the insight that I needed into their personalities, their people skills, and ultimately, whether or not they were in education for the right reasons and were potentially a good fit for Hartsville High School.

61

You've Got to Figure Out the Damn Game

In May 1985, I was fired after seven years as the head boys' basketball coach at Hartsville High School. Several years later I was doing some reading and came across a quote from Geoffrey Ward in *Baseball: An Illustrated History* that hit me right square between the eyes. The quote was this:

> Sometimes it seemed like the entire subtext of our game was self-knowledge . . . that when good effort is met with repeated failure, that isn't bad luck. And it doesn't mean that deep down, you're winning. It means that deep down, you haven't figured out the damn game.

I had gained enough perspective by that time to understand that quote described my basketball coaching career perfectly. That deep down, I hadn't figured out the damn game. Following are the thoughts that I shared with our faculty and staff about the correlation between the status of Hartsville High School in 2009 and those events that occurred almost twenty-five years earlier in my life.

So, what's the connection between that quote and The Red Fox Renaissance at Hartsville High School in 2009-2010? Our test data, for the most part, is improving. Our graduation rate is improving, and our school report cards have been good. Our IB Programme has been very successful. Last spring, one hundred percent of our IB English and math students did well enough on their IB exams to earn college credit. Hartsville High School is becoming a great school again. We are winning, but we aren't winning everywhere, and that is what this is all about today. When we look at ourselves, there's part of the game that we still haven't figured out, and that is the achievement gap between our white students and our black students. We can't continue to talk about offering the finest college preparatory program in the world to our students and have that many others not performing at a better level. We can't just keep saying that we're going to work harder and keep making general statements about getting better. We've got to figure out how to work smarter, and we've got to establish a more specific focus on exactly what we need to be doing to get better. That is what will enable us to teach our black students more effectively and close the achievement gap. That is when Hartsville High School will truly be a great school again . . . for ALL of our students.

We're going to address this issue in two ways. One will be an increased focus on using the data that we collect from MAP and HSAP. We'll have data on the individual strengths and weaknesses of students, and we will use that data to address the weaknesses and improve in those areas with each student. We'll be using that "self-knowledge" to figure out what is working with our students and what isn't working, and we will make the necessary improvements in instructional strategies. The second thing that we'll emphasize is nothing new; it's something that we just need to continue to work on and improve. It's a good deal easier than what we just talked about because there's not one bit of data analysis required. In another respect, though, it's a lot harder because it's all about negotiating that slippery slope of teacher-student relationships. It's summarized in a quote from Jason Dorsey: "The success of a school is directly determined by the relationships of adults in that school with the students." This is what is most important, and this is the key to the degree of effectiveness of our whole teaching-learning process.

Successful teachers sometimes have to take their students to places that they don't necessarily want to go. If they don't trust you, it's going to be like pushing a rope uphill. If you've got that appropriate, mutually respectful relationship with them - if they like you for the right reasons - they'll follow you anywhere. If your students see that you're working to find ways to teach them in an engaging manner all the time, they'll know that you truly care about them learning something, and they'll work just as hard as you do. If you make an enemy of a student, you've lost him or her forever as far as teaching anything is concerned, and you're just going to make each other miserable. If you reach out and figure out how to help a student who has been fighting you and can win him or her over, that student will become one of your best. And you'll have a friend for life.

Hartsville High School is going to become a great school again. There are about thirty-five of you in the room who heard me say that for the first time six years ago. If you've been around here that long, you know that we're a lot closer to our goal now than we were back then. There is work left to do though, and that's why we have to learn more about ourselves - in order to work more efficiently and more effectively, and with a greater sense of understanding and compassion as we demand more from our students. We have to continue to figure out the damn game. That's when we'll be a great school again.

Dr. Charlie Burry, Jr.

62

The Tipping Point and the Speed of Trust

Following are thoughts that I shared with the Hartsville High School faculty and staff at the beginning of the 2011-12 school year.

A couple of books that I read this summer helped me with the thoughts that I want to share with you this morning, as a means of setting the tone for what we want to accomplish during the coming school year. One of the books, recommended to me by Brian Howell for pleasure reading, is *The Tipping Point* by Malcolm Gladwell. The other book, *The Speed of Trust* by Stephen M. R. Covey, was required reading for our principals' district-level staff development earlier this summer. These two books, I believe, provide a good picture of where we now are as a school, where we are poised to go, and what we can do to make it happen.

The Tipping Point, as defined on the back cover of the book, is "that magic moment when an idea, trend, or social behavior crosses a threshold, tips, and spreads like wildfire." It's when that fickle friend called momentum picks you up and sweeps you away. Gladwell says that the purpose of his book is this: to answer two simple questions that lie at the heart of what we would all like to accomplish as educators, parents, marketers, business people, and policy makers. Why is it that some ideas or behaviors or products start epidemics and others don't? And what can we do to deliberately start and control positive epidemics of our own?

Other individuals who offer acclaim for the book describe *The Tipping Point* in the following ways:

. . . a convincing case that, contrary to the prevailing wisdom of mass trends and focus-group marketing, a few individuals or a single haphazard event can set off a social epidemic that profoundly alters the culture, and

. . . the proposition that minor alterations, carefully conceived and adeptly enacted, can produce major consequences for individuals, organizations, and communities.

Do you see the significance of that idea for a school? Hold onto those thoughts for a few minutes while we move to *The Speed of Trust*.

The premise of *The Speed of Trust* is that when a high degree of trust is present in an organization, progress toward a goal happens much more quickly. The two formulas, more easily applied to the business world, which explain this idea are "low trust equals a low speed and high cost of operating, obviously in an inefficient manner, while high trust equals a high speed and low cost of doing business, and clearly greater efficiency." While Covey goes into quite a bit of detail about the various aspects of trust, the part that I think is most applicable to building efficiency in teaching and learning is what he calls "relationship trust." Covey puts it this way:

The truth is that in every relationship - personal and professional - what you do has a far greater impact than anything you say. You can say you love someone - but unless you demonstrate that love through your actions, your words become meaningless. . . . You can say that you will comply with the rules, that you won't engage in unethical practices, that you will respect a confidence, keep a commitment, or deliver results. You can say all of those things, but unless you actually do them, your words will not build trust; in fact, they will destroy it. As you think about behaving in ways that build trust, keep in mind that every interaction with every person is a "moment of trust." The way you behave in the moment will either build or diminish trust. And this opportunity is geometric.

Do you see the significance of that idea for a teacher? Continuing to improve test scores and graduation rates, having a fine arts program that excels, and winning more state championships in athletics will certainly help. However, what we need is a pervasive attitude - manifested in our behaviors and actions - which will cause us to cross that threshold and accelerate the momentum that we have now. That's where, in my opinion, *The Speed of Trust* comes in. As Covey explains, "it's the one thing that changes everything."

So, how do you get to that point with your students? First, you show them two critical things: one, that you're competent, and two, that you care. And, you do that by preparing a great lesson for them every day, a lesson that will engage and challenge them and help them learn. During a lesson, you continuously check for their understanding because it's about showing your students that you care about whether or not they're learning. Second, you hold your students accountable. You establish and communicate clear expectations, and you let your students know by your words and your actions that you are there to help them meet those expectations, whether it is in terms of academic success or acceptable behavior. You won't let them fail, and you won't let them act badly because you expect better from them. Finally, you treat your students with respect and with the inherent concepts of fairness and good judgment.

My message for you this morning is that I believe that the speed of trust can be the tipping point for Hartsville High School to become a great school again. Bank moments of relationship trust with each of your students. And, as that trust balance grows, get ready for the tipping point of a positive epidemic of learning in your classrooms.

63

The Courage To Change

I shared these thoughts with the Hartsville High School faculty and staff at the beginning of the 2010-11 school year.

At our graduation ceremony last May, I spoke to the Class of 2010 about change. One of the points made was that change is constant. Change is inescapable. We gain weight, and we lose our hair. People come and go in our lives. It can happen dramatically in the blink of an eye, or it can be almost imperceptible. Nothing stays the same. If we accept that premise, then we've got to accept this next one as well. If things never stay the same, if things are constantly changing, then we - as administrators and teachers, and as a school - are either getting better or we are getting worse every day. It is a choice that we have to make each day, and there is no middle ground. If we do not choose to get better, then we are choosing to get worse.

The further question, then, becomes the motivation for our choice. Why are you here? Why did you sign a teaching contract for this year? I hope you're here because you understand and accept the immense responsibility of helping young people prepare for their futures. I hope you're here because you have a passion for your subject matter. I hope you're here because you want to have a good influence on the character development of young people who are in some of the most formative years of their lives. If those are the things that drive you, then you are going to choose to get better every day. It's going to come naturally, it won't be painful, and it will be genuine and consistent. And years from now, your students will recall you as being someone who helped them change and helped make their lives better.

Last Thursday, South Carolina buried one of its true heroes - U. S. District Judge Matthew J. Perry. He would have been ninety years old this week. Judge Perry was described as being "a towering civil rights figure who used intellect, hard work and courage to end segregation in South Carolina and usher in a more just society," and as being "a transformative figure in the political history of our state." In an interview several years ago, Perry was recalling the height of the civil rights movement in the 1960s when he was jailed on numerous occasions and endured death threats to himself and his family. During that interview, he was asked if, during that time of controversy and social upheaval, he was ever afraid. Perry answered that question by saying, "I knew that if things didn't change for the better, that I would always be afraid."

Judge Perry understood that things had to change for the better, because the alternative was unacceptable to an entire race of people. He dedicated himself to bringing that change about. We must apply that premise to our situation at Hartsville High School if we are going to get better . . . that the alternative, not to stay the same but to get worse, is unacceptable. While the emotional intensity of our current challenge may not equal that of the Civil Rights Movement, I don't think it's a stretch to make a comparison. There is freedom at stake, just as there was in the 1960s, and it is the freedom that comes with each one of our students obtaining a quality education. We cannot be afraid, and we cannot be complacent. On Monday morning we get our first chance of the new school year to change some lives. How will you respond? As always, the choice is yours.

64

Every Kid Needs a Champion

During the summer of 2012, I was searching for an inspirational idea on which to anchor my Red Fox Renaissance keynote address for our August school-level staff development that would begin the 2012-13 school year. I found a TED Talk by Dr. Rita Pierson entitled *Every Kid Needs A Champion* - a part of which became a rallying cry for our students and teachers for a number of years. As I've mentioned before, a core part of Hartsville High School's philosophy about teaching and learning centered on student/teacher relationships. Pierson's TED Talk validated and reinforced our philosophy in a sometimes funny, yet remarkably inspiring manner founded in real world classroom experiences from her forty-year career in education. When we'd finished watching her eight-minute presentation, many of our teachers had tears in their eyes, both from laughing and from being deeply moved by her words.

Pierson's theories on teaching and learning centered on down-to-earth premises, such as "Kids don't learn from people they don't like." While she was not compromising in the areas of classroom discipline and student accountability, she was emphasizing the importance of relationships. She mentioned Covey's idea of "seeking first to understand," rather than pressing to be understood. With that idea, Pierson was emphasizing the importance of teachers understanding and having empathy for their students' personal life circumstances as a key to understanding classroom behavior and learning styles. She told of an instance in which she had won over an entire class by apologizing to them for a lesson that she'd taught incorrectly the day before. The real lesson for her students was that "We're all human, and we all make mistakes," and it deepened their connection. Pierson talked of another case in which a student had answered only two out of twenty questions correctly on a test, yet she was able to turn that into a positive motivational experience for the child. The point she was making with that story was the importance of somehow raising a student's self-esteem, and thereby giving him or her enough positive encouragement to try harder the next time.

In order to build self-esteem, she instilled the following mantra in her students that eventually became a part of their self-images:

> I am somebody!
> I was somebody when I came here today!
> I'll be a better somebody when I leave this afternoon!
> I am powerful, and I am strong!
> I deserve the education that I get here!
> I have things to do, people to impress, and places to go!

We had those words included in our student agendas one year, and the following year, they were printed on the back of our student ID cards. I wanted every student to have those thoughts readily available - at least in print if not in their minds - throughout the day. I'd go into two or three classrooms at the beginning of each day and have the students repeat each line after me, and we were loud enough so the other classes on that part of the hall could hear us. Many of the students probably thought I'd lost my mind, but I wanted them to hear it, and feel it, and - as Pierson hoped - for those positive and affirming words to become a part of them. I also believe that doing that helped my relationships with our students. Over a period of a few weeks, every student in the school got to see their principal first thing in the morning at least once. More importantly, most of them began to believe - through my leading them in those words - that I genuinely had their best interests at heart. If nothing else, it gave them a good laugh - or at least an eye-roll - to start the day.

Pierson closed her talk with a story about her mother's teaching career and the legacy of positive relationships that she had left with hundreds of students. She talked about how her mother had created that legacy by just being kind to her students and showing them that she cared about them. Pierson encouraged her audience to remember that at some point in their lives, every child would need a champion, and I challenged our teachers to be that champion for as many of their students as possible. It was one of the most meaningful staff development sessions we had during my time as principal. For a reason that you'll discover in a moment, we revisited *Every Kid Needs A Champion* at the beginning of the 2013-14 school year. If you've never viewed Pierson's video, I'd encourage you to do so.

Pierson's mother would be proud to know that her daughter also left quite a legacy. On June 28, 2013, a little more than a year after delivering her TED Talk, Dr. Rita Pierson died unexpectedly at the age of sixty-one. At the time I'm writing this, her *Every Kid Needs A Champion* video has more than 3.4 million views. Dr. Rita Pierson was, and continues to be, a true champion for children and educators everywhere.

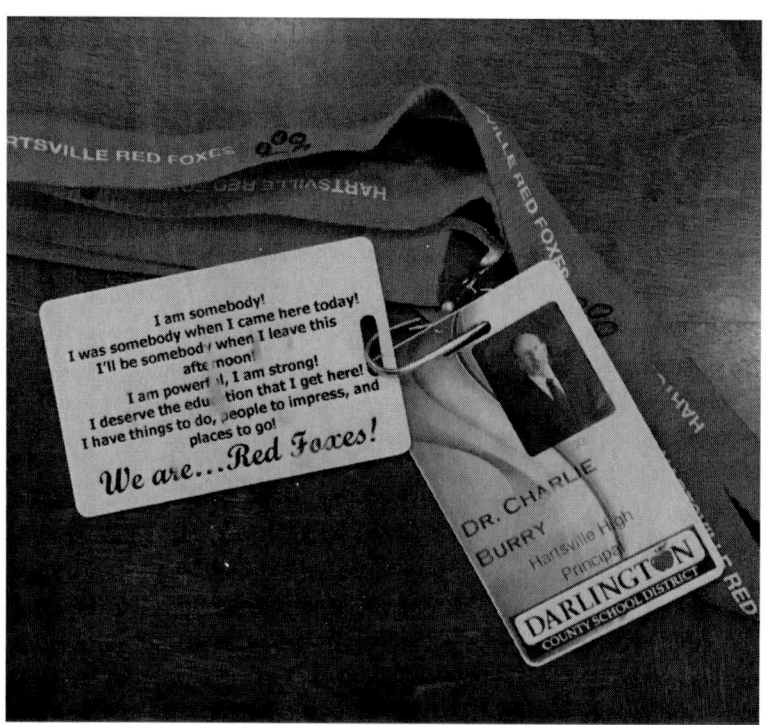

Dr. Rita Pierson Quote

Dr. Charlie Burry, Jr.

65

Elie Wiesel and the Kingdom of Night

Following are thoughts that I shared with the Hartsville High School faculty and staff at the beginning of the 2016-17 school year.

As much as I'm looking forward to the next few years of a Red Fox Renaissance at Hartsville High School, I've begun to think recently about the term "renaissance" a little differently. Most of you recall that the sports world lost two iconic figures this summer in Muhammed Ali and Pat Summit. I thought for a while about writing my beginning-of-the-year Red Fox Renaissance speech about one of them, and there was certainly plenty to draw from either of their lives. And while I still might write about one of them at some point this year, it was the death of another well-known person that inspired me more and got me thinking about renaissance in a different context. That person - who died on July 2, 2016 - was Elie Wiesel, survivor of the Holocaust and 1986 winner of the Nobel Peace Prize. His memoir *Night* described his experience in Auschwitz and Buchenwald, and some of our students at Hartsville High School have read this work. The Nobel committee called Wiesel a "messenger to mankind."

From an article written by Maria Popova found on the website *DailyGood*, hear some of the words from his Nobel acceptance speech thirty years ago at Norway's Oslo City Hall:

I remember, it happened yesterday or eternities ago. A young Jewish boy discovered the kingdom of night. I remember his bewilderment, I remember his anguish. It all happened so fast. The ghetto. The deportation. The sealed cattle car. The fiery altar upon which this history of our people and the future of mankind were meant to be sacrificed.

I remember, he asked his father, "Can this be true?" This is the twentieth century, not the Middle Ages. Who would allow such crimes to be committed? How could the world remain silent?

And now, years later, the boy is turning to me in my old age. "Tell me," he asks, "What have you done with your life? What have you done with my future?"

This is what I say to the young Jewish boy wondering what I have done with his future. It is in his name that I speak to you and that I express to you my deepest gratitude. No one is as capable of gratitude as one who has emerged from the kingdom of night. We know that every moment is a moment of grace, every hour an offering; not to share them would mean to betray them. Our lives no longer belong to us alone; they belong to all those who need us desperately.

My point is this. The Red Fox Renaissance that I talked about earlier is connecting with a lot of our students. They're winners in the classroom and with their extra-curricular activities, and they are preparing for good futures by learning every day. But we've got too many other students who, because of their life circumstances, live in their own kingdom of night. They come to us from the darkness of poverty. Their family structure and support system struck midnight long ago. There are other influences in their lives, regardless of their socio-economic status, that are keeping the window shades pulled all the way down. We talk with them about success, but they can't even imagine that because it's been night their whole lives. We wonder why they don't seem to care in the classroom, and it's because we can't imagine the intellectual, personal, and emotional holocaust they're in. Our society's kingdom of night.

Dr. Charlie Burry, Jr.

But, with every one of those students, there's a spark still in them somewhere. There's a hidden talent or a latent interest waiting to be discovered. They are the ones who need a renaissance in their lives. They need someone to understand their bewilderment and anguish and give them some hope. They are turning to us and asking, "Tell me, what are you doing with my future? What are you doing with your life?" And, because our life choice is the noble profession of education, our lives no longer belong to us alone: they belong to all those who need us desperately. They need us to awaken them, to inspire them, to challenge them, and to help them see the light of their own personal renaissance. Like Elie Wiesel in the Holocaust, they need someone to rescue them from their kingdom of night. They need hope and possibility.

Hope and possibility. I believe those are the most precious things that you can give to someone. And whether you ever hear it from them or not, remember that no one knows gratitude as much as one who has emerged from the kingdom of night. One day, like Elie Wiesel, they'll remember who helped them.

66

A Place of Hope and Possibility

I shared these thoughts with the Hartsville High School faculty and staff at the beginning of the 2015-16 school year.

How do you get young people to care? How do you reach more students and change the mindset of those students who still tell us, with their actions if not their words, that they just don't care. There is no magic pill, and I'm not sure that a reward system is the answer. A lot of times, tough consequences don't seem to matter either. How do you get young people to care?

Rick Reilly, eleven-time National Sportswriter of the Year and former columnist for *Sports Illustrated* and ESPN, helps us understand that with a chapter called *When Cheering for the Other Side Feels Better Than Winning* from his book entitled *Tiger, Meet My Sister, and Other Things I Probably Shouldn't Have Said*.

They played the oddest game in high school football history last month down in Grapevine, Texas.

It was Grapevine Faith vs. Gainesville State School and everything about it was upside down. For instance, when Gainesville came out to take the field, the Faith fans made a forty-yard spirit line for them to run through.

Did you hear that? The other team's fans?

They even made a banner for the players to crash through at the end. It said, "Go Tornadoes!" Which is also weird, because Faith is the Lions.

It was rivers running uphill and cats petting dogs. More than two hundred Faith fans sat on the Gainesville side and kept cheering the Gainesville players on - by name.

"I never in my life thought I'd hear people cheering for us to hit their kids," recalls Gainesville's QB and middle linebacker, Isaiah. "I wouldn't expect another parent to tell somebody to hit their kids. But they wanted us to!"

And even though Faith walloped them 33-14, the Gainesville kids were so happy after the game they gave head coach Mark Williams a side-line squirt-bottle shower like he'd just won state. Gotta be the first Gatorade bath in history for an 0-9 coach.

But then you saw the twelve uniformed officers escorting the fourteen Gainesville players off the field and two and two started to make four. They lined the players up in groups of five - handcuffs ready in their back pockets - and marched them to the team bus. That's because Gainesville is a maximum-security correctional facility seventy-five miles north of Dallas. Every game it plays is on the road.

This all started when Faith's head coach, Kris Hogan, wanted to do something kind for the Gainesville team. Faith had never played Gainesville, but he already knew the score. After all, Faith was 7-2 going into the game, Gainesville 0-8 with two touchdowns all year. Faith has seventy kids, eleven coaches, the latest equipment and involved parents. Gainesville has a lot of kids with convictions for drugs, assault, and robbery - many of whose families had disowned them - wearing seven-year-old shoulder pads and ancient helmets.

So Hogan had this idea. What if half our fans - for one night only - cheered for the other team? He sent out an email asking the Faithful to do just that. "Here's the message I want you to send," Hogan wrote: "You are just as valuable as any other person on planet Earth."

Some people were naturally confused. One Faith player walked into Hogan's office and asked, "Coach, why are we doing this?"

And Hogan said, "Imagine if you didn't have a home life. Imagine if everybody had pretty much given up on you. Now imagine what it would mean for hundreds of people to suddenly believe in you."

Next thing you know, the Gainesville Tornadoes were turning around on their bench to see something they had never seen before. Hundreds of fans. And actual cheerleaders!

"I thought maybe they were confused," said Alex, a Gainesville lineman (only first names are released by the prison). "They started yelling 'DEE-fense' when their team had the ball. I said, 'What? Why they cheerin' for us?'"

It was a strange experience for boys whom most people cross the street to avoid. "We can tell people are a little afraid of us when we come to the games," says Gerald, a lineman who will wind up doing more than three years. "You can see it in their eyes. They're looking at us like we're criminals. But these people, they were yellin' for us! By our names!"

Maybe it figures that Gainesville played better than it had all season, scoring the game's last two touchdowns. Of course, this might be because Hogan put his third-string nose guard at safety and his third-string cornerback at defensive end. Still.

After the game, both teams gathered in the middle of the field to pray, and that's when Isaiah surprised everybody by asking to lead. "We had no idea what the kid was going to say," remembers Coach Hogan. But Isaiah said this: "Lord, I don't know how this happened, so I don't know how to say thank You, but I never would've known there was so many people in the world that cared about us."

And it was a good thing everybody's heads were bowed, because they might have seen Hogan wiping away tears.

As the Tornadoes walked back to their bus under guard, they each were handed a bag for the ride home - a burger, some fries, a soda, some candy, a Bible and an encouraging letter from a Faith player.

The Gainesville coach saw Hogan, grabbed him hard by the shoulders and said, "You'll never know what your people did for these kids tonight. You'll never, ever know."

And as the bus pulled away, all the Gainesville players crammed to one side and pressed their hands to the window, staring at these people they'd never met before, watching their waves and smiles disappearing into the night.

Anyway, with the economy six feet under and Christmas running on about three and a half reindeer, it's nice to know that one of the best presents you can give is still absolutely free.

Hope.

So, how do you get young people to care? You care about them, and you give them hope. You care about them, and you give them hope by the way you teach them and the way you treat them. You treat them with respect, and you give them hope by understanding their life circumstances. You work hard for them, and you give them hope by coming to school every day prepared to teach a great lesson. You make your expectations clear, and you give them hope for becoming a better person by holding them accountable. You give them hope by being a good role model for them, by being somebody that they want to emulate for all the right reasons. You find a way to give that young person hope on the days that he or she needs a champion.

I challenge you to do all you can every day to make this another championship year of a Red Fox Renaissance. Let's all do everything we can to make Hartsville High School a place of hope and possibility for every student. That's why that phrase is under your name, as a reminder, outside the door of every classroom on this campus. Help your students to believe that when they see it on their way in, every day, all year - that your classroom is a place of hope and possibility.

67

The Shawshank Redemption

The Shawshank Redemption is a 1994 movie starring Tim Robbins (Andy) and Morgan Freeman (Red). It is the story of Andy Dufresne, who is sentenced to life in prison for the murder of his wife and her lover even though he is innocent of the crime. When he arrives at Shawshank State Penitentiary, he is befriended by Ellis "Red" Redding, a fellow inmate. After almost twenty years, Andy escapes from Shawshank and also executes a scheme to implicate the prison warden in a number of illegal activities while stealing his ill-gotten fortune. Red is eventually paroled, and he and Andy reunite in a town on the southern coast of Mexico. When I told a couple of my colleagues that I was going to use this movie as the theme for my annual Red Fox Renaissance remarks to our faculty and staff at the beginning of the 2017-18 school year, they were incredulous that I would use a prison movie for staff development with high school teachers. What they didn't understand was that *The Shawshank Redemption* isn't about prison. It's about hope. As a faculty, we watched four pivotal scenes from the film.

In the first scene we watched, Andy is taking a seat at the cafeteria table with his fellow inmates just after being released from solitary confinement. He'd done time in the hole because while acting as a trustee, he'd locked himself in the warden's office and played opera music over the loudspeaker system to the entire prison population. Andy tells his friends that music is important because it's something you have inside that "they can't get to, that they can't touch. It's yours." When Red asks Andy what he's talking about, Andy says, "Hope." Red's reply is, "Hope. Let me tell you something, my friend. Hope is a dangerous thing. Hope can drive a man insane. Got no use for it on the inside. Better get used to that idea." At that point, Red has no hope and leaves the table because he doesn't want any.

In the second scene we watched, Andy has escaped, and Red has been paroled. Red has made his way to a rock fence around a pasture at a location that Andy has told him about. There, marked by a single black rock, he finds a metal box containing money and a letter from Andy. In the letter, Andy invites Red to join him in a town on Mexico's Pacific coast that they talked about while they were in prison. Red also reads these words from his friend: "Hope is a good thing, maybe the best of things. And no good thing ever dies. I will be hoping that this letter finds you, and finds you well." Red contemplates those words and begins to feel a sense of optimism. He begins to find hope.

In the third scene, Red catches a bus to a Texas border town where he intends to cross into Mexico. As the Trailways bus rolls along, Red's silent monologue is this:

I find I'm so excited, I can barely sit still or hold a thought in my head. I think it's the excitement only a free man can feel, a free man at the start of a long journey whose conclusion is uncertain. I hope I can make it across the border. I hope to see my friend and shake his hand. I hope the Pacific is as blue as it has been in my dreams. I hope.

Red finally realizes what an incredibly wonderful and inspiring feeling it is to have hope.

In the final scene, Red finds Andy on a beach of the blue Pacific, affirming Andy's belief - and now Red's, too - that "Hope is a good thing, maybe the best of things."

High school students - regardless of culture, socio-economic background, or ability - need hope. Some need it more than others, and some need it more often than others, but they all need hope at some stage. Students need to believe in the possibility of success in the classroom and in life. Too many of them don't have that belief because they don't see it at home. They hear us talk about being successful, but they don't understand what we're saying because they have no reference point of success in their life experiences. On the other hand, too many of them don't understand success because they've been given everything all their lives and don't know what it takes to earn it. That's why it was so important for Hartsville High School to become "a place of hope and possibility for EVERY student." That phrase became our school's motto: it was posted outside the door of every classroom, and it's still on the marquee sign in front of the school. Our teachers give a lot of themselves. Every teacher does. What teachers have to give more than anything else, though - because it's foundational to every other thing that they're trying to give - is hope and possibility. Hope and possibility - the best thing that anyone can ever give or receive, because "Hope is a good thing, maybe the best of things." Just ask Andy and Red.

68

The Changing of the Guard

Several years ago, I reconnected with Steve McCammon, an old Furman friend who is retired from the newspaper business. He is a very intelligent guy, well-traveled and extremely well-read, and much more attuned to the cultural world - art, music, and theatre - than I am. Rumor has it that he used to be a pretty good athlete as well. He posts on Facebook regularly, and many of his posts are philosophical in nature, encouraging his readers to "pay it forward" and to be more cognizant of "being kind" and doing things "for the common good." Steve is also very supportive of education, and some years ago he made me aware of an episode of *The Twilight Zone* television series from the early 1960s. *The Twilight Zone* series, created by Rod Serling, included a variety of highly imaginative stories, usually with suspenseful themes and endings which teach life lessons.

Steve's recommendation was *The Changing of the Guard*, and it became the centerpiece of our August staff development and my Red Fox Renaissance address for the 2014-15 school year. I was looking for something inspirational as an emphasis to our faculty and staff about the importance that teachers have in the lives of young people and to remind them that their former students recall their instruction - and especially their relationships - throughout their lives.

The Changing of the Guard is about Professor Ellis Fowler, an elderly English teacher at a boys' prep school who is being forced into retirement after fifty-one years at the school. He is given this news by his supervisor on the day the students are being dismissed for the Christmas holidays. Depressed by this bleak holiday news and convinced that his career has amounted to nothing, Fowler decides to commit suicide on Christmas Eve. He plans to shoot himself next to a statue of the famous educator Horace Mann, with its quote, "Be ashamed to die until you have won some victory for humanity." As he's standing by the statue, though, he hears a class change bell in the night and is mysteriously drawn back to his old classroom. There Fowler is visited by the ghosts of several of his former students, some of whom died heroic deaths. One was a hero at the Battle of Iwo Jima, another saved the lives of twelve of his shipmates at Pearl Harbor, and another died from the effects of his research into cancer treatments. All of the boys tell Fowler about how his teachings inspired them to be better men and what a tremendous difference he made in their lives. The bell then tolls again, and the ghosts disappear. Professor Fowler, heartened by the visit from his former students and now convinced that he has "won some victory for humanity," decides that he is content with his retirement.

Teaching, especially in a public high school in today's society, is a difficult profession. Teachers face challenges each day that the good people who taught most of them would have never imagined. When you think about it, that makes the teaching profession even more important. A lot of young people have become better spouses, parents, and citizens because of the academic and life lessons learned from teachers who were also people of good character. That's more important today because teachers may be one of the few significant people in our students' lives who have had that kind of influence on them, and that influence ripples into eternity. Teachers should remember when it's time for the changing of the guard that they've touched many more lives than they realize and that they're appreciated in many more ways than they will ever know.

Lessons for Graduates

During the time that I was principal of Hartsville High School, we began each day - as most schools do - with morning announcements. That was also the time for the Pledge of Allegiance to our nation's flag and our own Red Fox Pledge of Honor. At the conclusion of these announcements, I presented a "Project Wisdom Thought for the Day" or a "Character Education Quote for the Day." The purpose of those thoughts or quotes was to have our students hear - and hopefully give some consideration to - ideas that would lead to self-improvement and making our school a better place. As a result of these early morning forays into the minds of our students, it also became my practice to ask the senior class to consider one last thought or quote - accompanied by my commentary - at their graduation ceremony. That lesson usually came from something that I'd run across in a movie, a book, some song lyrics, or sometimes an event that happened during the school year. My remarks were always tempered by advice from my wife, which was "Don't try to be witty, intelligent, or say something profound. Just be yourself." Anyway, the chapters in this section are the remarks that I offered during each of the commencement exercises in which I was privileged to participate from 2005 through 2018.

Dr. Charlie Burry, Jr.

O' Graduates, Where Art Thou?

While tonight's graduation ceremony marks the end of the high school experience for members of the Class of 2005, we should also be aware that Webster's Dictionary defines commencement as "the act or time of a beginning." Tonight, the end of one journey marks the commencement of another. While many of you have plans and are well-prepared for your next journey, no one really knows where it will lead.

The movie *O Brother, Where Art Thou* is a film loosely based on Homer's *The Odyssey*, and is about the adventures of three escaped prisoners from a chain gang. By the way, I hope you won't assume that there's any intended correlation between that scenario and your high school days. At the beginning of their escape odyssey, a blind prophet tells the three fugitives this:

You seek a great fortune. . . . You will find a fortune, though it will not be the one you seek. But first . . . first you must travel a long and difficult road, a road fraught with peril. You shall see things, wonderful to tell. You shall see a . . . a cow . . . on the roof of a cotton house. And, oh, so many startlements. I cannot tell you how long this road shall be, but fear not the obstacles in your path, for fate has secured your reward. Though the road may wind, yea, your hearts grow weary, still shall ye follow them, even unto your salvation.

As you go forth tonight to seek your fortunes, you should be aware that what you seek is not always what you'll find. On your journey, you'll see amazing things - "things wonderful to tell" - that your grandparents, or even your parents, never dreamed of. Your journey sometimes will be difficult and dangerous, with "oh, so many startlements." You should have no fear, but instead have faith that there is a plan for each of your lives that is known to no earthly being. And on your journey, above all else, you must continue on the road, even when it winds and "your hearts grow weary."

The next idea that I'll leave with you tonight may help you when your hearts grow weary. It's another quote, this one from Calvin Coolidge, the thirtieth President of the United States, and he was speaking about the idea of persistence. Persistence is the character trait of outlasting and overcoming difficulty, and carrying on no matter how hard life gets - the belief in never quitting. President Coolidge said these words:

Nothing in the world can take the place of persistence. Talent will not; nothing is more common than unsuccessful men with talent. Genius will not; unrewarded genius is almost a proverb. Education will not; the world is full of educated derelicts. Persistence and determination alone are omnipotent. The slogan 'press on' has solved and always will solve the problems of the human race.

People place a lot of value on talent, and that is one area where men are not created equal, physically or intellectually. But the talent and native intelligence of even those who are most gifted requires development and cultivation, and that requires plain old hard work and persistence. When that work ethic is not present, the result is what President Coolidge meant when he spoke about unsuccessful men with talent and unrewarded genius. He was talking about the unfulfilled potential of those who could have made so much more of their lives but didn't. He also cited education as being something of great value, but he also mentioned educated derelicts - those who fail to put what they've learned in school to any great use.

What President Coolidge spoke of is a truth that is as valid today as it was eighty years ago - you're going to have to use the achievement that we celebrate tonight to obtain further education, gainful employment, and personal satisfaction. While we celebrate education and talent and genius, the character traits of persistence and determination will be far more important as you seek the great fortune of a better life and contributing positively to society. In my experience, the real cause for celebration is the success of people whose exceptional work ethic maximized talent and ability that was less than others. Those people in life are called overachievers, and the difference between them and those who are more gifted but less successful is simply persistence - that dogged refusal to quit and their relentless pursuit of excellence.

What I have offered you tonight has been your last lesson at Hartsville High School. Rather than English, math, science, or social studies, it's been a lesson of life from a blind prophet in a movie and a United States President, and I hope will help each of you on your journey. Have a plan but expect the unexpected. See amazing things. Have faith, not fear. Persist through difficulty. Choose what you know is right. Respect yourselves and others. From the faculty, staff and administration of Hartsville High School, from your families and friends, and from all those who love you - we wish you Godspeed on the great odyssey that awaits each of you. Press on . . . for fate has secured your reward.

70

The Choice of Hercules

Tonight's graduation ceremony marks the end of the high school experience for members of the Class of 2006, but we also know that another part of your lives is about to begin. While many of you have plans and are well-prepared for your next journey, no one really knows where it will lead or what you'll encounter. To help you think about some of the choices you'll be making along the way, I'm going to tell you one of my favorite stories. It is from Greek mythology and is entitled *The Choice of Hercules*. The time of the story is when Hercules was a young man, probably about your age, preparing to go out into the world to seek his fortune. Let's walk along with young Hercules for a bit and see what happens to him.

One day, while wandering along in thought, Hercules came to a place where two paths met. He sat down to consider which path he should follow. One path led over flowery meadows, but toward a darkening distance; the other path, passing over rough stones and rugged, brown furrows, lost itself in a glowing sunset. As Hercules sat thinking about his choice, he saw two beautiful maidens coming toward him. The first was tall and graceful, and wrapped in a snow-white mantle. The other maiden hurried to outrun the first. She, too, was tall, but seemed taller than she really was. She, too, was beautiful, but her glance was bold. As she ran, a rosy garment floated like a cloud around her form, and she gazed in admiration at her own shadow as it moved along the ground.

When this maiden arrived, she began to try to convince Hercules to follow her path, the one over the flowery meadow. She promised him a delightful and easy road and great fortune. She promised him every kind of pleasure, and a life of never having to labor. When Hercules asked her name, she replied, "My friends call me Happiness, but my enemies name me Vice."

As this was happening, the white-robed maiden came near and said to Hercules, "My name is Virtue, and I have watched you and tended you from a child, and I know the fond care that your parents have bestowed upon you. Come now along the rugged path that leads to my dwelling. I will not seduce you with promises of vain delights; instead I will tell you that lasting fame and true nobility come only through pain and labor. I will tell you that if you seek the gracious gifts of Heaven, you must remain in constant prayer, and if you would be beloved by your friends, you must serve your friends. And I will tell you that if you are anxious to reap the fruits of the earth, you must till the earth."

The maiden called Vice then said, "Don't you see, Hercules, the difficult and tedious road that Virtue would have you travel? I will give you a short and easy path to perfect happiness."

The maiden called Virtue replied, "Why do you deceive this lad? You want to pamper him with riches and make him feeble with softness, and when he comes to a wretched old age, he shall lay himself down in melancholy death, and his name will be remembered no more. I am the companion of virtuous men. I, Virtue, am welcome in the homes of artisans and tillers of the soil, and am the guardian of industrious households. I am the promoter of the labors of peace, and no honorable deed is accomplished without me. When my friends have run their courses, and death overtakes them, their names are celebrated in song and praise, and they live on in the hearts of grateful countrymen. Come, then, O Hercules, son of noble parents, follow me and by your worthy and illustrious deeds secure for yourself exalted happiness."

Virtue stopped speaking then, and Hercules, withdrawing his gaze from the face of Vice, arose from his place, and followed Virtue along the rugged, brown path of Labor.

Graduates, just as Hercules had a decision to make that day, you will also be faced with choices. Each decision that you make, regardless of how insignificant it may seem at the time, could very well affect your future and your true, long-term happiness. Hercules chose wisely that day, and I hope that you will draw on the wisdom that you've accumulated from the experiences in your lives to also make wise choices. Your parents, teachers, and coaches have talked to you about sound judgment, and hopefully some of those conversations have been meaningful to you. The successes that have led you to tonight will reinforce your confidence in your talents and abilities to meet further challenges. As you face the temptation of wrong choices along the way, I hope you'll have the strength of character and courage to stick with your convictions. You'll become discouraged from time to time with the difficulties of your journey, and you'll need to persist and keep moving. Finally, I pray that, when there is no other light to be seen ahead, you'll have faith that there are plans for your lives known only to God.

Finally and simply, as Hercules did, choose what you know is right. Finally and simply. Is it really that easy? Most choices in life aren't really complicated. We sometimes think that they are because of the influence of others or the temptation of taking what appears to be an easier and more appealing way. And, while it is certainly helpful to seek the advice of trusted friends and listen to other voices of experience, there is really only one person whom you need to ask when you think you're faced with a tough choice. Ask yourself. Your conscience will tell you which path to take, just as it happened with Hercules. From the faculty, staff, and administration of Hartsville High School, from your families and friends, and from all those who love you - we wish you Godspeed along your rugged, brown path of Labor to a virtuous and honorable life.

71

Be Like Raymond and Jennings

High school graduation is a time of reflecting on and celebrating past accomplishments and a time of contemplating future dreams and ambitions. You know where you have been for the last twelve years, and many of you think you know where you will be for the next four years or so. But where will you be fifty years from now? In June of 2057, when you are at some stadium - maybe this one, or some gymnasium or auditorium watching your grandchildren graduate - what will your lives have been like?

In 1991 Gatorade came out with the first television commercial that encouraged us to "Be Like Mike." The message was that if we drank Gatorade, we could be like Michael Jordan, and that we could - at least in some small manner - associate ourselves with the man who would become arguably the best basketball player in the world. Was that a realistic assumption? Probably not, but those commercials sold a lot of Gatorade. Many of us have been fortunate enough to have role models in our lives who were a little closer to us than Michael Jordan. I am where I am today because of the way my parents raised me, because of men who coached me, and because of one who was my guidance counselor. I am where I am today because I respected and admired those people so much that I wanted to be like them.

Who are your role models? Who might be the people who lived their lives so well - and were so well known - that they could offer realistic inspiration to the entire Hartsville High School

Class of 2007? I'll offer a suggestion. Many of you knew these two people, and we've thought a lot about both of them in the last fifteen months or so. Some of you attended their funerals. Members of the Red Fox Family know, of course, that I'm talking about Raymond Davis and Jennings Smith. We missed Raymond this year, kicking field goals and shooting the three at halftime. And the one thing missing from the state championship baseball series with North Augusta a few weeks ago was Jennings' war whoop.

Raymond Davis - adopted coach, manager, and cheerleader for the Red Foxes for twenty years until he died of leukemia in March 2006. Jennings Smith - statistician for Red Fox athletic teams for more than thirty years until he died of cancer last October. Raymond and Jennings, men of different races who saw no color and treated everyone with the same degree of respect - like brothers and sisters. Raymond and Jennings, men whose loyalty to the Red Foxes was strong and unquestioned - in the good times and the bad. Raymond and Jennings - one mentally challenged and the other with a disease that physically crippled him at a young age, but men who never showed the first moment of feeling sorry for themselves. Raymond and Jennings - men who found a passion in their lives and gave it all they had. Raymond and Jennings - men who even in the last darkest hours of their earthly lives . . . had faith. Raymond and Jennings - ordinary men who provided extraordinary examples for us about how to live life.

Graduates, there are no real secrets to a successful life. You have achieved a significant level of education, one that will hopefully be the foundation for higher education and success in your chosen occupation, and that is very important. However, the things that will bring you true success in life are the things I've just mentioned - loyalty, persistence, passion, respect, and faith - and all of those things are right out in front of us every day, just like they were with Raymond and Jennings. The choice is yours.

So, graduates, I'd like to offer one last Thought for the Day to the Class of 2007. In the years ahead, if I were you, I wouldn't worry too much about trying to "Be Like Mike." First of all, you need to be yourselves, but that's a topic for another day. But if I were you, I'd try to remember to be a little bit like Raymond, and I'd try to remember to be a little bit like Jennings. And if you do that, by 2057 you'll have had lives that are happy, successful, fulfilling, and respected . . . by your grandchildren and everyone else who knows you. From the faculty, staff, and administration of Hartsville High School, from your families and friends, and from all those who love you - we wish you Godspeed.

Raymond Davis

Jennings Smith

Dr. Charlie Burry, Jr.

72

Dreams Can Come True

During the last two or three months of each school year, one of the things that is always in the back of my mind is trying to come up with a meaningful topic for the principal's remarks at graduation. Tonight, I'm going to tell you about one of my favorite country music songs. About three Saturdays ago I was on the walking trail at Byerly Park, and as I listened on my iPod, an old song by an old group called the Statler Brothers entitled *Class of '57* came up. I've probably heard that song a thousand times over the years, but I'd never thought about it as a topic for a graduation speech. It's kind of an upbeat tune, but the lyrics are a little bit melancholy . . . not really sad, but expressing some degree of regret about the reality of unfulfilled dreams. Some of it goes like this:

> The Class of '57 had its dreams,
> but living life day to day is never like it seems.
> Things get complicated
> when you get past eighteen,
> but the Class of '57 had its dreams.
> Tommy's selling used cars,
> Nancy's fixing hair,
> Harvey runs a grocery store,
> and Margaret doesn't care.
> Jerry drives a truck for Sears,
> and Charlotte's on the make,
> Paul sells life insurance,
> and part-time real estate.

And the Class of '57 had its dreams,
we all hoped we'd change the world
with our great words and deeds.
Maybe we all thought the world
would change to fit our needs,
but the Class of '57 had its dreams.

What the Statler Brothers are saying in that song is that a lot of our dreams that we have when we're young don't come true. When I began my teaching and coaching career thirty-five years ago, I was going to be the next John Wooden, Bob Knight, and Dean Smith all rolled into one. Obviously, that didn't happen. We all can't be Hall of Fame athletes, live in the White House, or be the next American Idol. The fact of the matter is that most of us are going to be average people living ordinary lives. That's what average is.

Understand this, though. I don't mean to say - and I don't think that the Statlers meant to say - that there's anything wrong with being average. I would suggest that most ordinary people live very fulfilling lives and make solid contributions to the world by practicing their faith, being loving husbands and wives, raising their children the right way, being good citizens in the community, doing some kind of productive work, serving others, and simply enjoying life. I think what I've just described would be a life well-lived by anyone's standards.

Here is the point that the Statler Brothers were making, though, and this is one of the main points that I want to make to you tonight. What was important - and what the Statlers keep repeating in that song - was that the Class of '57 had its dreams. It doesn't matter that most of them didn't come true. It doesn't matter that Tommy ended up selling used cars and that Harvey ran a grocery store. The important thing was that they dreamed, that they had goals, and that they had enough ambition to work toward them. What matters most is that they

Dr. Charlie Burry, Jr.

dreamed and that they tried, whether they accomplished all of their goals or not.

Some of you may remember the movie *Thelma and Louise*. Susan Sarandon and Geena Davis play two ordinary women whose lives and marriages haven't turned out well. Through a series of poor choices and bad luck they become fugitives from the law in a wild, cross-country chase, and end up driving a convertible off a cliff into the Grand Canyon. At one point in the movie Louise, thinking back on their lives of unfulfilled promise, says to Thelma, "You get what you settle for." She was saying that sometimes life - if we allow it to - can beat our expectations down, and what we end up with is just that for which we're willing to settle. Thelma and Louise didn't start dreaming again until it was too late.

So, to the Class of 2008, here is your very last Thought for the Day: The important thing is that you have dreams and that you go after them. As we acknowledged a minute ago, most of you will live good, average lives, and that will be fine. On the other hand, it's impossible for any earthly being to know what potential greatness lies ahead for some of you. At this moment in time it doesn't matter what your last name is, whether your class rank is in single or triple digits, or where you live. It doesn't matter whether you're male or female, black or white, rich or poor. What matters is that you dream, and that you do not settle. Every one of you here in front of me tonight has taken a first step toward greatness by earning a high school diploma. Some of you may have dreamed of that, and if you didn't, I'd be willing to bet that your parents did. Now it's come true. And if that dream has come true, why can't others? You'll never know unless you try.

Graduates, from the faculty, staff, and administration of Hartsville High School, from your families and friends, and from all those who love you, we wish you Godspeed on your life's journey. And if you don't remember anything else that I've said tonight, remember these two simple things - these three words - from the Statler Brothers, and Thelma and Louise to you: Dream ... don't settle. Because dreams can come true.

Where Have You Gone, Joe DiMaggio?

Graduations are generally bittersweet times of mixed emotions: joy and a sense of great satisfaction in the culmination of twelve years of school work; maybe some sadness, as you realize that you won't be seeing some of your closest friends on a daily basis anymore; and possibly some apprehension, as the uncertainty of college, the military, the world of work, and the question of "What am I going to do with my life?" is suddenly a lot closer than it's ever been before. For me, and probably some people in our audience, tonight is a bit special, too. You see, a little more than forty years ago on May 26, 1969, I sat here with my classmates and then walked across the stage to receive a Hartsville High School diploma from our principal, Mr. David Johnson.

You're stepping into quite a different world today than we did forty years ago, though. We're in an economic situation that is unprecedented in most of our lifetimes. Statistics say that more than one of every ten employable adults in our audience tonight is out of work. There are some wonderful teachers sitting with our faculty tonight for the last time who would love to come back to work at our school next year and can't because budget cuts had to be made, and their jobs were eliminated. The uncertainty of what's around the corner for us in our lives is probably more ominous than most of us have ever known.

In thinking about this uncertainty and trying to relate it to tonight, I remembered a movie that came out in 1967 entitled *The Graduate*. It was Dustin Hoffman's breakthrough role in his career as he played Benjamin Braddock, a young college graduate who had no idea about what he was going to do next in his life. Sound familiar? In the movie, he ultimately falls in love with a girl named Elaine, and they presumably live happily ever after. The catch to the whole thing, though - and the plot of the movie - is that in the months before he met Elaine, Benjamin has had an affair with her mother. The soundtrack of that movie introduced one of the biggest hit songs of the 1960s, performed by Paul Simon and Art Garfunkel . . . *Mrs. Robinson*. Some of the most memorable lyrics of the song are

> Where have you gone, Joe Dimaggio?
> Our nation turns its lonely eyes to you.
> What's that you say Mrs. Robinson?
> Joltin' Joe has left and gone away."

I suppose I need to add here, for those of you who don't know Joltin' Joe Dimaggio, that he was one of the greatest professional baseball players of all time. He was with the New York Yankees; his fifty-six-game hitting streak is still the major league record; and he played centerfield, swung the bat, and ran the bases with a rare athletic skill and grace that can be recognized even in old game films from the 1950s. Joe Dimaggio was a superstar of his time, but perhaps his most memorable characteristics were the class, humility, dignity, and respect with which he played the game. Joe Dimaggio didn't take steroids or performance-enhancing drugs, he would have never chest-bumped a teammate or taunted an opponent, and all he did after each of his three hundred and sixty-one home runs was politely tip his cap to the crowd. His life wasn't lived under the microscope of today's media coverage. Joe Dimaggio was, to all Americans, the ideal: a true, bigger-than-life - yet quietly humble - hero.

I know you're wondering by now, "Where in the world is he going with all this - *The Graduate*, *Mrs. Robinson*, and Joe Dimaggio?" I'll try to pull it all together, and conclude, now.

Life, in good times and bad, is filled with uncertainty. Forty years ago was an uncertain time as well. The Vietnam Conflict, the Civil Rights Movement, and the assassinations of President John F. Kennedy, Senator Robert F. Kennedy, and Dr. Martin Luther King, Jr., shook our faith, challenged our ideals, and changed people's thinking. While we can never know what tomorrow holds, economically or otherwise, in uncertain times it helps us to have goals, to have something on which to anchor our hope, and to be able to look up to heroes. But what Paul Simon was doing with the words, "Where have you gone Joe Dimaggio?" - while paying tribute to Joltin' Joe - was to comment on how the popular culture and changing times of the 1960s had magnified and distorted how our heroes were perceived. I think the question being posed by Paul Simon in 1967 was whether or not our society had become too cynical and judgmental to have any real heroes. That question is even more pointed today as the media constantly gives us disturbing accounts of the imperfect lives of professional athletes and celebrities from the entertainment world. The question is especially pertinent to those of us who are baseball fans when we learn that of the fifteen players who hit the most home runs in the major leagues between 1993 and 2004, ten of them have tested positively for performance-enhancing drugs. Where have you gone, Joe Dimaggio? Can there be any real heroes left in today's society?

My message to you tonight, finally, is to answer Paul Simon and tell you that Joe Dimaggio has not left and gone away. A nation can still turn its eyes to his legacy, and we can still have ideals and heroes in our lives today that provide inspiration and help us through the difficult times. As we go through life, we all have experiences that provide bitter doses of reality, but we don't have to let those things destroy our faith. We can still be positive and approach life with humility, respect, and dignity - just like Joe Dimaggio played baseball. Some of you may know that Joe Dimaggio dealt with tragedy in his personal life, too. He was married for a short time to one of Hollywood's most beautiful movie stars, Marilyn Monroe. Even though they'd divorced, after her shocking and mysterious death in 1962, he sent roses to her grave twice a week for the next twenty years. Even Joltin' Joe was devoted to an ideal, although Marilyn herself was far from perfect.

As you can see from our little history lesson this evening - or by opening the newspaper tomorrow morning - our heroes won't always be perfect. There has been only one who lived that kind of life. We sometimes find that even some of the ones closest to us are flawed. As you leave here tonight though, diploma in hand and with an education that no one can take away from you, be determined never to lose your sense of idealism. Find a hero - the right kind - to admire. And by the way, there are some good ones sitting just to your left. I'm doing what I'm doing today because forty years ago there were two men on the Hartsville High School faculty and coaching staff whom I admired. Never lose your faith in doing things the right way. Continue to believe in fairness and equality. Stretch your ambitions and don't accept what may or may not be your limitations. Never give up. Always believe in yourself. Rich or poor, black or white - the ideal, your Joe Dimaggio - still exists, as long as you keep it in your mind. And as long as it's there, it can be achieved. At the end of the movie, at least in one respect, that even came true for Benjamin Braddock.

On behalf of the faculty, staff, and administration of Hartsville High School, and all those who love you, I'll close with

Dr. Charlie Burry, Jr.

a few of the words that Paul Simon said to Mrs. Robinson in the rest of the lyrics to that song:

> Here's to you, graduates . . .
>
> God bless you, please . . . .

The Distance from Yesterday

Those of you who have been in my office during the last four years, for whatever reason, have probably noticed that I have a quote wall that is filled with thoughts that, for one reason or another, have been meaningful to me. They've come from movies, song lyrics, books, magazine or newspaper articles, or from people that I've heard speak at one time or another. The quotes have, at different times over the last thirty-seven years, become part of my educational and life philosophy. They've also provided me with inspiration and guidance, correction and rebuke when I haven't measured up, and occasionally, a topic for the principal's graduation remarks. Because of the threat of bad weather at last year's graduation, the Class of 2009 was spared from having to listen to my speech; we cut it out of the ceremony, and I just mailed it to them. This year, it appears that you won't be so lucky. So, just bear with me for a few minutes, and as you listen . . . take time to think about it.

One of this year's quotes is from a man named Robert Nathan, an American novelist and poet, who once said, "There is no greater distance on this earth than yesterday." Listen once more, closely: "There is no greater distance on this earth than yesterday." At first, his mixing of two different types of measurement, distance and time, may seem a little puzzling. After all, yesterday, as of this moment, was only a little more than nine hours ago, and it can never, ever be more than twenty-four hours ago. The circumference of the earth, in case you don't remember this fact from your social studies or science classes, is 24,901.55 miles at the equator. What Mr. Nathan was expressing by comparing a relatively short amount of time with a tremendous distance was a future-oriented philosophy of life, and that makes it the perfect topic for a commencement speech. You see, while this morning marks the end of your high school career as our Class of 2010, it is also a new beginning. That's what the word "commencement" means.

What Mr. Nathan was saying can be applied in a lot of different ways, and - as with most things in life - the key is applying those words in the most appropriate and productive manner. He was not saying that past accomplishments are unimportant because what we accomplish in the past does lay the foundation for future achievements. You are receiving a hard-earned high school diploma this morning, and that's a wonderful accomplishment that we'll all rightfully celebrate. More importantly though, that diploma represents the educational foundation and structure for what you're going to do with the rest of your life. And that, as Mr. Nathan says, is much more important than yesterday.

We're building a new gymnasium on the Hartsville High School campus right now. The foundation for that beautiful building has been laid, and it's a good one; all of you have seen the concrete, steel rebar, cement blocks, and mortar that have gone into it. Some of the walls have gone up now. There's been a lot of the construction - and the most important part so far - that has been accomplished. But what if everything just stopped right there? What if Edison-Foard Construction just said, "Well, we built a great foundation and some walls for the gym yesterday, we really don't need to do anymore," and walked off the job? The wonderful facility that might accommodate our PE classes, student body assemblies, athletic and community events, and maybe even next year's graduation ceremony would never be. That foundation and those raw concrete block walls would just sit forever out behind Building 7 as an ugly monument to what might have been. So, applying Mr. Nathan's philosophy to the new gym, we can correctly say that what is most important on that site will happen tomorrow, and the week after, and in the coming months, and in the coming years as that building is being used to its fullest capabilities - not yesterday. Not in the past.

There's another way of looking at Mr. Nathan's quote that also pertains to the importance of putting the past behind us and looking ahead to the future. All of us make mistakes in our lives, do things that we regret, and let opportunities slip away. And while it's important to learn from our mistakes, it is also important to remember that, according to our Thought for the Day, there is quite a bit of distance between where, and what, and who we are now and yesterday. Some of you have taken tremendous advantage of the opportunities that you've had in the last four years at Hartsville High School. Others of you, let's just say, could have done better. Regardless of how you handled it, what we're talking about is yesterday. Tomorrow is a different day, with new opportunities that are much more important than those that are gone forever. What Mr. Nathan is telling us is that the most important part of our journey of life lies ahead of us, not behind us.

The concluding thought that I'd like to offer you, and tie to our perspective on yesterday, is this. This quote was given to me by a dear friend, and it hangs on the wall behind my desk in my office: "The people who share the journey of life with you are more important than the destination." I've tried to get you to think this morning about where you're going, not where you've been. But I'd also like to tell you that the most important thing - on any journey - is not where you are, but the people who have been with you along the way. We talk a lot about the importance of relationships at Hartsville High School, and those are the things, even forty or fifty years from now, that the

Class of 2010 will recall about your time together. That is what will be most important in your spiritual life as a child of God. That is the part of your future that will be most important in your family life, as a son or daughter, brother or sister, in your marriage, as a father or mother, and even as a grandparent. It will be what is most important in whatever career you chose, and especially if you happen to become an educator. What we will all cherish most in life, sooner or later, will not be our accomplishments or possessions. It will be our relationships with the people who have been a part of our lives.

So, with those two thoughts in mind, on behalf of the faculty, staff, and administration of Hartsville High School, and all those who love you, we wish you Godspeed on your journey of life. We wish for you yesterdays - no matter how far away they are - that will be good memories. We hope that you will have futures filled with accomplishment, fulfillment, and happiness. And we pray that you will be blessed with some very special people in your life with whom to share your journey.

Tradition and Giving to the Future

You might know that commencement speeches were born in the idea that graduates are not fit to be released into the world until they are properly sedated. Putting you to sleep is not really what I have in mind tonight; my intent is to take less time than you might ever dream. So, for one last time, bear with me for a few minutes, and - take time to think about it.

A traditional graduation ceremony is an interesting mix of past, present, and future. It's an occasion when we reflect on the past and realize how far we've come in the last twelve years. Can you remember who your teacher was in the first grade? Graduation is also when, in the presence of celebration, we suddenly realize that this might be the last chance for us to be with some of our best friends, maybe forever. I've recently used Facebook to connect with some of my high school classmates whom I haven't seen in more than forty years. Finally, graduation is a rite of passage when we look at our futures with both positive anticipation and nervous anxiety. Do you know what you'll be doing and where you'll be three months from now instead of just reporting to Hartsville High School as you've done for the last four years? In thinking about this coming together of different aspects of time, here - from an unknown source - is one of our quotes for the day: "Tradition is not so much holding onto the past as it is giving to the future."

Tradition is important in all societies, to institutions, and to families. Tradition is based on how things have been done in the past and gives us a foundation on which to stand. We have traditional holidays - Christmas and Easter and Thanksgiving. There are traditions in the athletic world - singing *Take Me Out to the Ballgame* during the seventh inning stretch at Wrigley Field, rubbing Howard's Rock before running down the hill at Clemson's Death Valley, and The Masters golf tournament. We have the traditional hymns that we sing in church - *The Old Rugged Cross*, *Amazing Grace*, and *How Great Thou Art*. There is the traditional family structure, there are traditional values, and we're all now familiar with what educators call the traditional seven-period school day. In recent years, there are traditions that have faded away in politics, the military, business, industry, and even religion. We appreciate tradition, though, because it values our history, as well as giving us a sense of comfort and security. Sometimes we become uneasy or even angry when tradition is threatened.

The difficulty with tradition is that it is often in direct opposition with one of life's absolutes, which is change. Few things stay the same, and that brings us to two other quotes, the first from Denise McCluggage and the second from Esther Dyson. Ms. McCluggage said: "Change is the only constant. Hanging on is the only sin." Ms. Dyson said: "Change means that what was before wasn't perfect. People want things to be better."

So, change is just as interesting a concept as tradition. There are times when we want change so badly that we can hardly stand it until it happens. The stoplight stays red forever, money burns holes in our pockets, and we can't wait for graduation. At other times, we may be so afraid of change that it almost paralyzes us, especially when the change involves close personal relationships, even on such a joyous occasion as a wedding day. In whatever manner we view change, there is one absolute truth: it is going to happen. Circumstances change. People change. Stuff happens.

What is important then, as with all things in life, is how we respond to it. We can try to escape change, which is usually futile and is described - maybe a little too harshly by Ms. McCluggage - as a sin. Or, on the other hand - as Ms. Dyson proposed - we can embrace change as an attempt to make something better, an effort to improve the way we do things. In recent years, I think technology is the best example of this. In terms of accepting those changes - particularly in the area of communication - some of us older folks are unrepentant sinners and will remain that way the rest of our lives. Others of us, especially the younger generation, have dived into the baptismal pool of technology headfirst. In whatever manner we do it, we do it that way because we're comfortable with it. The big question, which I'll leave for you to answer yourselves, is this: Is comfortable better?

In whatever manner we choose to answer that question, our task is creating a compatible relationship between tradition, which tries to remain constant, and change, which is constant in a very different way. In thinking about this, a good analogy to use is that of a ship's anchor. An anchor can hold a ship in a safe position during a storm, just as traditional values, especially those of a spiritual nature, can keep us steady in times of trouble in our lives. But for a ship to travel from port to port and fulfill the purpose for which it was created and given life, its anchor has to be pulled up from the bottom of the ocean. The ship carries the anchor, using it properly and at the appropriate times, and the same is true of tradition. As our quote said, tradition is not about holding us to the past, and keeping us in one place forever. It is about giving to the future while keeping us steady from time to time as we navigate our way through life. It seems to me that the key to having tradition be a positive influence in our changing culture, as with many other things, is having it placed in the proper time and context, and used for the benefit of society. That, graduates - and this is my challenge to you this evening - is what educated people do.

Finally, with that challenge, here we are at the point of all this. Each of you has earned a traditional South Carolina High School Diploma. The one you'll be getting shortly is pretty much like the one I got in 1969, and closely resembles the diploma that many of your parents and brothers and sisters have received. The challenge, as I said a minute ago, lies in what you're going to do with it. You've been preparing for the future by learning every day for the last four years. How will you use your education to impact your future? Will you stow it away in the trunk of tradition and never use it again as the storms of life toss you about and finally crash you against the rocks? Will you throw it overboard and never pull it up again, while you sit anchored in port all your life and never see the world? Or will you use it wisely as you go through life, balancing the reasonable weight of tradition with the constant winds of change?

With those thoughts in mind, on behalf of the faculty, staff, and administration of Hartsville High School, and all those who love you, we wish you Godspeed on your life's voyage. My hope for you is that you'll see the world - and that you won't ever become too comfortable.

Time Is a Tree with Many Branches

My thoughts for the Class of 2012 come from a recent book by Stephen King entitled *11/22/63*. It is a book about time travel, and the main character - a high school teacher named Jake - has the opportunity to go back in time and change history. Jake's quest in *11/22/63* is to go back in time almost fifty years and prevent Lee Harvey Oswald's assassination of President John F. Kennedy that occurred on November 22, 1963, in Dallas, Texas. He believes that by saving Kennedy's life and thereby altering the course of our country's foreign policy, he will - among other things - prevent the loss of thousands of American lives and other casualties that resulted from the involvement of the United States in the Vietnam Conflict. In a thrilling race to the Texas School Book Depository building on November 22, 1963, Jake arrives in the nick of time to keep Oswald from firing the rifle shots that killed President Kennedy. The problem with his heroic act, as he discovers in his further time travels, is that when Kennedy fulfills the remaining years of his Presidency, he puts our country on course for an apocalyptic nuclear war, as well as the failure of the Civil Rights Movement. In short, by saving Kennedy's life, Jake alters the course of history in ways that are infinitely worse for our country and the world than what actually did happen as a result of Kennedy's death. To make things even more interesting for Jake when he travels back to 1963, he falls deeply in love with Sadie, who is the librarian at the high school where Jake gets a job teaching English. The point of my remarks tonight, and what I believe is Stephen King's central idea in *11/22/63*, is expressed in this quote from page 648: "Time is a tree with many branches."

As each of you commence your life's journey after Hartsville High School, you'll be blessed with opportunities, faced with challenges, and given choices to make. If you haven't already, you'll make a decision about furthering your education. You will decide on an occupation and figure out where to live. You may choose a spouse and decide to have children of your own. You'll decide on how to express and practice your religious faith. You'll make many other choices that will affect the directions in which your lives will go.

As the years go by, you'll go further and further up your tree of time, choosing which branches to try, each of them leading to another, and another, and another. And, the interesting idea is, each branch that you choose leads to an entirely different set of branches than another one. One decision that you make can take you, over the course of a lifetime, on an entirely different path to an entirely different future. For example, in 1976, I accepted a job as the head basketball coach at Gilbert High School in Lexington County. A few days after I accepted that job, I was offered a job as an assistant coach at South Florence High School. The decision was a no-brainer because I wanted to be a head coach, right? Well, the catch was that my wife and I had just bought a house in Florence, and taking the job at South Florence would mean that we wouldn't have to sell the house and move. I chose to honor the contract that I'd signed at Gilbert, and I taught and coached there for two years before coming back to my alma mater, Hartsville High School, as the head basketball coach in 1978. I've wondered occasionally over the years what would have happened if I'd gone to South Florence instead of Gilbert. Would I have ever come back to Hartsville, or would I have been a Bruin instead of a Red Fox for the last thirty-four years? Who knows? Time is a tree with many branches.

So, the big question that I hope you're thinking about right now, and the one that we all face throughout our lives, is "How do I make the right choices?" You might choose branches that will take you to the top of your tree, and from that vantage point you'll be able to see the world. Or, you might stay close to the trunk of your tree, never venturing onto its outer branches to see what wondrous things might be the reward of a little courage or curiosity. There will be a tree that will have a branch with some hidden weakness or crack, without enough strength to hold your weight, and fate will have you choose that branch - or not. Or, if you make really unfortunate choices, your tree might be ravaged by the hurricane forces of alcohol, drugs, or other vices. Who knows? Time is a tree with many branches.

What I've said so far makes life seem like a game of chance, but that's not entirely the case. First, it is important to sustain our tree with the proper nutrients of integrity, understanding and respect for our fellow man, and lifelong learning so that its roots grow deep and strong. It is also important to have some ambition and a plan for reaching our goals so that we recognize the branches that are most likely to take us in the direction that we want to go. Finally, the most important thing we must remember is our faith in a higher being who has a plan for our lives even though that plan sometimes seems to be hidden by the leaves. That faith will allow us to hold on tight when the stormy winds of life are whipping our tree so hard that it seems to be on the verge of being blown over.

My closing thought gets back to 11/22/63 and our friend, Jake. He has the opportunity to go back in time and change history - his history, our country's history, and the history of the world. The question that he wrestles with throughout King's tale is whether or not that is the right thing to do. In the end, Jake

Dr. Charlie Burry, Jr.

finds out that it is best not to disturb what happened nearly fifty years ago even if it means giving up Sadie, the one great love of his altered past. He learns that it is best to live with the past as it was, the present as it has been brought to us, and the future as we can best determine it. He learns that - time is a tree with many branches.

One of the great truths of our existence is that we live life looking forward, and we understand it looking backward. A simpler way to put it is "Hindsight is 20-20." Are there things in our lives that we'd like to go back and change? Most of us would say, "Yes." But, if we could do that, are we sure that everything else that would play out differently since that change of course would be for the better? After reading *11/22/63*, my opinion is that it's best that we don't have the opportunity, and the torment, that Jake did. It is best that we can't go back down the tree of time as we could when we were climbing real trees in the backyards of our childhoods. We make the best choices in life that we can, we live with those decisions, we don't dwell on regrets, and we move on. We need to learn from experience, but the most important thing is that we look forward, unburdened by the past, and see how we want our lives to be in the future with the clear eyes of hope, faith, and optimism. Because, time is a tree with many branches.

Graduates, you cannot change your past, and you must not resign yourselves to, or be content with, anything based on what is behind you. What you must believe is that you do have the opportunity, the responsibility, and the power - from this moment on - to shape your future. Tonight, each of you has good reason to be excited and optimistic about that. Your high school graduation is a worthy accomplishment, a strong branch that can lead to many others. With that thought in mind, on behalf of the faculty, staff, and administration of Hartsville High School, and all those who love you, we wish you Godspeed as

you look upward at your tree of time. My hope for each of you
is that you'll climb high.

It Is When It Is Supposed to Be

My thoughts for the Class of 2013 come from a book by Mitch Albom called *The Timekeeper*. You may not have heard of this title, but perhaps you've heard of other books by Mr. Albom, such as *Tuesdays with Morrie*, *The Five People You Meet in Heaven*, or *Have a Little Faith*. If one of the purposes of good writing is to cause the reader to think deeply about a topic, then - at least in my opinion - Mitch Albom is one of the best at doing that, and certainly he is one of my favorite authors. So, as you are eagerly anticipating the conclusion of my remarks tonight, keep this quote from *The Timekeeper* in mind: "It is never too late or too soon. It is when it is supposed to be." If you understand what that means by the time I walk away from the podium this evening, you'll have gotten my point, and maybe you'll have learned something that will help you along a bit in the future, too.

In *The Timekeeper*, Albom's fable takes us back in history to a time when, well, there was no such thing as time - to the first man on Earth to count the hours, to a man named Dor - who became Father Time. The discovery of time turns out to be a curse for Dor, and he must serve his penance by listening for centuries to the pleas of all those who come after him seeking nothing but more hours, more days, more time. In the last year, how many of us have wished for more time, for ourselves, for a classmate or a teammate, for a loved one? Eventually, Father Time is granted a chance to redeem himself by teaching two earthly people the true meaning of time. In the fable, Dor returns to the present world, now dominated by the hour-counting that he so innocently began. His redemption involves two very different people: one a heart-broken teenage girl who thinks she wants her life to end and the other a wealthy old businessman who believes that he wants to live forever. Father Time, in order to redeem himself, must save them both from their tragic obsession with time. Dor must convince Sarah Lemon not to take her life and help Victor Delamonte let his go. They must reach the understanding that "it is never too late or too soon. It is when it is supposed to be."

I thought long and hard about what to say tonight. We certainly want this to be a joyous occasion, and I do not want my remarks to cast a somber tone. But the truth of the matter is that for all of us, the memories of the three students that we've lost in the last year - especially Ronald - are close at hand. Two of the funerals were in this very arena. For the Hartsville High School Class of 2013, like it or not, that is part of your legacy. So, I didn't have a choice as to what I would talk about tonight. It wouldn't have been right - for Jy'Meke, or for Bayy, or especially for Ronald - to do it any other way. I ask you again, in this last year, how many of us have wished for more time - for ourselves, for a classmate or a teammate, for a loved one? How many of us, like Dor, have numbered our days?

What I learned from *The Timekeeper*, and the point that I want to make to you tonight, is that too much focus on time - time spent, time gained or lost, and time left - robs us of the joy in our lives. Part of Father Time's curse was that man will count all his days, and then the smaller segments of the day, and then smaller still - until the counting consumes him, and the wonder of the world he has been given is lost. Had Dor been wiser, he might have marveled at the beauty of the sunrise and given thanks for being able to witness it. But he was not focusing on the miracle of the day, only on measuring its length. Dor had to learn; and in order to redeem himself in Albom's fable, he had to teach Sarah and Victor that "it is never too late or too soon. It is when it is supposed to be."

Before anyone jumps to any rash conclusions about what I'm saying, let me issue a disclaimer by pointing out that time does have its place in our world, and we have to pay attention to that. Businesses and airports still run on time. Television shows still have time slots, even though the commercials seem to last forever. We're still going to put eight minutes on the scoreboard for each quarter of a basketball game, and the school day is still going to be from 8:00 until 3:11 next year. Punctuality is still a virtue. So, I'm a step ahead of our underclassmen who already are plotting tonight when I tell you that as you're walking in from the parking lot next year after the tardy tone sounds, if you tell me that "it is never too late or too soon," that is not going to help you escape Sunset School.

What Albom does suggest for our consideration is this: Try to imagine a life without time. We probably can't. We all know that it is Wednesday, June 5, 2013, and it's a little after seven o'clock. We've all got something to do later tonight or tomorrow. Yet all around us, timekeeping is ignored. Birds and animals aren't ever late. A dog doesn't worry about how old he is. Albom reminds us that "Man alone measures time. Man alone chimes the hour. And, because of this, man alone suffers a paralyzing fear that no other creature endures. A fear of time running out."

A lot of the stress and anguish in our lives is the fault of our human perception of time. During the last year, we have searched our hearts and our minds for answers about loved ones gone too soon. We have questioned why the lives of those so young, with so much time seemingly ahead of them, ended so suddenly. We want to know why time ran out on Jy'Meke, and Bayy, and Ronald. There are no answers to those questions, any more than we can reach out and grab time and hold it still.

What we have to put our faith in is the admonishment that Dor received at the beginning of his journey toward redemption, that "the length of your days does not belong to you. You will learn that as well." In other words, rather than leaning on our own knowledge and understanding, and tormenting ourselves with questions and doubts, we must accept the fact that "a clock ticks for all of us, silently, somewhere." We simply must have faith that "it is never too late or too soon. It is when it is supposed to be."

I am always concerned with my commencement remarks - and particularly so tonight - that someone will be only half-listening or will take something out of context, and misunderstand what I'm really trying to get across to our graduates. Tonight of all nights - a time filled with happiness and hope for the future - the last thing I want to convey is a simple sense of resignation that things are just going to happen to us in our lives, and there's nothing we can do about it. All of our graduates celebrate a significant achievement tonight, and have every reason to be optimistic about the next step in their lives, whether it's going to be college, the military, or the world of work. Each of you should plan, set goals, have faith, and continue to work toward accomplishing what you want from life. What I want you to have as the foundation of your ambition, though, is a sense of comfort with the true meaning of time as Dor, and Sarah, and Victor finally understood it. I want you to believe that there is a plan for your life - not of anyone's earthly making - and that in time you'll discover that plan, not all at once, but bit by bit. I want you to have faith that whatever happens in your lifetime - personally, professionally, or spiritually - "It will never be too late or too soon. It will be when it is supposed to be."

With that thought in mind, on behalf of the faculty, staff, and administration of Hartsville High School, and all those who love you, we wish you Godspeed. It is my hope that wherever your journey leads, that you'll occasionally be at a point in your life where you'll marvel at the beauty of the sunrise and give thanks for being able to witness it, where you'll focus on the miracle of the day . . . because time never crosses your mind.

78

A Tale of Misplaced Love and Irony

Tonight, I'm going to tell you a story. The story is not mine: I got it from an Indian writer and film-maker named Pavithra Mehta. From her home in the San Francisco Bay area, she contributes to a website called *DailyGood*, which is devoted to sharing inspiring and positive news from around the world. I have changed the story some so that it better relates to our graduates, but much of it is closely paraphrased from Ms. Mehta's original article. The story, from the July 12, 2013, edition of *DailyGood*, is called *A Tale of Misplaced Love and Irony*. Here it is. Listen closely to see if you recognize anyone.

When the world began, there was a place for everything in the human heart, and everything was in its place. Everything in people's hearts was orderly and organized, and this meant that one never, ever had to look for anything. Which sounds awfully convenient, and that is exactly what it was. Awfully . . . convenient. In fact, far too convenient. In this precise order of things, everything happened on a schedule. Opportunity, for instance, got the 2:00 o'clock slot on Tuesday afternoons, which meant of course, that people always snoozed through it. Everything under the sun was totally reliable and terribly boring.

People soon began to think of little games for themselves to make life more interesting. As a result of this, they sent love deep into the forest, and they hid happiness in a mountain cave. They left contentment stranded on a desert island, and they buried fulfillment in the backyard. People also made up of elaborate costumes and disguises for themselves so that no one was quite sure of who they really were anymore.

All of this activity caused lots of authors to begin writing books about how to discover oneself. These self-help writers also invented a series of ten-step shortcuts to true love, purpose in life, becoming an enlightened person, and so on and so forth. A few of the authors actually knew what they were talking about, but most of them just made it up as they went along. This resulted, as you might expect, in countless misunderstandings, lots of wild goose chases, widespread confusion, and considerable disillusionment.

Meanwhile, love got lonely in the forest, and happiness got cold in the mountain cave. Contentment was starving on the desert island, and fulfillment was afraid of the dark underground. So, they all sneaked back home one day, without anyone noticing. They used their spare keys to let themselves back into the chambers of the human heart and moved back into their old homes with sweet sighs of relief. Their return, however, continued to go completely unnoticed by all of the world's people. All people, by this time, were totally consumed with their own selfish desires. They were off four-wheeling through the forests, snow skiing in the mountains, cruising across the oceans, and barbequing in their backyards. It was at this point that irony - that strange twist of circumstances - entered the world.

Here's what happened. Very soon technology began to serve as a substitute for all that people were having trouble finding. When truth could not be located, humanity made itself feel better with wonderful inventions like the GPS. Instead of finding honesty, one could always pull up directions to the nearest shopping mall. Text messages and tweets began to substitute for real conversation and understanding. Who had time anyway for more than byte-sized helpings of relationships and real feelings? People who were searching for answers to

Life's Big Questions just started using Google, which usually had a much faster response rate than the power of prayer.

And so the years rolled on, like wave upon wave. People's lives got bigger, brighter, faster, and louder. A seemingly infinite number of ice cream flavors appeared at Ben & Jerry's. Yet underneath the fast pace and the glittering exterior and the availability of all that ice cream, ironically, people were more exhausted, frightened, and lonely than they had ever been since the dawn of history.

Every once in a while, though, a few people would grow so sick and tired of their fake and shallow lives that they resorted to drastic measures. They shut off their cell phones, turned away from their computer screens, and took out their earbuds. They stopped texting and tweeting and shopping and seeking. And, they settled back comfortably and sweetly into the skin of their skins, the heart of their hearts, and the soul of their souls. At which point love would rush over to greet them with a hug, happiness would put on the kettle for a cup of tea, contentment would tend to the fireplace, and fulfillment would begin to sing a familiar song.

So, that's what happened in *The Tale of Misplaced Love and Irony*. Did you recognize anyone? How and why did most of those people end up being exhausted, frightened, and so very lonely? As the convenient distractions of our modern world become more and more appealing, people get busier with what they think are higher priorities, and what is really most important in life just fades into the background. That is what happened to most of the people in Ms. Mehta's story. It happens to us, too - slowly and quietly over time - so that we don't even realize it.

But remember that a few people in the story lived happily ever after. You see, they noticed that love was missing from their important relationships. They figured out that happiness had slipped away from their true and lasting friendships. They recognized that they no longer felt any satisfaction or real contentment from their accomplishments. And they realized that they had fooled themselves into thinking they had lives that were truly fulfilling. Those few people woke up, and it dawned on them that they had misplaced what was really important in life. Love. Happiness. Contentment. Fulfillment. And they understood again how all of those things belong in the truly meaningful relationships and worthwhile activities that we have in life, instead of being hidden away in a forest or a mountain cave, buried in the backyard, or stranded on a desert island that was once our consciousness.

Finally, here are the questions, and the challenges, that I want to leave with the Class of 2014 tonight. Will you live a life so filled with material distractions and false priorities that you, too, become exhausted, frightened, and lonely? Or, will you love life and people every day so that when you open your memory book of family and friends at the end of your time on earth, every page will be filled? Will you come to understand true and genuine happiness so that when you're old like me, you can honestly say that you've enjoyed your life? Will you slow down enough so that contentment has a chance to catch up with you at the end of the day and put its feet up on the front porch rail to relax? Will you find a career that holds the true reward of doing something that contributes positively to society and our world and fulfills your own wonderful potential? Will you value and work enough at relationships with your friends and loved ones so that those blessed ties that bind will stay fresh and alive through the test of time? I challenge you to do these things: Be vigilant against the numbness and shallowness that technology fosters. Refuse to allow the fast pace of today's world - hidden by the distractions of instant gratification, selfish materialism, and social media - to rob your relationships of the love, happiness, contentment, and fulfillment that make them truly meaningful and lasting. Remember that those are the things that are most important in life.

With those challenges in mind, on behalf of the faculty, staff, and administration of Hartsville High School, and all those who love you, we wish you Godspeed. Our hope for each of our graduates is that at some point in your own Tale of Love and Irony, love will greet you with a hug, happiness will put the kettle on for a cup of tea, contentment will tend to the fireplace, that you'll hear the familiar song of fulfillment, and that you, too, will live happily ever after.

Dr. Charlie Burry, Jr.

79

Loving Hands

Most of you know that it has been my practice to ask the senior class to endure one last Thought for the Day during the principal's remarks at their graduation ceremony. Many of you are probably thinking right now the same thing that the church congregation thought when the preacher stepped to the pulpit and said, "I've got so much to say that I don't know where to start," and a voice from the back of the church responded, "Somewhere near the end would be good." Well, I won't start somewhere near the end, but I will try to be brief and to-the-point with my message to you.

Tonight, as I did at last year's graduation, I'm going to tell you a story. The story is not mine; I got it from a Facebook post by a friend of a friend. My research revealed that its author is Angel Chang on a website called *LittleThings.com*. I have changed the story just a bit to suit my writing style, but most of it is closely paraphrased from the original post. So, give it a listen and maybe you'll see a little of your past - and your future - somewhere in it. The story goes like this.

A young man who had just graduated from college was applying for an important position with a large company. He did well in the first interview and had been called back to meet the company president for the final interview that would determine whether or not he got the job. The company president looked at the young man's resume' for a few minutes and was pleased with what he saw. Then he asked him, "Did you receive a scholarship to help you pay for college?" The young man replied, "No." The older man continued, "So, it was your parents who paid for your studies?" "Yes," the young man replied. "Where do your parents work?" the company president asked. The young man answered, "My father has his own shop, and he's a carpenter. My mother is a housewife, and she keeps a big garden for our family." The older man then asked the young man to show him his hands. The young man's hands were soft and perfect. The company president asked, "Have you ever helped your father in his shop or worked with your mother in her garden?" The young man replied, "No, sir - never - my parents always wanted me to study so that I could go to college." The company president said, "I have a request. When you go home today, ask your parents to let you wash their hands for them. Then come back to see me tomorrow morning." The young man left feeling that his chances of getting the job were good, but he was puzzled about the company president's request.

When the young man returned home, he first asked his mother if she would allow him to wash her hands. His mother thought it was a strange request, but she agreed, so with mixed feelings she showed her hands to her son. The young man slowly washed his mother's hands. It was the first time he noticed that they were rough and hard, that they had so many scars, and that her fingernails were torn and ragged. Then he went to his father and asked if he would allow him to wash his hands. That's when he saw that his father's hands were much rougher, with big callouses, and even more wounded than his mother's hands.

After washing his father's hands, the young man went to his room in silence and in deep thought. He thought about why his parents' hands were so rough and hard and what had made them that way. It was the first time that the son had ever realized what it had meant for his parents to work hard every day to pay for his education, his school activities, and his future.

Dr. Charlie Burry, Jr.

Later that night, the young man and his parents talked for a long, long time.

The next morning the young man went back to the office of the company president. The older man noticed tears in the young man's eyes when he asked him what he had learned when he went home the night before. The young man replied, "I learned that without my parents, I would not be where I am today. I learned of the hard work and the sacrifices that my parents made for me and that a person does not get anywhere in life without the help of others. I gained a greater appreciation for family and teachers and others who have helped me throughout my life." Then the company president said, "That is what I look for in my employees. I want to hire people who appreciate the help of others, people who are grateful for the hardships of others on their behalf, and people who are willing to help others in return. The job is yours."

As you're maybe taking a look at your own hands right now, we should keep in mind that in today's world of work, this story is not a perfect analogy. In our present economy, there are many jobs that require long, hard hours in difficult working conditions that might not involve real physical labor. Instead of rough and wounded hands, the labor might manifest itself in mental fatigue or emotional stress. That kind of work, so demanding over a period of many years, also takes a harsh physical toll on a person in ways not as easy to see as a pair of calloused hands.

Keeping that in mind, let's think for a minute about the people who have had a hand in bringing us to where we are tonight. None of us got where we are by ourselves. We had biological parents who gave us the genes and the characteristics that made each one of us a uniquely talented person in an interestingly diverse population. We are products of our experiences with those who cared for us throughout our childhood years. We have been influenced by those in our extended families, church groups, educational experiences and extra-curricular activities, and maybe even the world of work. We have had people in our lives who set examples for us and inspired us. There are those in our lives who disciplined us to be who we should be and challenged us to be better than we thought we could be.

How have your parents' hands or the hands of others - literally or figuratively - helped you to be the person you are now, and the person that you will be in the future? In addition to working for your well-being, did they also work on your character? Did they insist that your behavior meet their expectations with your personal and social life, and have there been consequences when you failed to do that? If you got in trouble at school, did they encourage you to accept the responsibility and learn from it? Did they ever take away any of your privileges or restrict what you were allowed to do? Did your parents teach you the value of money by setting limits on your spending and telling you to get a part time job if you wanted more? Did they insist that you show them proper respect, and by doing that did they also teach you to respect your teachers and other adults? Did they encourage you come to school on time, have good attendance, and do the best that you could in your schoolwork? Here at school, did your teachers have high expectations of you in the classroom? Did they require a strong work ethic and encourage you to read and write and think when you really didn't want to? Did your coaches and instructors push you to be more successful than you thought you could be? Looking forward, the most important question is this: What kind of person, citizen, spouse, parent, employee and life-long learner will those hands have helped you to become? And finally, when I asked a minute ago if those who helped you worked for your well-being as well as on your character, are those two things really any different?

Tonight, when you meet your parents and other family members after the ceremony, take a look at their hands. They may or may not be visibly wounded or rough to the touch, but I hope they will always remind you - as the young man seeking the job in tonight's story learned - to appreciate the help of others, to be grateful for the hardships endured on your behalf, and to be willing to help others in return. If you live your life based on those ideals, you will help make our world a better place, which is what a truly educated person should do. Now, as you commence on the next leg of your life's journey, remember whose rough - and loving - hands helped to set you on your way. Tonight, those hands applaud you, wish you Godspeed, and they are folded in silent prayer that a greater being will continue to hold you in the palm of His hand.

80

If I Could Have Just Seen the Shore

Tonight, as I've done at the last couple of graduations, I'm going to tell you a story. This one is about swimming, so I hope your attention span will be able to stay afloat during the next few minutes. This true story is about a young woman named Florence Chadwick, who was a long-distance swimmer.

One morning in 1952, she stepped into the waters of the Pacific Ocean off Catalina Island, determined to swim to the shore of mainland California, a distance of about twenty-six miles. That's about the same distance as it is from here to downtown Florence, and the distance of a marathon. Can you imagine swimming that far? In the ocean? Ms. Chadwick had already been the first woman to swim the English Channel both ways, so she was an experienced swimmer. The weather that day was foggy and cold; she could hardly see the safety boats that were accompanying her: the men in some of them were occasionally shooting at sharks to keep them from attack-ing her. Still, she swam - for fifteen hours. When she began to struggle and begged to be taken out of the water so she could quit, her mother, in a boat alongside her, told her that she was close and that she could make it. Finally, though - physically and emotionally exhausted and despite her mother's encour-agement - Florence stopped swimming and had to be pulled out of the water. It wasn't until she was on the boat and her mind began to clear that she realized she'd swum twenty-five and a half miles, and the shore was less than half a mile away. At a news conference the next day Florence Chadwick said,

Dr. Charlie Burry, Jr.

"All I could see was the fog. I think if I could have just seen the shore, I would have made it."

The lesson that we can learn from the Florence Chadwick story is two-fold. First, we need to have shorelines - or goals - in our lives. There has to be a goal in place in order for us to make progress towards it. We have to know where we want to go so we can plan how to get there. All of you have fulfilled your goal of meeting graduation requirements, and you reach the shore tonight when you walk across this stage and receive your high school diploma. That goal was always there even when you thought the water was too rough in math class or when you felt like the Periodic Table was pulling you under or when it seemed that your senior year was an ocean away. Some of you know where you're going to be and what you're going to be doing this fall because you've set an additional goal. You're going to reach that goal in August or September because you identified it some time ago and purposefully worked toward it, and soon you will be within sight of that shoreline. If you're in the productive habit of setting goals for yourself, that's going to lead you to even more achievements and success in life. On the other hand, if you haven't set any goals for yourself, you need to get busy doing that and stop just drifting around anywhere the current happens to take you.

The second thing that we can learn from Florence Chadwick is a lesson about faith. All of us have the fog roll into our lives from time to time. That fog might come in the form of an illness or an accident, a financial misfortune, a mistake that we've made, a broken relationship, the death of a loved one, or sometimes the darkness of depression may creep into our minds. Those kinds of things can cloud our vision of the future and cause us to feel lost and hopeless. But the Bible tells us two things. One, to lean not on our own understanding; and two, that faith is the belief in that which we cannot see. If we've set a goal and believe that we can accomplish it, self-doubt won't pull us under the water when we can't understand the hard, seemingly unfair circumstances that sometimes wash over us. If we have faith that the goal is there, we don't have to be able to see it all the time in order to believe in it and keep working toward it when misfortune clouds our vision. Florence Chadwick didn't run out of strength or stamina; she ran out of faith. She admitted that when she said the next day, "I think if I could have just seen the shore, I'd have made it." That was proven in a nice sequel to the Florence Chadwick story about two months later. She returned to Catalina Island for another attempt and, her faith restored, swam the entire twenty-six-mile distance to the California shore. She said that one thing that helped her make it on the second attempt was that she pictured the shoreline in her mind the whole time she was swimming. She had a vision of her goal, and it gave her the belief that she needed to accomplish it.

So, to the Class of 2016 - from the faculty and staff of Hartsville High School and all those who love you - we wish you Godspeed and bright blue skies on your life's journey. But, on the days when it's dark and rainy, and when all you can see is the fog, have faith that the goals you've envisioned are still there and that you can make it to the shore. Remember Florence Chadwick. Don't look back with regret on anything in your life and say, "If I could have just seen the shore . . . ." It's there. Have faith. Believe in it. Persist. Give yourself a chance. The shore - and the fulfillment of your vision - might be closer than you think.

81

The Crossroads of Should and Must

Tonight, during my commencement remarks we'll be taking a trip and passing through some busy intersections. I want you to keep up with me, so I hope that your attention span has a full tank of gas. I found the thought for our Class of 2017 on a website called *DailyGood.com*, which is devoted to sharing inspiring and positive news from around the world. It was on the October 6, 2016, edition of that website that I read an essay entitled *The Crossroads of Should and Must* by a designer, painter and writer named Elle Luna. Ms. Luna cites this quote from Mark Twain as one of the central themes in her essay: "The two most important days in our lives are the day we are born, and the day we find out why."

There are many important days in a person's life. Today is certainly one for our graduates and their families. Other things like your first date, getting your driver's license, and your first day of work at a new job are pretty important in a teenager's life, too. There will be other firsts that will come later in your lives - your first day of college or being sworn into the military, your wedding day and the birth of your own first child. But the day we find out why we were born is what I'm going to talk about tonight. Hartsville High School's mission of "Preparing for the Future by Learning Everyday" is primarily focused on getting an outstanding education. Many of you have done that. Next, you can use that education as a means to achieve the kind of job and career that you'd like to have. But, much more important - and sometimes much different - than our job and our career is our calling, and our true calling is why we were born. Our calling is what Mark Twain was talking about when he said, "The two most important days in our lives are the day we are born, and the day we find out why."

With that thought in mind, we have arrived at what Ms. Luna refers to as The Crossroads of Should and Must. She says that choice - between an average life and an extraordinary life - is ours, every day. And, if you'll allow me this one piece of advice tonight, I believe that in order to be truly fulfilled and happy - and I'm talking about more than money and material things - a person has to find a passion in life. Your passion is not what you happen to end up doing just by chance, unless you're exceptionally lucky. It's not something you settle on doing just because that's the best option you happen to have, unless you're really easy to please. It's not even what you should do, unless you're content to do what other people expect you to do. Your passion is what you must do. Your passion is what you were born to do. It's the choice that your complete fulfillment and true happiness depend on when you get to The Crossroads of Should and Must.

By this point, if you've been paying attention, you're asking me, "So, when I get to this crossroads, how do I know which way to go?" According to Ms. Luna, this is what you consider. Listen closely.

Must is who we are, what we believe, and what we do when we are alone with our truest, most authentic self. It's our instincts, our cravings and longings, the things and places and ideas we burn for, the intuition that swells up from somewhere deep inside of us. Must is what happens when we stop conforming to other people's ideals and start connecting to our own. Because when we choose Must, we are no longer looking for inspiration or approval from other people. Instead, we are listening to our own calling from within, from some luminous, mysterious place. Must is why Van Gogh painted his entire life without ever receiving public recognition. Must is why Mozart performed *Don Giovani* and Coltrane played his new sound, even as the critics called it ugly. Must is why a Mississippi lawyer in his thirties spent three years writing his first novel only to be rejected by three dozen publishers. But he stayed true to his calling, eventually received a 'yes,' and that is why John Grisham is a household name today and the author of thirty best-selling novels.

A little closer to home, choosing Must is what led Shannon Johnson, a 1992 graduate of Hartsville High School and currently the head women's basketball coach at Coker College, to an Olympic gold medal. Choosing Must is what Dr. Robert Gilliard, a 2005 graduate of Hartsville High School, did to begin his journey toward becoming a world-renowned chemist. Those two members of our Red Fox Family chose Must, and they followed their passion.

It is however, important to understand that choosing Must doesn't have to come at the expense of everything else in your life. As Ms. Luna said, we make these choices every day of our lives. We come to The Crossroads of Should and Must over and over again. There are times when we'll make the safe, practical choice of Should in order to maintain relationships, preserve our health, or stay out of trouble. Those things can be pretty important to a person's happiness, too. The problem we face is being able to tell the difference between Should and Must and knowing when that choice really makes a crucial difference in the direction of our lives. To that end, Ms. Luna gives us this additional advice:

If you want to know Must, get to know Should. This is hard work. We unconsciously and comfortably imprison ourselves to avoid chancing our most basic fears of loss. We choose Should because choosing Must is terrifying and incomprehensible, and choosing Should is safe. The walls of our prisons are constructed from a lifetime of Shoulds, the bricks of choices we've unwittingly agreed to, the walls that separate us from our truest, most authentic selves. How often do we place blame on the other person, job, or situation when the real problem, the real pain, is within us? And we leave and walk away, angry, frustrated, and sad, unconsciously carrying the same load of Shoulds into the next relationship, the next job, the next friendship - hoping for different results. Should is the doorkeeper to Must. Once you recognize that, just as you created your prison, you can open that door and set yourself free.

Shannon Johnson and Robert Gilliard stepped through that door into a wide world of opportunity and have experienced amazing things in their lives. That door is somewhere on your life's journey for each of you, too. And, I hope that you will soon come to that second most important day in your life, the day when - as Mark Twain said - you discover why you were born. On that day, when you arrive at The Crossroads of Should and Must, my prayer for you is that you'll have the awareness, the self-knowledge, and - most importantly - the courage to open the door to your real passion, your true calling in life, whatever that might be. The faculty and staff of Hartsville High School and all those who love you wish you Godspeed, and we hope you'll choose Must.

82

One Last Story

Each morning during this school year we have had a Project Wisdom Thought for the Day that we included with the Pledge of Allegiance and our Red Fox Pledge of Honor. It also has been my practice to ask the senior class to consider one last thought for the day during the principal's remarks at their graduation ceremony. Tonight, I'll be telling you a story by Barbara Diamond from *LittleThings.com* about a grandmother's wisdom.

The story begins with a young woman whose once wonderfully promising life had become extremely difficult. She and her husband had separated, and in addition to the heartbreak of a failed marriage, the emotional stress of the separation had begun to cause health problems for her, as well as financial hardship. The young woman had always had the good fortune of a close relationship with her grandmother, though, so she went to her looking for sympathy and advice. She told her grandmother about her seemingly ruined life, how things had become so hard for her, and that she just didn't know what to do or where to turn. She told her grandmother that she did not know how she was going to make it, and that she just wanted to give up. She was tired of fighting and struggling. Her life was a mess, and it seemed as soon as one problem was solved, a new one arose.

Her grandmother said nothing, but took her into the kitchen. She filled three pots with water and placed each one on an eye of the stove with the heat turned on high. Soon the water in each of the pots was boiling. The grandmother then put a couple of carrots in one pot, in the second pot she placed two eggs, and into the third pot she spooned some ground coffee beans. The young woman and her grandmother sat at the kitchen table silently and watched the pots boil.

In about twenty minutes the grandmother turned off the burners. She fished the carrots out and placed them in a bowl. She picked the eggs out and placed them in another bowl. Then she ladled some of what had become a dark brown liquid out of the third pot and poured it into a cup. The older lady turned to her granddaughter and said, "Tell me what you see." The young woman replied, "I see carrots, eggs, and coffee."

The grandmother brought her granddaughter closer and asked her to take one of the carrots out of the bowl. She did and noticed that it had become soft. The grandmother then asked her granddaughter to take one of the eggs out of the bowl and break it. The young woman did that, and when she peeled off the shell, she found a hard-boiled egg. Finally, the grandmother asked her granddaughter to take a sip of the coffee. The granddaughter smiled at its rich aroma and pleasant taste. The young woman then asked, "What are you trying to tell me, grandma?"

The grandmother then explained that each of the three things - the carrots, the eggs, and the ground coffee beans - had faced the same harsh circumstance, the boiling water. Each one reacted differently, though. The carrot went into the boiling water tough, hard, and unrelenting, but after a while it softened and became weak. The water in the pot, after cooling, was still water. The egg originally had been fragile with its thin outer shell protecting its yolk and liquid interior, but after being boiled, it became hard on the inside. The water in that pot, after cooling, was still water. The coffee beans were different, though. While they had been subjected to the same kind of heat, the coffee beans instead had changed the water in the third pot into something with a much more pleasing flavor.

After offering that explanation, the grandmother asked her granddaughter, "Which one are you? When adversity comes into your life, how do you respond? Are you a carrot, an egg or a coffee bean?"

As we finish the story, ask yourself that same question. Which one are you? Are you like the carrot that seemed strong, but then with pain and adversity do you wilt and become soft and lose your strength and resolve? Are you like the egg that had a fluid, adaptable spirit, but then do you change with the heat of a broken relationship, a financial problem, or some other trial, so that your heart becomes hard and unforgiving? Or are you like the coffee beans that actually change the hot water - the very circumstance that brings the pain - into something better? When you find yourself in life's hot water, does that release your full potential to make the circumstances in your life better? How do you meet adversity in your life? Are you a carrot, an egg, or a coffee bean?

The important thing to remember from this story is that - unlike the carrot, the egg, and the coffee bean - we have been given the free will to make choices in our lives. The fate of the carrots, the eggs, and the coffee beans was predetermined because they are what they are, for better or for worse. On the other hand, we determine our own futures by how we choose to respond to the things that happen to us. When we face adverse circumstances, we can choose to see them as either problems or opportunities. When we're faced with challenges in our lives, we can choose to let them whip us down, or we can rise to the occasion, conquer them, and end up on higher ground. Every day, we can choose to become better, or worse, than we were the day before. We can choose how to write our life stories.

I've told you a story tonight about a grandmother's wisdom that I hope will be of some help to you as you meet the challenges in your own lives. You see, all of our lives are like books made up of short stories - some of the chapters are good, and maybe some are not so good. And, it's important to remember that some of the worst chapters can be followed by some of the best. In the end, it's all of those chapters lined up through the years that make up the history book of a person's life.

Grove McCord, one of the characters in Clyde Edgerton's book *In Memory of Junior*, said it this way: "In the end, all you have is your history. And, it better be good, because you're history longer than you're fact." What Grove McCord was saying is that when your life - or maybe your career - ends, your history lives on, and that's what people remember. It's a fact that Abraham Lincoln's life was only fifty-six years, but his history - now going on one hundred and fifty-three years - is that of one of our country's greatest presidents. It's a fact that the life of Dr. Martin Luther King, Jr., was only thirty-nine years, but his history - now fifty years after his death - will always be that of a man who is the face of the American Civil Rights Movement. It's a fact that Amelia Earhart's life was only forty-one years, but her history - now seventy-nine years after she disappeared and was declared dead - is that of the first female aviator to fly solo across the Atlantic Ocean. It's a fact that Aristotle, a Greek philosopher and scientist, lived only sixty-two years, yet he has a history of being one of the greatest intellectual figures of Western culture more than twenty-three hundred years after his death. I think that we can all agree that these people met Grove McCord's standard of a life well-lived and well-remembered.

While the likelihood of our becoming iconic historical figures like Lincoln, King, Earhart, or Aristotle might be slim, we can all choose to create admirable and worthy histories in our own families, occupations, and communities that will be well-remembered. No matter what kind of hot water we find ourselves in, we can choose to have faith in our abilities, choose to persist through the hard times, choose to be kind and compassionate to others, and choose to do what we know to be right. We can choose to be coffee beans.

So, to the Class of 2018 - from the faculty and staff of Hartsville High School and all those who love you - we wish you Godspeed as you write the rest of your life's history. And remember what Grove McCord said - that in the end, we're all just history. I hope you'll make yours a good one.

Charlie Burry

Epilogue

I've always enjoyed writing, and many times when I spoke publicly at a school, church, or community function, I pretty much read from a script of remarks that I'd prepared beforehand. I certainly attempted to achieve an engaging and genuine delivery with my audience, but I liked the security of having my words in front of me instead of just in my head or on note cards. I'm also a wordsmith, and I wanted to be able to communicate my message exactly as I'd written it - word for word - instead of trusting it to my memory or having it compromised by a case of nerves. Writing also helped me to think through a topic more thoroughly and achieve better content. While I was principal, I was always a proponent of having our students read. I also wanted them to write because I knew that made them think even if they didn't want to go to the effort. For those reasons, I believe that attempting a book was sort of a natural evolution for me. It's also been important in my attempt to deal with retirement in a positive manner as I search for new purpose in my life.

Maybe I've discovered a new purpose because I've enjoyed tweaking and pulling the already existing parts of this book together, and I've found myself fully immersed in writing new parts of it during the past eighteen months. I'm hopeful that people will enjoy reading what I've written and that they'll learn from my life lessons. Am I truly a writer, as I claimed to be in the prologue? Maybe it's a possibility.

If you think so, then I'm glad this book found you, and I hope it found you well.

List of References

Chapter 1

Faile, Jim. *Charlie Burry Is at Home in Hartsville*. Florence Morning News, 1998.

Brokaw, Tom. *The Greatest Generation*. Penguin Random House LLC., 1998.

Travis, Merle. *Folk Songs of the Hills*. Capitol Records, 1947.

Chapter 4

John 20:21-22. *Life Application Study Bible*. Tyndale House Publishers, Inc. and Zondervan Publishing House, 1991.

Hatch, Edwin. *Breathe on Me, Breath of God*. Privately published, 1896.

Chapter 8

Schuller, Robert. *Tough Times Never Last, but Tough People Do*. Bantam Press, 1984.

James 1:2-3. *Life Application Study Bible*. Tyndale House Publishers, Inc. and Zondervan Publishing House, 1991.

Chapter 10

Williams, Margery. *The Velveteen Rabbit*. George H. Doran Company, 1922.

Chapter 11

Koch, Howard (Producer), & Saks, Gene (Director). *The Odd Couple* [Motion Picture]. Paramount Pictures, 1968.

Davis, John (Producer), & Petrie, Donald (Director). *Grumpy Old Men* [Motion Picture]. Warner Brothers, 1993.

Mitchell, Fritz (Director). *SEC Storied: Maravich* [Television documentary]. ESPN, March 12, 2018.

Abbey, M. E. *Life's Railway to Heaven*. Public Domain, 1890.

Kadison, Joshua. *Painted Desert Serenade*. Universal Music Group, 1993.

Chapter 13

Lewis Carroll Quotes. BrainyQuote.com, BrainyMedia, Inc, 2019. 9 November 2019. https://www.brainyquote.com/quotes/lewis_carroll_165865.

Zimmerling, Charles. *Pin the Tail on the Donkey*. Public Domain, 1899.

Woody Allen Quotes. BrainyQuote.com, BrainyMedia, Inc, 2019. 9 November 2019. https://www.brainyquote.com/quotes/woody_allen_136686.

Chapter 14

Kenneth Blanchard Quotes. Goodreads.com, GoodReads, Inc, 2019. 9 November 2019. https://www.goodreads.com/quotes/kenneth_blanchard_56863.

Yogi Berra Quotes. BrainyQuote.com, BrainyMedia, Inc, 2019. 9 November 2019. https://www.brainyquote.com/quotes/yogi_berra_125285.

Chapter 15

Weldon, Anthony. *The Court and Character of King James I.* Public Domain, 1651.

Chapter 16

Haft, Steven; Witt, Paul Junger; Thomas Tony (Producers), & Weir, Peter (Director). *Dead Poets Society* [Motion Picture]. Touchstone Pictures, 1989.

Chapter 17

Psalm 139:1-5. *Life Application Study Bible.* Tyndale House Publishers, Inc. and Zondervan Publishing House, 1991.

Grizzard, Lewis. *If Love Were Oil I'd Be a Quart Low.* Grand Central Publishing, 1987.

Mark Twain Quotes. TwainQuotes.com, TwainQuotes, Inc, 2019. 9 November 2019. https://www.twainquotes.com/quotes/mark_twain_morals.

Psalm 32:5. *Life Application Study Bible.* Tyndale House Publishers, Inc. and Zondervan Publishing House, 1991.

Chapter 19

Matthew 7:12. *Life Application Study Bible.* Tyndale House Publishers, Inc. and Zondervan Publishing House, 1991.

Chapter 20

Proverbs 3:5. *Life Application Study Bible.* Tyndale House Publishers, Inc. and Zondervan Publishing House, 1991.

Brokaw, Tom. *The Greatest Generation.* Penguin Random House LLC, 1998.

Brokaw, Tom. *The Greatest Generation Speaks*. Penguin Random House LLC, 1999.

Bush, George. *Congressional Record*. US Government Publishing, 2001.

Matthew 7:12. *Life Application Study Bible*. Tyndale House Publishers, Inc. and Zondervan Publishing House, 1991.

Chapter 21

1 John 4:12. *Life Application Study Bible*. Tyndale House Publishers, Inc. and Zondervan Publishing House, 1991.

Chapter 22

Pride, Charley. *Charley Pride Sings Heart Songs*. RCA Records, 1971.

Carpenter, Mary Chapin. *Come on Come on*. Columbia Records, 1992.

Brooks, Garth. *No Fences*. Capitol Nashville, 1990.

Schuller, Robert. *Tough Times Never Last, but Tough People Do*. Bantam Press, 1984.

Chapter 23

Matthew 8:26. *Life Application Study Bible*. Tyndale House Publishers, Inc. and Zondervan Publishing House, 1991.

Spafford, Horatio. *Gospel Songs No. 2*. Library of Congress, 1896.

Williams, Margery. *The Velveteen Rabbit*. George H. Doran Company, 1922.

Chapter 24

Psalm 23:1-6. *Life Application Study Bible*. Tyndale House Publishers, Inc. and Zondervan Publishing House, 1991.

Chapter 25

Ecclesiastes 2:4-11. *Life Application Study Bible*. Tyndale House Publishers, Inc. and Zondervan Publishing House, 1991.

Travis, Merle. *Folk Songs of the Hills*. Capitol Records, 1947.

Philippians 4:7-9. *Life Application Study Bible*. Tyndale House Publishers, Inc. and Zondervan Publishing House, 1991.

1 Corinthians 15:54-57. *Life Application Study Bible*. Tyndale House Publishers, Inc. and Zondervan Publishing House, 1991.

Chapter 26

Soren Kierkegaard Quotes. BrainyQuote.com. BrainyMedia, Inc, 2019. 9 November 2019. https://www.brainyquote.com/quotes/soren_kierkegaard_105030.

Chapter 27

Vince Lombardi Quotes. BrainyQuote.com, BrainyMedia, Inc, 2019. 9 November 2019. https://www.brainyquote.com/quotes/vince_lombardi_786490.

Chapter 28

Stark, Ray (Producer), & Ross, Herbert (Director). *Steel Magnolias* [Motion Picture]. TriStar Pictures, 1989.

Chapter 29

Anonymous. Public domain, nd.

Chapter 30

Sidney J. Harris Quotes. Inspiringquotes.com. InspiringQuotes, Inc, 2019. 9 November 2019. https://www.inspiringquores.us/quotes/sidney_harris_parenting.

Chapter 31

Leonard, Sheldon (Producer). *The Andy Griffith Show* [Television series]. CBS, 1960-68.

Chapter 32

Will Durant Quotes. BrainyQuote.com, BrainyMedia, Inc, 2019. 9 November 2019. https://www.brainyquote.com/quotes/will_durant_145967.

Aristotle Quotes. BrainyQuote.com, BrainyMedia, Inc, 2019. 9 November 2019. https://www.brainyquote.com/quotes/aristotle_379604.

Chapter 33

James Carlos Blake Quotes. Goodreads.com, GoodReads, Inc, 2019. 9 November 2019. https://www.goodreads.com/quotes/james_carlos_blake_amusement.

Chapter 34

Deford, Frank. *The Rabbit Hunter.* Sports Illustrated, January 26, 1981.

Chapter 35

The Washington Post. Public domain, October 25, 1911.

Chapter 36

Mark Twain Quotes. BrainyQuote.com, BrainyMedia, Inc, 2019. 9 November 2019. https://www.brainyquote.com/quotes/mark_twain_414009.

Chapter 37

Oppenheimer, Jess (Producer). *I love Lucy* [Television series]. CBS, 1951-57.

Leonard, Sheldon (Producer). *The Andy Griffith Show* [Television series]. CBS, 1960-68.

Chapter 38

McCarey, Leo (Producer), & McCarey, Leo (Director). *Love Affair* [Motion Picture]. RKO Radio Pictures, 1939.

Chapter 39

Don Meyer Quotes. AZquotes.com, AZQuotes, Inc, 2019. 9 November 2019. https://www.azquotes.com/quotes/don_meyer_peace.

Chapter 40

Schlitz, Don. *The Gambler*. United Artists Records, 1978.

Chapter 42

Anonymous. Public domain, 1999.

Ethel Waters Quotes. AZquotes.com, AZQuotes, Inc, 2019. 9 November 2019. https://www.azquotes.com/quotes/ethel_waters_1358962.

Mitchell, Fritz (Director). *SEC Storied: Maravich* [Television documentary]. ESPN, March 12, 2018.

Chapter 43

John Wooden Quotes. BrainyQuote.com, BrainyMedia, Inc, 2019. 9 November 2019. https://www.brainyquote.com/quotes/john_wooden_380232.

Chapter 44

Bill Watterson Quotes. Goodreads.com, GoodReads, Inc, 2019. 9 November 2019. https://www.goodreads.com/quotes/bill_watterson_calvin-and-hobbes.

Shelton, Ron (Director) and Mount, Thom (Producer). *Bull Durham* [Motion Picture]. Orion Pictures, 1988.

Chapter 45

Anonymous. *The Story of Ralph Beard*. Sports Illustrated, November 30, 2007.

Monk, John and Dulaney, Cody. *The Twisted Journey of Child Killer Tim Jones*. The State, June 23, 2019.

Chapter 50

Muhammad Ali Quotes. BrainyQuote.com, BrainyMedia, Inc, 2019. 9 November 2019. https://www.brainyquote.com/quotes/muhammad_ali_145945.

Anonymous. *The Ghost of Might Have Been*. Greatexpectations. org, nd.

Chapter 51

Radmacher, Mary Anne. *Courage Doesn't Always Roar*. Red Wheel Weiser, 2009.

Chapter 52

Ferdinand Foch Quotes. BrainyQuote.com, BrainyMedia, Inc, 2019. 9 November 2019. https://www.brainyquote.com/quotes/ferdinand_foch_158850.

Chapter 53

Fincher, David (Director) and Chaffin, Cean; Kennedy, Kathleen; Marshall, Frank (Producers). *The Curious Case of Benjamin Button* [Motion Picture]. Paramount Pictures, 2008.

Chapter 54

Maya Angelou Quotes. BrainyQuote.com, BrainyMedia, Inc, 2019. 9 November 2019. https://www.brainyquote.com/quotes/maya_angelou_392897.

Chapter 56

Bo Schembechler Quotes. AZquotes.com, AZQuotes, Inc, 2019. 9 November 2019. https://www.azquotes.com/quotes/bo_schembechler_754065

J. J. Watt Quotes. AZquotes.com, AZQuotes, Inc, 2019. 9 November 2019. https://www.azquotes.com/quotes/j.j._watt_642795.

Chapter 57

Hartsville High School. *Mission Statement*. Hartsville High School 2004-05 SACS Report, 2004.

Chapter 60

Glasser, William. *The Quality School Teacher*. Harper Collins, 1990.

Chapter 61

Ward, Geoffrey. *Baseball: An Illustrated History*. Penguin Random House, LLC, 2010.

Dorsey, Jason. *50 Ways to Improve Schools for Under $50*. LITL, 2005.

Chapter 62

Gladwell, Malcolm. *The Tipping Point*. Little, Brown and Company, 2000.

Covey, Stephen M. R. *The Speed of Trust: The One Thing That Changes Everything*. Simon and Schuster, 2006.

Chapter 63

Hinshaw, Dawn. *S. C. Mourns Death of Civil Rights Giant*. The State, July 31, 2011.

Chapter 64

Pierson, Rita. *Every Kid Needs a Champion* [Video file], 2012. Retrieved from http://www.ted.com/talks/rita_pierson_every_kid_needs_a_champion.

Stephen R. Covey Quotes. Goodreads.com, GoodReads, Inc, 2019. 9 November 2019. https://www.goodreads.com/quotes/steven_covey_understand.

Chapter 65

Popova, Maria. *Elie Wiesel's Nobel Acceptance Speech*. July 4, 2016. Retrieved from dailygood.org.

Chapter 66

Reilly, Rick. *Tiger, Meet My Sister . . . and Other Things I Probably Shouldn't Have Said*. Blue Rider Press/Penguin Group, 2014.

Chapter 67

Darabont, Frank (Director) and Marvin, Niki (Producer). *The Shawshank Redemption* [Motion Picture]. Columbia Pictures, 1994.

Chapter 68

Miller, Robert Ellis (Producer) and Serling, Rod (Writer). *The Twilight Zone: The Changing of the Guard* [Television series]. CBS, June 2, 1962.

Horace Mann Quotes. BrainyQuote.com, BrainyMedia, Inc, 2019. 9 November 2019. https://www.brainyquote.com/quotes/horace_mann_133541.

Chapter 69

Commencement. *Merriam-Webster's Online Dictionary*. 2011. Retrieved from http://www.merriam-webster.com/dictionary/commencement.

Coen, Joel (Director) and Coen, Ethan (Producer). *O Brother Where Art Thou?* [Motion Picture]. Touchstone Pictures, 2000.

Calvin Coolidge Quotes. BrainyQuote.com, BrainyMedia, Inc, 2019. 9 November 2019. https://www.brainyquote.com/quotes/calvin_coolidge_414555.

Chapter 70

Xenophon. *Memorabilia, Trans. Henry Graham Dakyns*. MacMillan, 1897.

Baldwin, James. *Hero Tales Told in School*. Charles Scribner's Sons, 1914.

Chapter 71

Gatorade. *Be Like Mike* [Television commercial]. ESPN, 1991.

Chapter 72

The Statler Brothers. *Country Music Then and Now*. Mercury Records, 1972.

Scott, Ridley (Director) and Scott, Ridley and Gitlin, Mimi Polk (Producers). *Thelma and Louise* [Motion Picture]. MGM, 1991.

Chapter 73

Nichols, Mike (Director) and Turman, Lawrence (Producers). *The Graduate* [Motion Picture]. United Artists, 1967.

Garfunkel, Art and Simon, Paul. *Bookends*. Columbia Records, 1968.

Joe DiMaggio Biography. Biography.com Editors, Biography, Inc, 2019. 14 April 2019. The Biography.com.

Simon, Paul. *Joe DiMaggio*. New York Times, 1999.

Deford, Frank. *Take Your PEDs: Fans No Longer Care About Steroid Usage in MLB*. Sports Illustrated, July 15, 2009.

Chapter 74

Robert Nathan Quotes. Goodreads.com, GoodReads, Inc, 2019. 9 November 2019. https://www.goodreads.com/quotes/robert_nathan_yesterday.

Ralph Waldo Emerson Quotes. Goodreads.com, GoodReads, Inc, 2019. 9 November 2019. https://www.goodreads.com/quotes/ralph_waldo_emerson_journey.

Chapter 75

Michael Kadoorie Quote (paraphrased). WiseOldSayings.com, WiseOldSayings, Inc, 2019. 9 November 2019. https://www.wiseoldsayings.com/quotes/michael_kadoorie_tradition.

Denise McCluggage Quotes. BrainyQuote.com, BrainyMedia, Inc, 2019. 9 November 2019. https://www.brainyquote.com/quotes/denise_mccluggage_397659.

Esther Dyson Quotes. BrainyQuote.com, BrainyMedia, Inc, 2019. 9 November 2019. https://www.brainyquote.com/quotes/esther_dyson_352101.

Chapter 76

King, Stephen. *11/23/63*. Charles Scribner's Sons, 2011.

Soren Kierkegaard Quotes. BrainyQuote.com, BrainyMedia, Inc, 2019. 9 November 2019. https://www.brainyquote.com/quotes/soren_kierkegaard_105030.

Anonymous. Public domain, 1950 appx.

Chapter 77

Albom, Mitch. *The Timekeeper*. Hachette Books, 2012.

Chapter 78

Mehta, Pavithra. *A Tale of Misplaced Love and Irony*. July 12, 2013. Retrieved from dailygood.org.

Chapter 79

Chang, Angel. *Son Learns True Meaning of Hard Work by Looking at His Father's Hands*. (nd). Retrieved from LittleThings.com.

Chapter 80

Channel Swimming Association. *Queen of The Channel: Florence Chadwick*. (nd). Retrieved from QueenOfTheChannel.com.

Chapter 81

Luna, Elle. *The Crossroads of Should and Must*. October 6, 2016. Retrieved from dailygood.org.

Mark Twain Quotes. Goodreads.com, GoodReads,Inc, 2019. 9 November 2019. https://www.brainyquote.com/quotes/mark_twain_reasons-why.

Chapter 82

Diamond, Barbara. *Grandmother Teaches Important Life Lesson Using a Carrot, Eggs, and Coffee*. (nd). Retrieved from LittleThings.com.

Edgerton, Clyde. *In Memory of Junior*. Algonquin Books, 2012.